U.S.-JAPAN
Relations *in a* Changing World

U.S.-JAPAN
Relations *in a*
Changing World

Steven K. Vogel
editor

BROOKINGS INSTITUTION PRESS
Washington, D.C.

Copyright © 2002
THE BROOKINGS INSTITUTION
1775 Massachusetts Avenue, N.W., Washington, D.C. 20036
www.brookings.edu

Library of Congress Cataloging-in-Publication data

U.S.-Japan relations in a changing world / Steven Vogel, editor.
    p. cm.
Includes bibliographical references and index.
    ISBN 0-8157-0630-8 (cloth : alk. paper) — ISBN 0-8157-0629-4 (pbk. : alk. paper)
    1. United States—Relations—Japan. 2. Japan—Relations—United States. I. Vogel, Steven Kent.
    E183.8.J3 U745 2002   2002003957
    327.73052'09'045—dc21   CIP

9 8 7 6 5 4 3 2 1

The paper used in this publication meets minimum requirements of the American National Standard for Information Sciences—Permanence of Paper for Printed Library Materials: ANSI Z39.48-1992.

Typeset in Sabon

Composition by Oakland Street Publishing
Arlington, Virginia

Printed by R. R. Donnelley and Sons
Harrisonburg, Virginia

Contents

Acknowledgments

This volume represents the culmination of the U.S.-Japan 21st Century Project, a conference, commemoration, and research project marking the fiftieth anniversary of the signing of the San Francisco Peace Treaty and the U.S.-Japan Security Treaty on September 8, 1951. Christopher Sigur of the Japan Society of Northern California was instrumental in launching this effort, in partnership with the Berkeley Roundtable on the International Economy (BRIE) at Berkeley and the Asia/Pacific Research Center (A/PARC) at Stanford. Many others helped with planning, including Barbara Bundy, Alexander Calhoun, Stephen Cohen, William Fuller, Daniel Okimoto, James Raphael, Robert Scalapino, Hitoshi Tanaka, Nobuaki Tanaka, Haydn Williams, and John Zysman. George Shultz served as honorary chair, and Bruce Pickering as executive director. The project featured a major conference highlighting the research compiled in this volume in San Francisco on September 6 and 7, and a ceremony attended by Secretary of State Colin Powell and Foreign Minister Makiko Tanaka on September 8, 2001.

The authors are especially grateful to the U.S.-Japan Foundation for sponsoring this research project, and to James Schoff of the foundation for his guidance. Keith Nitta served as project coordinator. Sigur and Pickering worked closely with the editor and authors throughout the project. Meredith Kummell, Lydia Mendoza, and Kristin Nelson of the Japan Society offered critical logistical support. The authors enjoyed a superb team of research assistants: Gene Park and Naoko Sakaue (various tables), Saori Nishida (chapter 3), Hiro Yamamoto (chapter 5), Florence Sanchez (chapter 6), and Michelle Clark, Yasuyuki Motoyama, and Susan Jong (chapter 9). Joseph A. Grimes provided helpful comments on chapter 3. Laurie Freeman thanks the Abe Fellowship Program for financial support for related research.

The authors' greatest debt goes to the workshop commentators (listed opposite) who gave critical input at an early stage in the research. The project organizers felt that it was important to incorporate the views of the real world practitioners in the relationship, and to do so as an integral part of the research rather than as a last-minute check on the findings. In this spirit, the authors presented initial thoughts and received feedback from these experts. This experiment paid off tremendously, and the authors are very grateful to the commentators for taking the time to participate. Jim Raphael helped to arrange two workshops at Stanford and Mari Miura coordinated one workshop in Tokyo.

The authors formed an all-American team of researchers, but felt strongly that there should be input from counterparts in Japan, so some of Japan's leading young scholars were asked to comment on individual chapter drafts. Kōji Murata (Balance of Power), Yoshiko Kojō (Macroeconomic Performance), Masaki Taniguchi (Domestic Politics), Saori Katada (Paradigms), Masayuki Tadokoro (Media), Keisuke Iida (International Organizations), and Jun Kurihara (Finance) all provided excellent comments, greatly strengthening the final result.

Finally, the authors thank Christopher Kelaher at Brookings Institution Press for guiding the manuscript through the process of review and revision, three anonymous reviewers for comments, Randi Bender for editing, Janet Walker for overseeing the editorial process, Carlotta Ribar for proofreading, and Julia Petrakis for providing an index.

Workshop Commentators

SECURITY

Kurt Campbell, director, International Security Program, Center for
    Strategic and International Studies, and former deputy assistant secre-
    tary of defense for Asia and Pacific affairs
Noboru Yamaguchi, defense and military attaché, Japanese Embassy
Paul Giarra, senior analyst, Strategic Assessment Center, Science Applica-
    tions International Corporation

MACROECONOMICS AND FINANCE

Bowman Cutter, managing partner, Warburg Pincus, and former deputy
    assistant to the president for economic policy
Kiyoto Ido, minister, Japanese Embassy
Mark Sobel, deputy assistant secretary for monetary and financial affairs,
    Treasury Department
Dan Tarullo, visiting professor of law, Georgetown University, and former
    assistant to the president for international economic policy

PARADIGMS

Thomas Rohlen, senior fellow, Institute for International Studies, Stanford
    University
John Nathan, Department of East Asian Languages and Cultural Studies,
    University of California, Santa Barbara
Robert Myers, research fellow, Hoover Institution, Stanford University

DOMESTIC POLITICS

James Foster, minister, U.S. Embassy, Tokyo
Glen Fukushima, president and chief executive officer, Cadence Design
    Systems, Japan, and former deputy assistant U.S. trade representative
    for Japan and China
Yoshihiko Nakamoto, Department of Law and Government, Shizuoka
    University
Keizō Takemi, member, House of Councilors

MEDIA

Orville Schell, dean, School of Journalism, University of California,
    Berkeley
Leslie Helm, correspondent, *Los Angeles Times*

Tato Takahama, freelance correspondent and executive director, Pacific Research Institute U.S.-Japan Media Center

INTERNATIONAL ORGANIZATIONS
Nobuaki Tanaka, consul-general of Japan, San Francisco
Takeshi Isayama, visiting scholar, Asia/Pacific Research Center, Stanford University, and former director general of the International Trade Policy and Trade Department, Ministry of International Trade and Industry
Masaki Taniguchi, Graduate School of Law and Politics, Tokyo University

TECHNOLOGY
François Bar, professor of communications, Stanford University
Martin Beversdorf, Department of Political Science, University of California, Berkeley
Martin Kenney, Department of Human and Community Development, University of California, Davis
Emily Murase, Department of Communications, Stanford University
George Scalise, president, Semiconductor Industry Association

CHAPTER ONE

Introduction:
The San Francisco System
at Fifty

STEVEN K. VOGEL

On September 8, 1951, Japan signed a peace treaty with forty-eight nations in San Francisco and forged an alliance with the United States under the Treaty of Mutual Cooperation and Security. In doing so, it formally accepted an arrangement—the San Francisco system—that would define its relationship with the United States, and thereby its place within the world, for more than fifty years. Under this arrangement, the United States incorporated Japan into the heart of its cold war strategy. Japan effectively committed itself to military, diplomatic, and economic dependence on the United States. Japan allowed the United States to station troops on Japanese soil and to maintain control over Okinawa. Japan acted as a member of the Western camp, following the U.S. lead on critical foreign policy issues. The United States protected Japan from external threats, but Japan developed military forces to help defend itself and to support U.S. forces in regional conflicts. The United States also supported Japan's economic recovery by allowing Japan to limit the reparations paid to war victims, by creating a liberal international trade regime, and by maintaining open markets at home while tolerating Japanese trade protection and an undervalued yen.[1]

This volume reviews the past fifty years of the U.S.-Japan relationship and speculates about how it will evolve in the years to come. The continuities over the past fifty years are as striking as the changes. Since 1951

Japan has risen from military defeat to economic power and then plunged into financial crisis, and the cold war system has solidified, transformed, and then collapsed. Yet the core features of the San Francisco system have survived. The United States and Japan maintain an unequal security alliance, American military bases remain in Japan, and Japan defers to the United States on many foreign policy issues.[2] The United States exerts global leadership, while Japan plays a much smaller role than one would expect based on its economic and technological strength.

This situation is not likely to continue. The San Francisco system remains intact, yet it is gradually losing its grip over the relationship. In the future, therefore, various pressures—such as changes in the regional balance of power—will have a greater impact on the bilateral relationship than they have in the past. This argument is elaborated in the chapters to follow, and predictions for the future are presented in the conclusion.

This volume is organized around a single analytical framework, with chapters devoted to developments in eight issue areas: the balance of power, economic performance, foreign policy paradigms, domestic politics, the media, international organizations, finance, and technology. In each case two central questions are addressed:

—How have developments in this area affected U.S.-Japan relations over the past fifty years?

—How are they likely to affect U.S.-Japan relations in the future?

Thus the chapters in the volume are not simply essays on different substantive topics, but explorations of how changes in specific factors (the independent variables in this study) affect the bilateral relationship (the dependent variable). Rather than analyze how many different factors have combined to shape one particular facet of U.S.-Japan relations, each chapter assesses how one specific factor affects the relationship as a whole. By proceeding in this way, the chapters develop clear causal arguments and specify what each factor can and cannot explain. Although any one chapter can provide only a partial analysis, the eight chapters combined offer a fairly comprehensive survey of the most important factors that have affected the U.S.-Japan relationship over time, and that will continue to define it in the future.

Each chapter addresses major intellectual debates that transcend the confines of U.S.-Japan relations. Michael Green, for example, stakes out a novel position on the fundamental debate over the nature of international relations. Green is a realist in that he stresses the primacy of the balance of power: military power defines international relationships more than other forms of power, and nations tend to define their core interests in relation to the international balance of power. Yet he explicitly parts company with structural realists who focus almost exclusively on the structure of the international system as a whole, such as a bipolar or multipolar system structure.[3] Instead, he stresses the multiple dimensions of the balance of power, including the U.S.-Japan bilateral balance of power and the Asian regional balance of power as well as the global system structure.

William Grimes demonstrates how changes in economic balances of power affect international relations. Specifically, he argues that rapid economic challenges to dominant powers generate severe tension. He combines a subtle analysis of how objective economic factors affect interstate relations with an innovative argument about how perceptions of economic performance can have an even greater impact than the underlying reality. Grimes suggests that perceptions often lag reality, and that this can fuel international conflicts as countries misinterpret economic trends and develop inappropriate foreign economic policies.

Keith Nitta contends that ideas matter even in the anarchic world of international relations, and he specifies how they matter. He argues that ideas can both enable or constrain political leaders, depending on how deeply embedded they have become. They first emerge as programs that expand leaders' freedom of action by presenting new options, but then they crystallize into paradigms that constrain leaders' discretion. As the San Francisco system became embedded in the postwar paradigms of the United States and Japan, for example, it became an increasingly powerful constraint on foreign policy. This contributed to stability in the relationship in two ways: it locked the two countries into fixed roles, and it harmonized expectations on both sides. Nitta warns, however, that the postwar paradigms are eroding in both countries, giving rise to a more volatile period of paradigm drift. Interestingly, Green and Nitta both explain the resilience of the San Francisco system and its increasing vulnerability in recent years, yet they do so in quite different ways.

Leonard Schoppa looks at how domestic politics interacts with international relations through the lens of "two-level games."[4] That is, international negotiators bargain simultaneously with two different parties: the other country and their own domestic political constituents. The two-level game approach highlights the ways in which the interaction between negotiators and domestic constituents affects negotiation outcomes. Schoppa adds a new twist to this approach by demonstrating how domestic political divisions can actually facilitate, rather than impede, bilateral cooperation.

These divisions foster cooperation because a negotiator representing a united front of domestic interests will be less willing to compromise than a negotiator representing divided interests. A negotiator representing divided interests will also be better positioned to arrange a domestic bargain that will accommodate the partner country's position. Schoppa applies this insight by showing how the United States and Japan have achieved high levels of cooperation despite intense domestic conflict within both countries over the terms of the relationship.

Laurie Freeman shows how media coverage itself reflects the broader context of international relations. She suggests that U.S. and Japanese media coverage not only affects the bilateral relationship, but is itself a product of that relationship. She specifies the ways in which changes in the relationship have transformed the quantity, quality, and tone of coverage in the two countries. Nevertheless she suggests that media coverage does have some independent effect on the relationship as well. The media can increase bilateral tensions by failing to offer sufficient coverage, by presenting biased coverage, or by stressing negative images over positive ones.

Amy Searight highlights the ways in which international organizations such as GATT, the World Bank, and the United Nations facilitate cooperation between countries and reduce tension. She does not stop there, however; she shows how their impact varies across different issue areas. Specifically, Searight argues that international organizations have a much greater impact on economic relations than on security relations. This variation between economic and security issues is especially pronounced in the case of U.S.-Japan relations, because Japan has much greater leverage and fewer political constraints in economic organizations such as GATT and the World Bank than in diplomatic and security organizations like the United Nations. Furthermore she demonstrates how Japan uses international organizations to bind the United States, that is, to pull the United States toward international cooperation while restraining it from unilateral action. Thus Green (realist), Nitta (constructivist), and Searight (liberal institutionalist) represent the three most prominent schools of thought in international relations theory today, and yet all three push their respective paradigms in promising new directions.

Adam Posen develops an innovative argument about how the globalization of finance redefines international relations. He contends that it drives international convergence in certain key institutions, such as government regulatory systems and corporate governance structures. This reduces structural asymmetries between countries and thereby eases the tensions that arise from these asymmetries. Likewise, financial change reshapes domestic political dynamics by forging cross-national coalitions among interest groups with common goals, and by augmenting the freedom and influence of these private sector actors vis-à-vis national governments.

Steven Vogel and John Zysman build on a considerable literature on how national governance systems interact with technological change, but they disaggregate this argument in new ways. They show how the impact of national institutions on technological development varies over time, across sectors, and across functions (such as production versus innovation) within sectors. They use this framework to explain the shift from U.S. technological dominance in the early postwar period, to Japanese challenge in the 1970s and 1980s, to U.S. resurgence in the 1990s. In addition they analyze how these shifts in technological power affect international relations, stressing that Japan's sudden challenge to American dominance created an unprecedented level of tension between the two countries.

This volume strives to depict the U.S.-Japan relationship in its full multidimensional complexity. Special emphasis is placed on the distinction between cooperation versus conflict, on the one hand, and harmony versus tension, on the other. Cooperation is defined in terms of the outcome of bilateral interaction: Did the interaction benefit the two countries (or benefit one without hurting the other)? Harmony is defined in terms of the process of interaction: How contentious was the interaction? This distinction is critical because the United States and Japan have so often combined high levels of cooperation, in the sense of working out agreements that benefit both sides, with high levels of tension, in the sense of elite-level hostility, public distrust, and the politicization of disputes. When it comes to specific episodes, of course, the authors of this volume may differ in their individual assessment of the balance of cooperation and conflict. When Leonard Schoppa looks at bilateral trade relations in the 1980s, he is struck by the ability of the two countries to achieve a high level of cooperation by working out compromises on highly contentious issues. When Steven Vogel and John Zysman review the same period, they stress conflict and tension: the inability of the two sides to reach agreements that effectively addressed their differences, and the enormous friction that this generated. In table 1-1 general assessments are reported about how the levels of tension and cooperation have fluctuated with various high points and low points in bilateral relations over the postwar period. Others might characterize the levels of tension and cooperation differently in specific cases, but this table should suffice to illustrate the general point: that cooperation (as opposed

Table 1-1. *High Points and Low Points in the U.S.-Japan Relationship, 1951–2001*

Date	Highlight	Cooperation	Tension
1951	**San Francisco Peace Treaty** U.S.-Japan Security Treaty also negotiated and signed.	High	Medium
1951–58	**U.S. technology exports** U.S. firms (RCA, Dupont, Motorola) sell rights to Japanese companies.	Medium	Low
1952	**Japan-China trade restraints** U.S. officials force Yoshida to agree.	Low	Medium
1954	**Lucky Dragon incident** Japanese fishing boat exposed to radiation from U.S. atomic bomb testing.	Low	Medium
1956	**U.S. nuclear basing in Japan** Japan resists U.S. attempts to move nuclear weapons and nuclear-powered ships into Japanese bases.	Low	High
1956	**"Voluntary" export restraints (VERs)** Japanese officials reduce exports of textiles, tuna, and electrical goods to the United States.	Medium	Low
1958–60	**U.S.-Japan Security Treaty revision** Renegotiated and renewed.	High	High
1968	**Vietnam War escalates** Japanese government questions U.S. policy. United States uses bases in Japan.	Medium	High
1969	**Satō-Nixon communiqué** United States returns Okinawa to Japan. Japan confirms that South Korea and Taiwan are essential to its security.	High	Medium
1971	**Textile dispute** Nixon threatens to impose quotas on Japanese textile imports.	Low	High
1971	**Nixon visits China** Nixon begins normalization without consulting Japan.	Low	High
1971	**Nixon shock** Nixon unilaterally devalues the dollar, ends fixed exchange rate regime.	Low	High
1977	**Television VERs** Japan restricts television exports to the United States	Medium	Medium
1978	**U.S.-Japan defense guidelines** Guidelines for security cooperation.	High	Low
1983–87	**Japan breaks GNP 1% defense spending limit** Nakasone breaks unofficial 1% GNP limit, strengthens security alliance.	High	Low

Table 1-1. *High Points and Low Points in the U.S.-Japan Relationship, 1951–2001 (continued)*

Date	Highlight	Cooperation	Tension
1985	**Plaza Accord** G-5 countries manipulate currency values, lower the dollar, and raise other currencies.	Medium	Medium
1986	**Semiconductor Trade Agreement** Regulates semiconductor pricing, sets target of 20% foreign market share in Japan in a side letter.	Medium	High
1986–93	**GATT Uruguay round** Japan pressures U.S. to accept legal language restricting unilateral action in trade disputes. Japan agrees to allow limited imports of rice.	High	High
1988–90	**Structural Impediments Initiative (SII)** Talks on structural issues, including distribution, industrial groups, macroeconomic balances.	Medium	Medium
1987, 1989	**FS-X codevelopment** Agreement to codevelop support fighter aircraft in 1987, renegotiated in 1989.	Low	High
1990	**Persian Gulf war** Japanese government unable to respond to U.S. demands for active Japanese participation.	Medium	High
1994–96	**Structural Framework talks** United States demands numerical targets for opening Japanese market sectors, Japan refuses.	Low	High
1995–96	**Okinawa crisis** U.S. marine rapes 12-year old girl. U.S. agrees to remove 11 air bases and return approximately 20% of its leased land on Okinawa.	Medium	High
1996	**U.S.-Japan defense guidelines** United States and Japan agree to revisions.	High	Medium
1997	**Asian Monetary Fund (AMF) proposal** Japan drops AMF plan to resolve Asian financial crisis in favor of U.S.-backed IMF bailout.	High	Medium
2000	**NTT interconnection agreement** NTT lowers interconnection fees by 20% over two years.	High	Low

to conflict) does not necessarily correlate with harmony (as opposed to tension). Figure 1-1 shows American and Japanese attitudes toward the other country, one rough indicator of the level of bilateral tension.

This book looks not only at fluctuations in cooperation and tension, but also at other dimensions of the relationship, such as shifts in the relative power of the two countries, the transformation of the substantive agenda, and the proliferation of relevant actors (citizens, leaders, organizations, countries). Green, for example, analyzes the shifting balance of responsi-

Figure 1-1. *Public Opinion Poll Data on U.S.-Japan Relations, 1978–99*

Percent

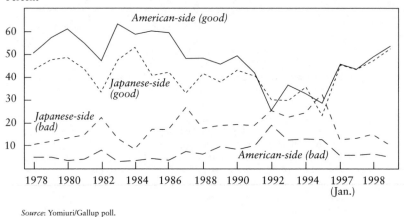

Source: Yomiuri/Gallup poll.

bilities within the U.S.-Japan military alliance; Grimes evaluates economic interdependence; Nitta interprets national roles; Searight examines arenas (bilateral versus multilateral); Freeman characterizes media coverage; and Posen addresses the convergence between U.S. and Japanese financial systems. By surveying many different dimensions of the U.S.-Japan relationship, this volume develops a more comprehensive picture of what has changed and what has not changed over the past fifty years. That, in turn, provides a first step toward understanding where that relationship is headed in the years to come—a question to which this book returns in the conclusion.

Notes

    1. John Dower, "Peace and Democracy in Two Systems: External Policy and Internal Conflict," in Andrew Gordon, ed., *Postwar Japan as History* (University of California Press, 1993), pp. 449–64.

    2. Kent Calder, "Japanese Foreign Economic Policy Formation: Explaining the Reactive State," *World Politics*, vol. 40 (July 1988), pp. 517–41.

    3. Kenneth Waltz, *Theory of International Politics* (Random House, 1979).

    4. Robert Putnam, "Diplomacy and Domestic Politics: The Logic of Two-Level Games," *International Organization*, vol. 42 (Summer 1988), pp. 427–60; and Leonard Schoppa, *Bargaining with Japan* (Columbia University Press, 1997).

CHAPTER TWO

Balance of Power

MICHAEL J. GREEN

Fifty years after the signing of the San Francisco Peace Treaty, the U.S.-Japan security relationship remains locked into the essential parameters of that strategic bargain. The United States maintains 37,000 troops in Japan and a monopoly on power projection and nuclear deterrence. Japanese defense spending is still hovering at about 1 percent of GDP and Japan's Self-Defense Forces (JSDF) continue to arm only for exclusively defensive self-defense (*senshubōei*), with the exception of tightly constrained participation in UN peacekeeping operations and expanded responsibilities for rear area support for U.S. forces in regional contingencies under the 1997 revision of the bilateral Defense Guidelines. This continuity is particularly striking when contrasted to U.S. security relations with the other enemy-turned-ally, Germany. In recent years Germany has formed a joint military corps with France, led the establishment of an independent European Defense Policy and the Organization of Security and Cooperation in Europe (OSCE), and participated in military bombings of Serb targets during the Kosovo air campaign. Few observers of the U.S.-Japan alliance could imagine Japan forming the core of an Asian defense policy or participating in a massive air campaign against a neighboring state.

At the same time, however, very few observers of the U.S.-Japan alliance expect that the security relationship will not change over the coming years.

As one State Department official with expertise in U.S.-Japan relations has noted, "there will probably be more change in Japanese security policy over the next decade than there has been over the previous five."[1] An influential report on U.S.-Japan security relations by a bipartisan group of American experts in October 2000 echoed this theme: "Japanese society, economy, national identity, and international role are undergoing change that is potentially as fundamental as that Japan experienced during the Meiji Restoration."[2]

This anticipation of change has been fueled by a convergence of international and domestic trends. Japan's economic engine has stalled and this has reinforced insecurity about the rise of Chinese power and the growing threats in Northeast Asia from both Chinese and North Korean missiles. The breakdown of Japan's economic model has also brought a greater fluidity to domestic politics and combined with generational change to shake loose many of the old taboos on defense issues. In March 1999, for example, the Japanese Maritime Self-Defense Forces (MSDF) were authorized to intercept North Korean spy vessels intruding in Japanese territorial waters for the first time in the postwar period. The MSDF vessels fired warning shots, and opinion polls taken subsequently showed support for an even more robust response. In April 1999 the Japanese government approved the development of indigenous spy satellites, breaking Tokyo and Washington's long-standing ban on Japanese strategic capabilities in space. In the same period, the Japanese Diet convened two commissions to investigate the modalities of revision of the Japanese Peace Constitution. Meanwhile, since the mid-1990s opinion polls have shown a growing pessimism about relations with China and North Korea and the prospects for peace in Northeast Asia.

Despite all the evidence of nonchange in the structure of the U.S.-Japan alliance, there is mounting evidence to suggest that Japan's strategic culture and the regional security environment are in transition. This chapter aims to identify how the U.S.-Japan alliance might change in the years ahead as a result. But as Yogi Berra warned, "prediction is difficult—especially about the future." The best approach, therefore, may be to reexamine the past. This is appropriate not only because the alliance has reached its fiftieth birthday (and many happy returns), but also because a careful look at the past shows that the U.S.-Japan security relationship has undergone important transitions before. Assessing what accounted for these transitions will provide a useful guide to what variables might shape the alliance in the years to come.

This chapter focuses specifically on the following periods of change in the alliance:

—1960 revision of the U.S.-Japan Security Treaty,

—1969 Sato-Nixon communiqué to the 1972 Nixon shocks,

—1978 U.S.-Japan Defense Guidelines to the Roles and Missions Agreement in the early 1980s,

—Gulf war, and

—Nye Initiative in the 1990s.

In each case the chapter isolates those independent variables that led to the adjustment in security relations. Did a change in the structure of the international system reshape the alliance, or was the most important variable change in the bilateral power structure between the United States and Japan? Was the adjustment in the alliance predictable based on these changes in power, or was it the result of specific individuals, institutions, or ideas within each country? What the case studies in this chapter reveal is that shifts in the balance of power have been the critical drivers of change in the structure and management of the U.S.-Japan alliance. Most important have been shifts in the international distribution of power that have highlighted the bilateral imbalance between the United States and Japan or created opportunities for mutually beneficial adjustments to the bilateral strategic bargain. Domestic politics and institutions, as well as ideational or cultural factors, have been important—but they have usually been secondary factors that have delayed or diverted the adjustment of policies as shifts have occurred in the international distribution of power. In other words, it is important to understand the role of domestic institutions and ideas, but these have changed only as power relations have changed. Weighing these factors will give some clues about the relative impact of such variables on the future of the security relationship as well as the overall durability of the alliance.

What changed at each point must also be measured. None of the changes to the alliance listed above were a win for one side only. Indeed, these changes in the alliance led to greater integration of security relations. But these changes in the alliance were also contentious because the burdens of risk and benefit were being recalibrated—even if in a mutually beneficial way (though never in a way that changed the fundamental parameters of the security relationship as it was defined in 1951 and 1960). Before accounting for the changes in the alliance over the past five decades, therefore, this chapter must return to San Francisco in the fall of 1951 to dissect the original strategic bargain struck by Shigeru Yoshida and John Foster Dulles.

Peace Treaty and the U.S.-Japan Strategic Bargain

When representatives of Japan and twenty-three allied nations gathered in San Francisco from September 4-8 to sign the peace treaty formally ending the Pacific war, the theatrics were captured for television by the cameras of the U.S. Army Signal Corps. The highlight was Soviet Foreign Minister Andrei Gromyko's repeated interruptions, which ended with the chief representative of the communist bloc storming out of the session together with his Polish counterpart on the last day. The magnanimous and conciliatory closing comments of Secretary of State Dean Acheson were also powerful, echoing President Abraham Lincoln's famous call for "malice toward none and charity toward all" at the end of the American Civil War. But the most revealing speech of all at the peace conference was probably that of the principal U.S. negotiator over the previous year, John Foster Dulles.

Dulles outlined to the delegates the American view of the strategic bargain that had now been struck with Japan. First, Japan would remain firmly in the community of democratic nations. Second, Japan would not develop offensive capabilities, though it retained the sovereign right of self-defense under the UN Charter. Third, the United States would retain bases in Japan. Although Dulles repeatedly spoke of Japan's rights as a sovereign nation, these three points were clearly nonnegotiable.

Dulles also put forward a vision of how the alliance with Japan might evolve—or, more precisely, what the peace treaty did not preclude. Dulles argued, for example, that Japan was not renouncing the right of collective defense. That left open the possibility that the United States could someday draw on Japanese military capabilities in the future or even bring Japan into a multilateral alliance relationship in Asia, a vision captured in NSC-125. Dulles also stressed that this would not be a punitive settlement. Japan would not be burdened with reparations. Indeed, the door would be open for Japan to reemerge as an economic engine in Asia, though no one in San Francisco had any idea how miraculously that recovery would occur or how much friction it would eventually create in U.S.-Japan relations. Finally, Dulles argued that U.S. military forces were staying in Japan based on a sovereign decision of the Japanese government. Japan was still under occupation, however, so this left open the possibility that a truly sovereign Japan might change its mind about the U.S. military presence in the future. The strategic bargain left both room for growth in military cooperation as well as unresolved asymmetries.

In the months before San Francisco, Prime Minister Shigeru Yoshida articulated the Japanese vision of the strategic bargain. What later historians would call the Yoshida Doctrine was threefold: Japan would remain in the Western camp, make the minimal military effort necessary to secure a defense relationship with the United States, and leave the hard security problems to Washington as Japan focused on economic recovery. In fact the Yoshida Doctrine was more of a political compromise. Within the conservative ranks of early postwar Japanese politics there were those who: wanted Japan to move toward unilateral rearmament; wanted a military relationship with Washington simply because it brought dual-use technology and economic assistance; wanted pure pacifism but American military protection; could not make up their mind and preferred not having to debate defense issues before a war-weary electorate (see chapter 5 by Schoppa in this volume). The strategic bargain with the United States brought all of these diverse camps together. Those who wanted rearmament would not achieve it without U.S. *gaiatsu* (pressure) and technical assistance. Those who wanted pacifism could not risk it in a dangerous Northeast Asia without a U.S. security guarantee. Those who wanted the recovery of heavy industry needed the mutual security assistance programs promised by Washington. And those who did not want the conservative camp divided over defense policy needed a clean compromise. As John Dower notes in his biography of Yoshida, "The reconsolidation and recentralization of conservative authority during the Yoshida era was inseparable from the strategic settlement reached between the United States and Japan."[3]

Yoshida also left ambiguous the eventual evolution of the alliance. He certainly did not expect the asymmetries in the strategic bargain to last forever. As the prime minister himself noted, "Japan should not continue to remain at a level where it depends on another country for its defense."[4] Whether Japan would reassert its autonomy through economic power, unilateral military capabilities, multilateral diplomacy, or a more equal partnership with the United States was still not clear. All were tested to some extent in subsequent years, though never enough to undermine the essential parameters of the original strategic bargain.

The strategic bargain was created at a time of vast difference in power between Japan and the United States, and it was established in the midst of the Korean War, when the struggle between East and West was at its bloodiest in Asia. Neither of these conditions would persist. Japan would grow in power relative to the United States. The sharp divisions of the early cold war would break down with the emergence of the nonaligned movement, the Sino-Soviet split, détente, and then the collapse of the Soviet Union itself. At the time Yoshida's view that the asymmetries would not last seemed reasonable. Indeed, subsequent observers from Herman Kahn to Henry Kissinger have argued that Japanese economic recovery would lead to an independent military capability.[5]

Yet most of the asymmetries in the strategic bargain persisted. One reason was Japan's "entrapment versus abandonment" dilemma. Pushing for more autonomy would increase the risk that Japan would be abandoned by the United States. Relying too much on the United States for security, on the other hand, would increase the prospects that Japan would become entrapped (*makikomareru*) in U.S. cold war adventures.[6] This classic dilemma has plagued smaller allies since Thucydides and the Peloponnesian Wars. Many Japanese have argued that the solution to the dilemma is revision of Japan's constitution so that Tokyo can develop more autonomous defense, but Yoshida—himself a fierce guardian of Japanese autonomy—argued that the constitution was a critical firewall against entrapment. In many respects the changes in the U.S.-Japan security relationship after 1951 were the result of Japan attempting to maximize both autonomy and security commitments from the United States, while minimizing the risks of either abandonment or entrapment. At the same time, the United States had its own dilemma. Washington was often attempting to maximize Japanese security contributions to the alliance without undermining the asymmetries of the strategic bargain: U.S. bases, no Japanese offensive capabilities, and no Japanese defection. These were contradictory objectives for both sides that explain both the persistence of the original strategic bargain and the deep ambivalence about change in both countries to this day.

Nevertheless, there was pressure on the alliance for change as bilateral power imbalances eroded and the international system changed. And these are the variables we must account for in the years after 1951.

First Adjustment: 1960 Security Treaty Revision

The 1951 Peace Treaty was a document of unprecedented magnanimity and forethought. The subsequent U.S.-Japan Security Treaty, however, had one critical flaw. On September 8, 1951, Japan signed the treaty while still under military occupation and, arguably, agreed to the continued stationing of U.S. forces in Japanese territory under duress. Moreover, the treaty contained within it clauses authorizing the United States to use force to maintain domestic stability. For Japan, which had embraced modernization in the Meiji period to shuck off the unequal treaties, this was an intolerable situation. Shigeru Yoshida's successor and nemesis, Ichirō Hatoyama, had attempted in 1957 to reassert Japanese autonomy vis-à-vis the United States with constitutional reform and outreach to the Soviet Union, and he failed on both counts. His successor, Nobusuke Kishi, instead turned to revision of the Security Treaty itself.

The United States also had reasons to revise the treaty. Washington had provided massive technical and financial assistance to Japanese rearmament through the 1953 Mutual Security Assistance Agreement and had encouraged Japan to transform its National Police Force (*keisatsu yobitai*) into the JSDF and Japan Defense Agency (JDA) in 1954. The United States no longer needed to play a role in Japanese domestic security and wanted Japan to develop some military capabilities to resist external attacks so that U.S. forces in Japan could focus more explicitly on regional security as communist insurgencies spread throughout Asia.

The adjustment to the strategic bargain in 1960, in other words, was primarily the result of restored Japanese sovereignty and a change in power relations between the United States and Japan. At the same time, however, Kishi also had a powerful domestic political motivation as well. As Hideo Ōtake has argued, the 1960 treaty revision became an ideological proxy war between industrialists and conservative politicians on the one side, and labor unions, radicals, and students on the other.[7] In the end Kishi succeeded in further consolidating the conservative-business axis in Japan and halting the growing influence of radical labor. That domestic result was as important as the changes in bilateral security, where the new treaty removed U.S. forces from any role in internal security; made explicit cooperation for the defense of Japan (increasing Japan's own role in self-defense under Article V of the treaty); and provided bases for the United States for the security of the Far East (Article VI).

Kishi's political victory was, however, short lived. The violent social collision caused by the Security Treaty debate put at risk the ruling Liberal Democratic Party (LDP) mandate. Kishi resigned and was replaced by the more moderate Hayato Ikeda, a protégé of Yoshida. Ikeda quickly shifted the national debate away from security and on to the core of the Yoshida Doctrine: growing rich. Ikeda promised in 1961 to double Japan's national income in ten years. It happened in about half that time. And with that came new pressures on the alliance for change.

Nixon-Satō Communiqué to the Nixon Shocks

The LDP's income-doubling strategy took the spotlight off the U.S.-Japan alliance for the rest of the 1960s with one important exception: the Vietnam War. Protests in Japan against the war grew after 1966 and earlier student radicals reemerged in groups like the *Beheiren* (Civilian League for Peace in Vietnam). The main impact on the alliance, however, was for Tokyo to introduce unilateral steps to insulate Japan from "entrapment" in the Vietnam conflict. While the war added as much a $1 billion to Japan's gross domestic product (GDP) because of the increased U.S. military presence flowing through Japan, the Diet pressed the government to guarantee that Japan would not become militarily involved. The result was a government statement in Diet interpolations that the "Far East" referred to in Article VI of the 1960 treaty applied only to the area north of the Philippines. That included by implication Taiwan and the Korean peninsula, but it drew a political line between Japan and Vietnam. It had little practical effect on the American war effort, however. B-52 pilots flying bombing missions against North Vietnamese targets from Japan simply "changed course" over international waters or took other steps to preserve the impression that Japan was not implicated in the war. The real adjustment to the strategic bargain came instead at the end of the decade, as a result of both American retrenchment after the 1968 Tet Offensive and the consequences of Japan's sudden economic explosion.

In January 1968 North Vietnamese forces attacked U.S. and South Vietnamese forces from Hue City to Saigon. In traditional terms of territory seized or casualties imposed, this Tet Offensive was a clear-cut American victory. In terms of the *Clausewitzian* "center of gravity," however, it became a decisive turning point in the Vietnam conflict and marked the beginning of American withdrawal. On July 25, 1969, President Richard Nixon outlined a security policy for Asia in a meeting with reporters on the island of Guam. Under the so-called Nixon Doctrine, or Guam Doctrine, the United States would be turning over more responsibility for security to American allies in East Asia. In the words of Nixon's predecessor, Lyndon Johnson, it was time for "Asian boys to fight Asian wars." Based on the Guam Doctrine, the Nixon administration pressed Japan to shoulder more of the defense burden, with Secretary of State William Rogers using the term "autonomous defense" to describe the stance Japan should take in the future.

This shift in the U.S. military strategy in East Asia coincided with a booming confidence in Japan after the doubling of national GDP in the

1960s. By the end of the decade Japanese industry had begun producing a full spectrum of indigenous jet trainers and warships, leading the JDA to report in 1969 that "Japan had reached the top level of defense-related technology and should emphasize autonomous development of weapons systems in the future."[8] Washington's call for Japan to shoulder more "autonomous defense" resonated with those in Tokyo who had wanted to pursue more independence back in 1951. Moreover, a greater emphasis on autonomy offered the promise of a significant boost to the defense industry, whose production accounted for about 0.50 percent of Japanese total industrial output, but critical inputs for aerospace and shipbuilding.[9]

The combination of American retrenchment in Asia and Japan's own growing economic and industrial power led to an unprecedented new debate about the security relationship in Tokyo. Industrial leaders, like Keidanren chairman Toshio Dokō, called for Japan to assume a greater burden for the defense of the entire region. Prime Minister Eisaku Satō had commissioned a study on Japan's nuclear option in 1967 and in 1969 told the U.S. ambassador to Japan that Japan's three nonnuclear principles were "nonsense."[10] Even in an influential economic report prepared by an advisory committee for the Ministry of Finance in 1970, senior business executives strayed from their macroeconomic policy messages to support an expanded budget for autonomous defense and to work for the repeal of Article 9 of the Constitution—to the shock of the Ministry of Finance.[11]

The prospects of a major adjustment to the strategic bargain increased in 1969 when the United States agreed officially to return Okinawa to Japanese sovereignty. In an implicit bargain, the Japanese side made gestures toward playing a larger security role in the region. This adjustment to the strategic bargain was articulated in the 1969 Satō-Nixon communiqué, in which Prime Minister Satō agreed with President Nixon on the return of Okinawa and the principle that the security of the Republic of Korea was essential to, and the security of Taiwan an important factor in, the security of Japan.

These trends were not lost on Yasuhiro Nakasone, an ambitious and nationalistic young politician who had emerged from Diet elections in 1969 as the head of his own faction. Nakasone was an ardent supporter of the autonomy school, and had even worn a black armband in the 1950s to mourn Japan's loss of sovereignty under Yoshida's accommodation with the United States. Nakasone saw the trends in domestic and international security policy, and sought to build both his ideological agenda and his financial support from industry as director general of the JDA. Nakasone introduced important reforms at the agency. For one thing, JSDF soldiers noticed that their rations began to improve. Industry's appetite was whetted as well. In his draft four-year defense plan for 1972–77, Nakasone proposed to realize "autonomous defense" by nearly doubling the JDA budget and procuring a range of new weapons systems that included fighters, airborne early warning aircraft, and missiles. These power projection capabilities were justified by the reversion of Okinawa and the need for Japan to play a larger regional security role under the Guam Doctrine.

Nakasone's aggressive defense plan provoked open battle between the LDP hawks and doves, but with the future U.S. commitment in Asia uncertain and Prime Minister Satō sympathetic with Nakasone's outlook, the battle remained indecisive. In the end the "autonomous defense" push was neutralized by another shift in the international system. Nixon had created the environment for autonomy with his Guam Doctrine in 1969. Two years later he sucked the oxygen out of "autonomous defense" with two new shocks to the international system. The first of these Nixon shocks was the president's decision to allow the dollar to free float in August 1971. That had the effect of increasing the value of the yen to the dollar and significantly raising the opportunity costs for indigenous development of weapons systems for the JDA. The more important shock came shortly thereafter when President Nixon opened dialogue with the People's Republic of China (PRC). Now the political and economic opportunity costs of autonomous defense shifted upward. Japan had quietly maintained low-level economic ties with the PRC through the so-called L-T trade in the 1960s, but Nixon's move cleared the way for Japanese corporations to rush into the promising China market for the first time since the war. Suddenly, the same corporate leaders who had favored autonomous defense (men like Toshio Dokō) were leading the calls for normalization of relations with Beijing and full economic relations with the mainland. Satō's successor as prime minister and leader of the LDP's most powerful faction, Kakuei Tanaka, also championed new ties to Beijing. Tanaka shelved Nakasone's controversial defense proposals and in 1972 proposed a new minimalist "peacetime defense" (*heiwa no toki no bōeiryoku*). With the onset of détente, Washington's pressure on Japan to increase its autonomous defense faded. With the oil shocks of 1973, the price tag for autonomous defense became even more problematic. Tanaka's successor, the dovish Takeo Miki, codified the peacetime defense concept in the 1976 National Defense Program Outline (NDPO)—which declared Japan would only maintain the military power necessary for defense against "small scale limited invasion"—relying on the United States for all the rest.

Instead of fading with the growth of Japanese economic power, the original strategic bargain between the United States and Japan was further institutionalized after the return of Okinawa. Satō's agreement that Taiwan was important to Japanese security was shelved within the Japanese government, and Foreign Minister Toshio Kimura declared in the Diet in 1972 that "there was no security threat to Japan from the Korean peninsula."[12] However, the asymmetries in the alliance relationship led to further pressures for change when the period of détente closed at the end of the decade.

1978 Defense Guidelines and Roles and Missions Approach

The 1976 NDPO institutionalized the strategic bargain in Japanese defense planning, but it had one weakness—it was a unilateral Japanese document that had no bearing on U.S. security policy. Concerns about the U.S. commitment and the viability of the strategic bargain grew with détente, particularly in the wake of the Carter administration's 1976 campaign pledge to withdraw U.S. forces from the Korean peninsula. To prevent the reemergence of autonomous defense arguments, the government of Prime Minister Miki needed also to lock in the U.S. side of the strategic bargain. For its part, the U.S. government wanted a reaffirmation of Japan's commitment to regional security in the 1969 Satō-Nixon communiqué. Moreover, by the mid-1970s the Pentagon had concluded that it needed Japan to take on a larger defense burden in order to bottle up the Soviets' newly expanding military capabilities in the Far East. It was particularly important to the U.S. Navy that Japan developed capabilities to defend the sea lanes around the Japanese islands. Détente was slipping and another adjustment to the strategic bargain was due.

The two governments addressed these problems through negotiations started in 1975 to establish bilateral Guidelines for Defense Cooperation. Predictably, Tokyo sought to maximize the U.S. commitment to the defense of Japan under Article V of the Security Treaty and Washington sought to maximize Japan's support for U.S. regional strategy under Article VI. Japanese political leadership was not willing at that point to assume responsibility for military missions beyond the narrow function of defending against a "small scale limited invasion." As the U.S. and Japanese governments negotiated the first Guidelines for Defense Cooperation, the Japanese side stuck closely to its doctrine of "exclusively defensive defense" (*senshubōei*) and refused to open the door to contingency planning for other conflicts in the region, even on Korea.[13]

Nevertheless, when the Defense Guidelines were signed in 1978, they did open the door to a more direct Japanese military role in the U.S. strategy of containment in the Far East. Two precedents included in the new Defense Guidelines opened the way for broader Japanese participation in U.S. containment strategy. First, the Defense Guidelines added sea lane defense as part of the defense of Japan against direct attack and therefore a legitimate area for U.S.-Japan military cooperation under Article V of the Security Treaty. Sea lane defense had been mentioned by the JDA as early as the 1960s,[14] but the guidelines document gave the mission the blessing of the Japanese government as a whole for the first time, stating that "the MSDF and U.S. Navy will jointly conduct maritime operations for the defense of surrounding waters and the protection of sea lines of communication."[15] Second, the Defense Guidelines legitimized military planning and exercises for the defense of Japan for the first time. This not only made it possible for the two militaries to "come out of the closet" about their cooperation, but it also brought the Ministry of Foreign Affairs and U.S. State Department clearly into the process of managing defense cooperation.

It must be emphasized, however, that this crack in the door was not widely accepted or appreciated even within the Japanese government. In the guidelines negotiations the Japanese side resisted all efforts by the U.S. government to include explicit terms for cooperation in the event of a regional contingency. In contrast to the detailed operational areas of cooperation listed under Section II for "Actions in Response to an Armed Attack against Japan," Section III only stated that the two governments would study the "scope and modalities of facilitative assistance" that might be provided to the United States in the event of a "situation in the Far East outside Japan which will have an important influence on the security of Japan." For almost two decades—until the Nye Initiative and the revision of the guidelines in 1996—there would be no legislation or deliberate planning in preparation for contingencies in the region. Moreover, the civilian leadership in the Carter administration, concerned about financial resources for maintaining U.S. forces abroad and Congressional pressure for allies to make a greater contribution, shifted its focus to the question of Japanese host nation support. At a time of rising trade problems, Japanese money was seen as the clearest measure of burden sharing for the U.S. Congress and media.[16] As a result, even the comparatively easy political problem of bilateral defense planning for the defense of Japan against direct attack was put on the back burner by the Carter administration.

Nevertheless, the legitimization of sea lane defense specifically and bilateral planning more broadly prepared the way for a dramatic move forward in strategic cooperation against the Soviet Union once Moscow itself raised the stakes by invading Afghanistan and supporting the Vietnamese invasion of Cambodia in 1979. The U.S. Navy had been growing concerned about the Soviets' use of the Sea of Okhotsk as an ocean bastion for the new submarine leg of its nuclear triad against the United States. When the Reagan administration came to power in January 1981, it quickly shifted the U.S. focus from financial burden sharing to the issue of assigning roles and missions to allies in the region. The Defense Guidelines provided the opening to do just that. Also, because cooperation on sea lane defense was considered "exclusively self-defense" in Japan, there was now a lower hurdle to bringing Japanese assets into the game of containing the Soviets' new naval expansion in the Sea of Okhotsk.

The opportunity to win political endorsement for sea lane defense came when Prime Minister Zenkō Suzuki traveled to Washington for his first meeting with President Reagan in May 1981. Suzuki was a dove and only became prime minister when his mentor, Masayoshi Ōhira, suddenly died in June 1980. Ōhira had studied defense issues carefully, commissioning the famous report on comprehensive security before his death in 1980 (comprehensive security focused on broader, nonmilitary avenues for Japan to consider its own defense). However, Suzuki was largely ignorant about defense and foreign policy issues. The Reagan administration asked him to accept certain "roles and missions" for the JSDF and Suzuki followed the Foreign Ministry's lead and acknowledged in the joint communiqué the "desirability of an appropriate division of roles and missions between Japan and the United States."[17] Afterward at the National Press Club, Suzuki announced that this meant Japan would defend its own sea lanes of 1,000 nautical miles. This, of course, was enough distance to help bottle up Soviet naval forces in the Sea of Okhotsk and to defend against Soviet bombers and submarines as far south as the Philippines. Suzuki himself probably did not fully digest the meaning of what he said, but he had been prepped to make the statement by key Ministry of Foreign Affairs (MOFA) officials and members of the Defense Zoku (caucus) in the Liberal Democratic Party who had worked closely with counterparts in the Reagan administration and knew exactly the implications of what Japan's acceptance of sea lane defense would mean.

The manipulation of Suzuki by his own party and MOFA reflected the Japanese side's recognition that the security alliance was the best vehicle for enhancing Japan's own status in Asia. The best and brightest in the Foreign Ministry gravitated quickly to the North American Affairs Bureau because that was where the action was and where Japan's new world role was being defined. In the LDP the close and cooperative relationship with the Reagan administration empowered a group of ambitious prodefense politicians who had been toiling in obscurity for decades. Where the Defense Zoku had represented only the hawkish Satō, Kishi, and Funada factions for decades, beginning in 1981 politicians from other, more moderate factions also began working on defense policy. This combination of nationalists and internationalists was united by their desire to see the defense budget increase. The Reagan administration gave them powerful "*gaiatsu*" against the fiscally conservative Ministry of Finance. Indeed, in 1981 the Defense Zoku sent a delegation to Washington to make certain that Reagan officials complained about insufficient defense increases just in time for budget negotiations in May and then December.[18]

Considerable progress was made, in other words, even under the dovish Suzuki. Then when Yasuhiro Nakasone took over as prime minister in November 1982, the close alliance relationship had its truest champion. Nakasone referred to Japan as an "unsinkable aircraft carrier" and a "member of the West" and told the Diet that heretofore "when Japan is under attack, the JSDF can assist U.S. naval vessels on their way to defend Japan," reflecting an expanded interpretation of Japan's carefully constrained right of "exclusively defensive defense."[19] His focus on the alliance relationship with the United States was captured by the famous "Ron-Yasu" relationship with President Reagan. Nakasone had championed autonomous defense ideas as JDA director general in 1970, of course, but like the Defense Zoku in the LDP, he came to realize that a close U.S.-Japan alliance was indispensable to his own political goals to increase Japan's defense and foreign policy profile in Asia.

The Reagan administration also got what it wanted. The U.S. Navy developed the "Maritime Strategy" for horizontal escalation against the Soviet Union, that is, to attack Soviet submarines in the Sea of Okhotsk as part of a global response to Soviet aggression in Europe. In close parallel, Japan and the United States began detailed studies on sea lane defense and the division of roles and missions. As the 1982 *United States Military Posture* stated, "it is no longer practical to design autonomous regional strategies, for a threat in one strategic zone will almost certainly have a serious impact on security of the others."[20] The Japanese government, of course, did not put its own defense efforts in such an explicit containment strategy. Sea lane defense, after all, was part of the exclusively defensive defense of Japan based on a rapidly increasing Soviet military threat in the immediate vicinity of Japan. However, those at the center of the alliance understood the implications of this arrangement: Japan was now an active player in the U.S. global strategy of containment against the Soviet Union. This new adjustment to the strategic bargain was consummated in a bilateral agreement made in 1986 for the deployment of F-16 fighters to Misawa, Japan. Officially, the fighters were being stationed in Japan to maintain the military balance against Soviet fighters on the Northern Territories. But the Pentagon and a handful of senior Japanese officials also understood that the deployment of nuclear weapons-capable tactical aircraft meant that the Soviets had to look at the U.S.-Japan alliance as part of global conventional and nuclear deterrence.

By 1987 there was no doubt that the 1983 Defense White Paper and Foreign Policy Blue Book claims that Japan was now a "Western ally" were true. For decades the U.S.-Japan alliance had been a vehicle for keeping the United States in Asia militarily and Japan on the side of the West. In the space of only a few years and with the planning of only a handful of people in Tokyo and Washington, the U.S.-Japan alliance had become much more than that. The alliance and Japanese military capabilities themselves were now central components of the global U.S. military strategy of containment against the Soviet Union.

Japan now also shared risk in the alliance more directly than at any point since the Korean War. But this adjustment to the strategic bargain also had a critical flaw. It was premised on the direct Soviet threat to Japan, which allowed Tokyo to play a role in U.S. regional strategy while maintaining the concept of "exclusively defensive defense" and defense against "small scale limited invasion." The collapse of the cold war and the eruption of conflict in Southwest Asia would leave the alliance exposed and bring new pressures for adjustment.

Gulf War

At the same time that the United States and Japan strengthened defense cooperation against a common and immediate Soviet threat, Japan also came under pressure to share the burden of leadership in other areas as well. Japan's expanding economic power—particularly after the Plaza Accord in 1985—increased bilateral economic tension and threatened to undermine the closer security cooperation now underway. Tokyo responded with massive efforts to recycle its capital surpluses through increased foreign aid, host-nation support for U.S. forces stationed in Japan, and contributions to the International Monetary Fund (IMF), World Bank, and United Nations. By the end of the decade, this economic power appeared as imposing as the military power wielded by the United States and the Soviet Union. Indeed, Japan's growing technological and financial clout suggested that the strategic asymmetries with the United States might be eased after the cold war as a new techno-economic paradigm defined international power.

These assumptions were proven wrong in the first security crisis of the post–cold war era. Japan provided over $13 billion to support the Gulf war, but received shockingly little gratitude for this contribution from the United States, Kuwait, or the international community. Under intense pressure to share "real" risk and not just so-called "checkbook diplomacy," Tokyo rushed to pass legislation that would allow the JSDF to be dispatched to the Gulf as peacekeepers. The first effort in 1991 failed in the Diet. A second bill in 1992 did pass, and opened the way for Japan to participate in carefully circumscribed and controlled peacekeeping activities. By that time, the Gulf war had ended. Japan's impressive efforts to share risk with the United States in the Roles and Missions approach of the 1980s were completely inapplicable to the Gulf war, where no direct and convenient threat to Japan could legitimize cooperation.

The Gulf war was a colossal diplomatic failure for Japan. More painfully, it highlighted the continuing asymmetries in the alliance after the cold war. Japanese burden sharing was insufficient from the U.S. perspective. Japanese influence on the United States was insufficient from Tokyo's perspective. As the Japanese Government pushed for permanent membership in the UN Security Council in the years after the Gulf war, it used the logic of Japan's international contribution to make its case, but UN Security Council membership was also about empowerment, hedging, and influence vis-à-vis the United States. The collapse of the Japanese economic bubble in the early 1990s only exacerbated the slide back to power asymmetries in the relationship. Tokyo continued focusing on multilateralism and integration with Asia as correctives, but the strategic bargain was ready for another adjustment on a bilateral basis.

Nye Initiative and Post–Cold War Redefinition

In the mid-1990s senior officials in Tokyo and Washington once again made an effort to adjust the U.S.-Japan security relationship, this time for a more fluid post–cold war setting. When Joseph Nye Jr. was named assistant secretary of defense for international security affairs in late 1994, he viewed the uncertain state of the U.S.-Japan security relationship since the Gulf war as an area requiring his personal and immediate attention. This was as much in order to shore up the alliance after years of high-level neglect, as it was to move the security relationship forward. From the beginning of what became known as the "Nye Initiative" there were subtle but important differences between those who focused on reaffirmation of the security relationship and those in both Tokyo and Washington who sought broader "redefinition" to give the alliance vitality in a new strategic setting. These differences reflected the continuing ambivalence in both capitals about altering the strategic bargain too much.

In the first half of the 1990s the alliance suffered both from neglect and from crises. The end of the cold war competition empowered those in the U.S. government who had wanted to focus on trade relations with Japan but had been constrained by strategic considerations. This shift became evident first when President George H. W. Bush brought senior U.S. auto executives with him to Tokyo in January 1992 in order to highlight trade relations with Japan. When Bill Clinton became president in 1993, he brought into government officials who were even more determined to place economic security on a par with traditional definitions of national security. As part of that strategy, the Clinton administration formulated a comprehensive Japan policy that focused its highest priority on establishing greater economic reciprocity in the bilateral relationship. The Office of the U.S. Trade Representative (USTR) and National Economic Council took the lead on the Economic Framework Talks with Japan. For its part the Pentagon's relationship with Japan was overshadowed by the Technology-for-Technology Initiative, which sought greater reciprocity in the flow of dual-use technology between the United States and Japan. Even with regard to the new mission of missile defense, senior officials told Japan in 1993 that the United States expected a cooperative development arrangement with Japan that would benefit the U.S. industrial base.[21] It appeared to skeptical Japanese officials that American jobs were now more important than protecting Japan against nuclear missiles from North Korea. By 1994–95 these various trade and technology initiatives had yielded modest agreements on sectoral areas such as auto trade and flat glass, but they had done so at the cost of unprecedented levels of acrimony between the two governments. Those responsible for "traditional" security relations with Japan in the National Security Council, the State Department, and the Pentagon took a back seat—and their counterparts in MOFA and JDA in Tokyo began focusing on areas other than the alliance.

With the U.S. definition of bilateral relations so adversarial, security policymakers in Japan began focusing on areas other than the alliance, in particular the United Nations, multilateral security, and Asia. These were not inimical to U.S. interests. Indeed, Japan's focus complemented the bilateral alliance in ways useful to Washington. However, given the acrimony in bilateral economic relations, Japan's wandering eye became a cause for concern. When Prime Minister Morihiro Hosokawa established a blue ribbon panel in 1993 to review Japanese defense policy for the new post–cold war setting, this concern took concrete form. The resulting Higuchi Commission report was actually quite bold and reaffirmed the importance of the U.S.-Japan alliance. But it also highlighted the multilateral theme as the new direction for Japanese security policy. The boldness of the report was appreciated in Washington, but the emphasis on multilateralism confirmed fears among many U.S. and Japanese officials that there was drift not only in Washington, but in Tokyo as well.[22]

To those who viewed security in traditional terms of the balance of power, this drift in the alliance was a serious problem. At a strategic level, the United States needed a solid U.S.-Japan alliance in order to manage the rise of Chinese power in the international system. The alliance was not necessary as an instrument of containment, but it was an essential backdrop to the policy of engagement. U.S. defense policymakers were also becoming concerned about the credibility of the U.S.-Japan alliance at the operational level after a crisis in 1994 over North Korea's putative nuclear weapons program. In June of that year it appeared possible that war might break out on the peninsula as the United States prepared to impose sanctions and a blockade on the North. Japan's rear-area military and logistical support was needed, but Tokyo was unable to promise anything concrete until North Korea used aggressive force. Once again, the absence of a direct offensive threat to Japan proved that the roles and missions approach of the 1980s was not fully applicable in a post–cold war setting.

In the fall of 1994 Nye won support for his effort to revitalize the alliance relationship from Secretary of Defense William Perry and Assistant Secretary of State for Asia Pacific Affairs Winston Lord, as well as from the Japanese government. The bilateral dialogue quickly produced a comfortable reaffirmation from both governments of the continuing importance of the alliance. The mutual suspicion caused over the previous three years was put largely to rest among the professionals. It helped that the Pentagon issued the East Asian Strategic Report in February 1995 declaring the United States intention to maintain approximately 100,000 troops in the Asia Pacific region for the foreseeable future.[23] It also helped that the JDA's revision of the original National Defense Program Outline (eventually completed in November 1995) was focusing on bilateral defense cooperation in "situations in the area around Japan that have a direct effect on Japanese security" and not just the multilateral themes of the Higuchi Report.

However, the question of explaining the alliance to the public in both countries was not yet resolved. In September 1995 that fundamental oversight became critical after three U.S. servicemen abducted and raped a young girl in Okinawa. Protests in Okinawa quickly turned national opinion in Japan against the desirability of U.S. forces in Japan and threw both governments into crisis mode. Private efforts at reaffirmation were no longer sufficient to sustain the alliance. The governments now had to signal their intention to at least partially redefine the alliance and adjust the U.S. military presence. They did so by establishing the Special Action Committee on Okinawa (SACO) in late 1995 to consolidate, realign and reduce U.S. bases, while maintaining current capabilities. That process did not prove easy, but it moved the alliance out of the crisis caused by the rape.

If the Okinawa crisis served any useful purpose, it was to focus national leadership on the drift in the alliance relationship. The Japanese reaction to the rape had been front page news in the United States. As a result no one in the White House objected when Defense and State Department officials proposed a U.S.-Japan joint security declaration to the president as a centerpiece for his next summit in Japan. The president was scheduled to hold that summit meeting with Prime Minister Tomiichi Murayama in Osaka on the edge of the annual Asia Pacific Economic Cooperation forum meeting in November 1995. But then fortune struck in the form of another political crisis, this time over the U.S. budget, which forced the president to postpone his visit to Japan until April 1996. The gap of four months made all the difference in the world. First, the extra time allowed U.S. and Japanese negotiators to agree on a dramatic centerpiece to the SACO realignment of bases in Okinawa—the return of the controversial U.S. Marine Corps Air Station at Futenma in return for a comparable facility elsewhere on the island. Second, Beijing provided a convenient reminder of the importance of the alliance and the potential for instability in East Asia by bracketing Taiwan with ballistic missiles in a clumsy attempt at intimidation in March 1996. Third, the pro-defense LDP hawk Ryūtarō Hashimoto replaced the Socialist Murayama shortly after the Osaka APEC

summit. Finally, President Clinton himself emerged from the primary sea-
son in the United States unchallenged for the presidency and in a strong
position to project an air of confidence and resolve in foreign policy.

With the political and geostrategic constellation now much more favor-
able than it had been in November, Clinton and Hashimoto were able to put
some substantial contents into the Joint Security Declaration they issued in
April 1996 in Tokyo. In addition to reaffirming the alliance and both countries' commitment to the U.S. forward presence, the two leaders now
suggested important areas of redefinition as well. Most important, they agreed
to revise the 1978 U.S.-Japan Defense Guidelines to address "situations in the
area surrounding Japan"—a pledge to fill in the third part of the original 1978
guidelines that had left the alliance so unprepared for the Gulf war and the
1994 Korean crisis. Though not deliberate, the implicit trade-off between
base consolidation and increased Japanese risk sharing was obvious.

The Nye Initiative broke through important obstacles to security cooperation, in spite of, and perhaps because of, new crises in Okinawa and the
Taiwan Strait. However, as many of the principals involved later acknowledged, the focus on the alliance dissipated in the years after the Joint
Security Declaration and the momentum of the initiative was lost. In part
this was because of the ad hoc nature of the Clinton administration's foreign policy process toward Japan and a lack of follow-through at senior
levels. In part, it was due to the onset of the financial crisis in Asia in the
summer of 1997. Confusion in Japan's domestic politics also undermined
implementation. Nevertheless, the Nye Initiative did shift the strategic bargain in important ways. Through the Defense Guidelines review, Japan
took on more risk in an explicit way. Through SACO, the United States
agreed to reduce base asymmetries. These were small steps, but they pointed
the way to a further round of bilateral negotiations and readjustments on
the grand bargain.

Accounting for Change and Nonchange in the Alliance

The strategic bargain penned in San Francisco in September 1951 locked in
asymmetries between the United States and Japan that few expected to last.
Yet the basic framework of the San Francisco Peace Treaty and the first U.S.-
Japan Security Treaty is remarkably intact five decades later. The
asymmetries in the strategic bargain led naturally to pressure for adjustment
as Japanese power increased relative to the United States. In simple terms,
Japan wanted greater autonomy and the United States wanted greater bur-

den sharing. However, neither side won these objectives based on shifts in the bilateral balance of power alone. That was because both sides feared a loss of the status quo. For Tokyo autonomy was not worth the risk of abandonment. For Washington burden sharing was not worth the risk of lost leadership and freedom of action in Asia.

As a result, the most significant adjustments in the strategic bargain occurred usually when shifts in the international distribution of power highlighted the bilateral imbalance or created opportunities for mutually beneficial adjustments to the strategic bargain. The bilateral balance of power was the driver, and domestic politics, institutions, and ideational or cultural factors mattered as secondary or tertiary variables. But it was acute changes in the broader international structure of power that usually led to the specific adjustments in a bilateral context.

In most cases these episodes began with Japan seeking both autonomy and a greater U.S. defense commitment and the United States seeking greater burden sharing. They usually ended with an alliance that was further integrated, with each side giving more explicit commitments under the original strategic bargain. This was not an irreversible dialectic toward integration. Japan hedged with indigenous military capabilities, independent diplomacy and legal determinations that insulated the nation against entrapment. Nevertheless, the trend has been one of incremental adjustments toward a more effective sharing of the burden, the risk and leadership, as we have seen in the case studies.

In the 1960 Security Treaty revision, the primary factor was Japan's increased power relative to the United States, but Japanese domestic politics were also important, as were U.S. efforts to redistribute some of the security burden to Japan. What changed, ultimately, was that the new alliance locked in the strategic bargain based now on full Japanese sovereignty. The strategic bargain itself remained in force for four reasons: the external environment was still too threatening for Japan to risk abandonment; Hatoyama's push for autonomy risked a split in the conservative ranks; the U.S. requirement for bases, Japanese strategic alignment, and a constrained but adequate Japanese defense capability did not change; and Ikeda refocused Japan on economic growth.

In the case of the 1969 Satō-Nixon communiqué and subsequent explorations of autonomous defense, the primary factor was also an increase in Japanese economic and technological power relative to the United States, but the Guam Doctrine created a permissive environment for autonomy. Moreover, it was ultimately changes in the international environment—

and particularly the Nixon shocks and the opening to China—that determined Japan's disposition and return to the strategic bargain. There was an adjustment, though, as Japan took a first toehold in regional security and regained sovereignty over Okinawa. It is also noteworthy that the divisiveness of autonomous defense in conservative ranks stalled more serious change. In spite of the Guam Doctrine, the United States had no intention to give up its forward bases in Japan or encourage Japanese power projection capabilities in Asia.

The Defense Guidelines began with U.S. and Japanese efforts to lock the other side into commitments that had become uncertain with détente. The Roles and Missions approach built on the guidelines to operationalize both Japan's backing for U.S. regional security policy and U.S. planning for the defense of Japan. The international factors were critical in this case, for Soviet expansion in the Far East blurred the distinction between the defense of Japan and the security of the Far East. Leadership in both capitals also mattered.

The Gulf war adjustments to the security relationship occurred more in Japan's security policies (peacekeeping) than in the mechanics of the bilateral alliance per se. Nevertheless, they reflected the untenable nature of the asymmetries in the alliance—asymmetries in the burden of risk that had been masked by the convenient Soviet expansion in the 1980s. The immediate impetus for change was clearly Saddam Hussein's invasion of Kuwait. However, few in Tokyo saw that as a serious security threat to Japan. The most important variable must therefore be recognized as the sudden growth in Japanese global economic power in the 1980s, the tensions that caused with the United States, and the inability of Japan to share concomitant risk. Peacekeeping and Tokyo's bid for a permanent UN Security Council seat represented both a symbolic increase in risk sharing and an attempt to empower Japan vis-à-vis the United States.

The Nye Initiative in the 1990s began as a corrective to badly distorted U.S. policies, but it took on a greater significance precisely because asymmetries in the security relationship were no longer tenable. The first of these asymmetries was the U.S. military presence, which was consolidated in the SACO agreement of 1996. The second asymmetry was Japan's willingness to share responsibility in regional security crises—revealed in the 1994 North Korean nuclear crisis—and corrected by the 1996 Joint Security declaration and the 1997 revision of Defense Guidelines. In Yogi Berra-like "déjà vu all over again," the adjustment to the strategic bargain in the 1990s had the same logic as the adjustment in the 1969 Nixon-Satō communiqué; that is, the return of U.S. bases in exchange for greater Japanese risk sharing.

These trends suggest several important lessons for the future of the U.S.-Japan alliance. First, the strategic bargain is highly resilient to changes in the bilateral and international distribution of power, but only as long as incremental adjustments are made to reduce domestic political pressures and keep the alliance relevant to emerging security challenges. Second, these adjustments succeed only when they lead to a reaffirmation of each side's commitment to the original strategic bargain and a modest trade of Japanese burden sharing (the Nixon-Satō communiqué, Defense Guidelines, and others) for Japanese autonomy (return of Okinawan sovereignty, SACO, and others). These adjustments have always been modest enough, however, so as not to undermine the original strategic bargain. Finally, none of these adjustments have yet led to fully integrated sharing of risk comparable to the U.S.-ROK alliance or NATO. There is no joint and combined command. Japanese forces would not serve under U.S. commanders in conflict, nor would the reverse occur. The United States still plans for military contingencies beyond the defense of Japan without assuming or depending upon full Japanese military support. There is still the psychological, legal, and operational separateness that Yoshida wanted.

That is the next great challenge for the alliance. Incremental adjustments have brought the alliance to the point where the separateness that Yoshida built into the strategic bargain must be confronted. Already the debate is intensifying about the right of collective defense in Japan. Theater missile defense and the revolution in military affairs will force greater integration of information sharing. Constrained U.S. budgets and expanding military requirements will force Washington to depend on allies like Japan more for backup in regional contingencies, particularly in low-intensity operations like peacekeeping and humanitarian relief. Tokyo will expect to be consulted earlier in international crises and the United States will expect Japan to do more. The United States will have to accept that increased integration means increased dependence on Japan in times of crisis and an increased Japanese capacity for independent action. The Japanese side will have to accept that empowerment in the alliance and the region requires Japanese action in times of crisis.[24]

The trends of the past fifty years suggest that the United States and Japan will be able to continue moving incrementally into this next stage of alliance relations. However, this cautious optimism must be tempered by recognition that the international system has not changed so dramatically that either

Japan or the United States would have incentives to dealign or end the strategic bargain. Thus far the two nations have passed each new test to the security relationship with restored confidence in the other side's commitment. Neither side has ever failed in its side of the bargain. However, we must watch carefully any changes in the distribution of power that might undermine the strategic bargain in the future. There are three scenarios that could be particularly devastating to the alliance, though all are unlikely. The first scenario is a continued implosion of the Japanese economy. In the short to medium term, this could lead to cuts in host-nation support for U.S. forces. However, history suggests that the strategic bargain could be adjusted to compensate for Japan's declining economic resources with relative increases in Japanese rear-area logistical support and expanded roles for the JSDF (based on removal of legal constraints rather than increased defense resources). The real danger of Japanese economic decline is over the long run. Concerns about the rise of Chinese power, common values, and other factors would serve as glue in the security relationship even as Japan's share of global GDP declined, but if China's GDP surpasses Japan's in the decades ahead, it is not inconceivable that the U.S.-Japan alliance could decline dramatically in importance to Washington. Hints of this future were evident in the way the Clinton administration emphasized "strategic partnership" with China at Tokyo's expense as Japan's GDP stalled in the late 1990s. This scenario depends on factors beyond Japan's own economic health. What role China plays will also be crucial to determining how closely the United States hews to the alliance with Japan or chooses accommodation with Beijing. A threatening China will require close alliance relations, even if Japan's relative weight continues to sag. In any case, the possibility of this future is precisely why the United States has increasingly emphasized Japanese economic growth as a matter of both trade and national security policy. U.S. strategic interests require a strong Japan.

The second scenario that could dramatically alter the alliance would be sudden and unexpected U.S. defeat in battle, perhaps in the Taiwan Strait. A U.S.-China military confrontation over Taiwan would not end well for either country, but one possible outcome would be a U.S. decision to stand down rather than risk nuclear war. This could create the unfortunate impression in the region that U.S. power has been eclipsed by China's. It is not at all certain how Japan would respond to this scenario. Realignment with China is not a commonly predicted outcome. More likely Japan would retain alliance with the United States while significantly increasing its own unilateral military capabilities as a hedge and independent deterrent against

China. That is certainly what the small precedents in the 1990s suggest (particularly Japan's response to the Taepodong launch in 1998). In any case, there is no predicting how a Taiwan scenario might unfold, and that ambiguity is itself an effective deterrent against China's use of force. No matter what the impact on the alliance and Japan, the consequences for China would be incalculable.

The third scenario that could undermine the strategic bargain is U.S. retrenchment, not from loss in battle, but from fatigue or economic decline. This possibility has been predicted for decades. However, the dependence of the United States on forward engagement in Asia is now well understood by the American people. Moreover, the scenario most often cited for an end to the strategic bargain—the growth of Japanese economic power relative to the United States— appears highly unlikely given the structural problems in the Japanese economy. Indeed, a decline in U.S. economic resources could now just as easily increase U.S. and Japanese interdependence on the strategic level, as the alliance becomes more important to safeguard each side's national interests. The negative impact of possible U.S. economic decline on the alliance cannot be dismissed, but history demonstrates that the two countries have been able to adjust the alliance when bilateral asymmetries became problematic; they did so in ways that strengthened and integrated the security relationship.

These three negative scenarios notwithstanding, then, the history of integration and empowerment still remains the best guidepost for the years ahead. On this fiftieth anniversary of the U.S.-Japan security relationship, there is every reason for optimism that this alliance can last another fifty years as a cornerstone of regional peace and stability in Asia.

Notes

1. Senior U.S. State Department official speaking on background. Center for Naval Analyses roundtable, March 2000.

2. Richard L. Armitage and others, *The United States and Japan: Advancing toward a Mature Partnership* (Institute for National Security Studies, National Defense University, 2000), p. 1. For further elaboration, see Michael J. Green, *Japan's Reluctant Realism: Foreign Policy Challenges in an Era of Uncertain Power* (Palgrave, 2001).

3. John Dower, *Empire and Aftermath: Yoshida Shigeru and the Japanese Experience, 1878–1954* (Harvard East Asian Monographs, 1979) p. 369.

4. Ichiro Ozawa, *Nihon Kaizō Keikaku (Blueprint for a New Japan)* (Kōdansha, 1993), p. 109.

5. See, for example, Herman Kahn, *Japan: The Emerging Superstate* (Prentice-Hall, 1970).

6. For elaboration on this theme see Michael J. Green, *Arming Japan: Defense Production, Alliance Politics, and the Post-War Search for Autonomy* (Columbia University Press, 1995).

7. For details see, Hideo Ōtake, *Nihon no Bōei to Kokunai Seiji (Japan's Defense and Domestic Politics)* (Sannichi Shoten, 1986).

8. Green, *Arming Japan*, p. 51.

9. Ibid., p. 18.

10. *"Hikaku 3 Gensoku wa Nansensu" (The Three Nonnuclear Principles Are Nonsense)*, *Kyodo Washington*, June 10, 2000.

11. Green, *Arming Japan*, p. 57.

12. Kōji Murata, *The Origins and the Evolution of the U.S.–ROK Alliance from a Japanese Perspective*, paper presented to the Conference on America's Alliances with Japan and Korea in a Changing Northeast Asia, Stanford University Asia-Pacific Research Center, August 21–23, 1998. See also, Kōji Murata, *Daitōryō no Zasetsu (A Setback of the President)* (Yūhikaku, 1998).

13. Then Chief of Naval Operations Admiral James L. Holloway argued in Congressional testimony on June 16, 1982 that "it is only with the assistance of the Japanese operating as a military ally, that the Japanese straits can be effectively denied to the Soviets." Cited in Eiichi Katahara, *The Politics of Japanese Defence Policy Making, 1975–89*, Doctoral Dissertation, Griffith University, Australia, April 1990, p. 192.

14. *Heisei Ninenpan Bōeihandobukku (Defense Handbook 1990)* (Asagumo Shimbunsha, 1990), p. 276.

15. "Guidelines for Japan-U.S. Defense Cooperation," report by the Subcommittee for Defense Cooperation, submitted to and approved by the Japan-U.S. Security Consultative Committee, November 27, 1978, Section II (Actions in Response to Armed Attack against Japan); (2); (i).

16. Interview with former Deputy Assistant Secretary of Defense for East Asia Morton Abramowitz, November 15, 1997. Cited in Michael J. Green and Kōji Murata, "The 1978 Guidelines for U.S.-Japan Defense Cooperation: Process and Historical Impact," Working Paper 17 (National Security Archives U.S.-Japan Alliance Project, June 2000).

17. "Joint Communiqué of President Ronald Reagan and Prime Minister Zenkō Suzuki," *Department of State Bulletin*, vol. 81, no. 2051, (June 1981), pp. 2–4.

18. Green, *Arming Japan*, p. 121; also described in "1982 *Bōei Yosan no Hensei Katei*" *(The Formation of the 1982 Defense Budget)*, a series in *Asahi Shimbun* that ran from February 16 to March 26, 1982.

19. Kiyofuku Chūma, *Saigunbi No Seijigaku (The Political Science of Rearmament)* (Chishikisha, 1985) p. 137.

20. U.S. Joint Chiefs of Staff, United States Military Posture FY 1982 (Department of Defense, 1982): p. 3.

21. *Mainichi Shimbun*, October 7, 1993, and interviews with JDA officials.

22. Advisory Group on Defense Issues, "The Modality of the Security and Defense Capability of Japan: Outlook for the 21st Century" (August 12, 1994—official English translation).

23. For details see Office of the Secretary of Defense, *East Asian Strategic Report*, February 1995.

24. See the conclusion to this volume for discussion of how the September 2001 terrorist attacks in New York and Washington may affect future U.S.-Japan security relations.

CHAPTER THREE

Economic Performance

WILLIAM W. GRIMES

The U.S.-Japan relationship in the postwar era has been distinctly asymmetrical, particularly in macroeconomic terms, with Japan far more dependent on the United States than the other way around. Japan's extraordinary rise as a world economic and techno- logical power changed the degree of asymmetry substantially, however, and created major frictions in the bilateral relationship. This chapter examines how the two countries' macroeconomic performance has affected bilateral relations over the past fifty years, and offers predictions about likely future effects. It finds that U.S.-Japan relations work most smoothly when Japa- nese growth does not exceed U.S. growth, and argues that foreseeable future trends in economic growth in the two countries are likely to contribute to less tense relations.

Macroeconomic performance affects the relationship directly by shifting the relative power of the two countries and determining the level and nature of economic interdependence.[1] It also affects the relationship indirectly by shaping perceptions on both sides regarding the two countries' relative eco- nomic strength, interdependence, and future prospects. In many cases perceptions have lagged reality. Americans were slow to recognize Japan's transformation into an economic superpower in the 1970s and Japan's turn toward stagnation in the 1990s, and they are likely to be late in recogniz- ing resurgence if and when it appears. Japanese were slow to grasp their own rising power in the world economy, at least until the 1980s, and they were slow to perceive the resurgence of the United States and their own economic crisis in the 1990s. When policymakers are slow to recognize meaningful change, they are likely to end up fighting the last war in domestic policies and in bilateral negotiations. U.S. policymakers have been particularly prone toward this type of misjudgment in their policy toward Japan.

Macroeconomic factors influence U.S.-Japan relations through both markets and policy. Their market effects include economic interdependence as seen in trade and financial flows. Although macroeconomic variables may appear apolitical in nature, however, they have probably had their most pronounced effects on intergovernmental relations. Over the past two decades, the two countries have increasingly focused their bilateral negotiations on macroeconomic issues, from exchange rates to budget deficits and fiscal stimulus plans. Moreover, both the reality and perceptions of the postwar period's massive shifts in macroeconomic variables have inevitably colored the overall bilateral relationship, in the worst cases contributing to substantial friction in the areas of trade, technology transfer, and security.

Measuring Friction

Unlike a number of the other topics covered in this volume, macroeconomic performance for the most part has not been the subject of specific negotiations or long-term agreements. Rather, differentials in macroeconomic variables form an important context for understanding other aspects of the relationship. For example, these variables underpin trade negotiations and the burden-sharing debate in security, in addition to the limited number of explicit attempts at macroeconomic policy coordination. For this reason, this chapter relies for the most part on indirect indicators of "friction." These include polling data on Japanese and U.S. public opinion toward each other and on the opinions of U.S. "leaders" toward Japan, in addition to sources on trade and policy coordination negotiations (see figure 1-1 in the introduction to this volume).[2]

While it is difficult to make categorical statements about levels of friction, one can make a few key generalizations. Most importantly, there have been two major troughs in U.S.-Japanese relations in the last two decades. The first appeared in 1987, followed by a plateau until around 1990, while the second ran from 1992 until 1995. In each, multiple quantitative and qualitative measures overlapped to produce much tenser relations than in the years before or since.

Overview

This chapter demonstrates how the reality and perceptions of macro-economic performance have affected U.S.-Japan relations in the postwar period, and makes some predictions about the future.

First, although Japan's rapid growth from early in the postwar period clearly complemented broad U.S. foreign policy goals, the concomitant rapid development of the Japanese economy proved to be politically disruptive within the United States. The speed with which Japanese firms swept into competitive or even dominant positions in a variety of sectors that had once been the exclusive province of the major Western economies led many in the United States (not to mention Europe) to view Japan as an adversarial trader. Japanese firms' entry into markets that had once seemed stable was so rapid that the industrial sectors of Japan's trading partners found adjustment difficult. This contributed to acute pain for both workers and management there (in some cases leading to fears of hollowing out of domestic industry), and then to political pressures to slow down the advance of Japanese products. While such changes were essentially micro-economic in nature and impact, they reflected the overall rise of labor and capital productivity in Japan in the postwar era.

Second, in the 1980s Japan and the United States executed an unprecedented macroeconomic *pas de deux*. Emerging current account deficits in the United States were financed largely by emerging current account surpluses in Japan, a situation that persisted through the 1980s and 1990s. Americans were able to consume and invest beyond their own income partly because of the thriftiness of Japanese savers, while Japanese firms and financial institutions with surplus funds got superior returns by investing their surplus outside the country—preeminently in the United States. There, the supply side of the great Keynesian experiment called Reaganomics would have been swallowed up by government deficits were it not for Japan's massive contribution to world savings. At the same time, high consumption in the United States kept workers employed in Japan, producing more than thrifty Japanese households were willing to consume. Similarly, the stagnation of the Japanese economy starting in the early 1990s was moderated by the voracious appetites of U.S. consumers and businesses caught up in the new economy. Since U.S. and Japanese business cycles have tended not to coincide completely, increased demand in one economy has often acted as a stabilizer for decreased demand in the other.

Third, despite the complementary nature of this *pas de deux*, current account and trade imbalances (particularly at the bilateral level) have fueled

Figure 3-1. *U.S.-Japan Trade Balance, 1950–99*

Millions of U.S. dollars

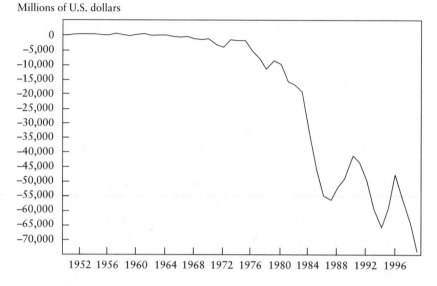

Source: U.S. Bureau of the Census, *Statistical Abstract of the United States*, 77th–120th eds., Washington, 1956–2000.

resentment, especially in the United States. One of the major bilateral stories of the past two decades has been the two governments' attempts to
reduce imbalances, for the good not only of the economic relationship, but
also of security and political cooperation. Bilateral trade and payments
imbalances have been at the core of some of the most contentious episodes
of the U.S.-Japan relationship, including trade frictions, exchange rate pressures, and attempts at macroeconomic policy coordination.

However, current account balances alone do not drive U.S.-Japan economic frictions. The United States has also focused on reducing trade and
current account imbalances for reasons of domestic macroeconomic conditions. U.S. public sentiment and government action have been most
concerned by international economic issues when the U.S. economy was suffering. This occurred in at least two ways.

To begin with, the very large U.S. trade deficits with Japan in the 1980s—
a period of high unemployment and weak growth in wages—led to strong
internal pressures to punish or contain Japan.[3] However, even larger deficits
(although not as a percentage of gross domestic product [GDP]) in the prosperous late 1990s had much less traction (figure 3-1). This observation
lends support to a scapegoating hypothesis: When the U.S. economy has

been weak, whether for reasons related to Japan or not, impatience with bilateral balances increases.

At the same time, U.S. fears of Japanese surpluses have closely tracked perceptions of the strength of the Japanese economy as a whole. The image of Japan as an economic juggernaut persisted well into the 1990s, even as Japanese economic growth fizzled. The Clinton administration took office with a strong disposition to try to contain Japan's allegedly predatory economy using any means necessary, from exchange rate manipulation to managed trade. While it soon stepped back from its most extreme statements, the actions of the new administration clearly reflected strong perceptions regarding Japan as an economic threat—presumably due to expectations that economic growth and technological transformation would remain significantly faster in Japan than in the United States.[4]

Macroeconomic Performance

In order to make this case, a brief review of macroeconomic performance in the two countries is in order.

Japan

Japanese economic growth for most of the postwar period clearly outstripped that of the United States (figure 3-2). This was to be expected under the standard growth model: in the postwar period the United States was consistently the most advanced (and thus most mature) economy, while Japan was playing catch-up. Therefore, it had large pools of underutilized factors of production and could benefit from improving its capital stock and by importing foreign technology. Japanese policies supported human capital development, savings, and a stable domestic macroeconomic environment to allow it to exploit the "advantages of backwardness."[5]

While Japan's investment remained very high as a percentage of income throughout the postwar period, savings were also extremely high. Since the mid-1960s, Japan has had a persistent surplus of savings over investment. That translated into first a trade surplus and then a current account surplus at the international level. By the mid-1980s, Japan had transformed itself from a poor debtor nation into a high-income creditor nation.

Notably, Japan continued to grow more rapidly than other economies at its level of development at any given point in time, and it succeeded in surmounting the challenges of the oil shocks and stagflation of the 1970s and

Figure 3-2. *Real GDP Growth Differential, 1956–98*[a]

Percent

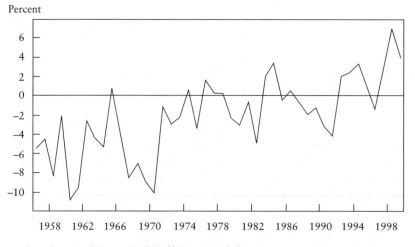

Source: International Monetary Fund, *World Economic Outlook*, various years.
a. Negative numbers show higher Japanese growth.

early 1980s. These achievements led to speculation that Japan had discovered a more effective means of economic management than other countries.[6]

The 1990s were a different story. Since 1992 Japan has been plagued by economic stagnation, mounting budget deficits, serious financial problems (including what can only be called a financial crisis in 1997–98), asset price deflation, and rising unemployment.[7] These economic woes have been accompanied by continuing high rates of household savings, and thus trade and current account surpluses. Unlike in previous years, when high savings were perceived as a strength, however, in the face of stagnation they have been problematic for Japan, since they imply depressed domestic demand. Income distribution appears still to be relatively equal, but this fact also carries a hidden irony. Japan's even distribution of income has at least partly been supported over time by government subsidies and protection to less productive sectors such as agriculture, which laid the groundwork for the expansion of unproductive investments and structural rigidities that now appear to be slowing economic recovery.[8]

United States

The United States began the postwar period as the world's preeminent economic power, and it has essentially stayed in that position in terms of total national income and per capita living standards. However, its relative lead in income has declined progressively. Looking at growth rates, despite obvious fluctuations, trend GDP followed a growth path that gently declined from 4.0 to 4.5 percent in the 1950s and 1960s to around 3 percent in the 1970s, 1980s, and 1990s.

From the mid-1990s, economic and productivity growth increased well above earlier trends, perhaps due to the impact of information technology. This led some to suggest that there had been an economic paradigm shift, dubbed the "new economy." Together with economic growth, asset prices and investment soared. Unexpected revenue gains contributed to the elimination of the central government deficit for the first time in decades, but private savings declined from their already low levels, perhaps due to wealth effects. The result was that current account deficits actually grew despite the elimination of the budget deficit.

In terms of its international impact, the United States' transformation into a debtor country is surely one of the most important stories of the postwar period. Though it started the postwar period as such an important creditor and supplier of capital and liquidity that economists in the 1950s openly fretted about the "dollar shortage," by 1986 it had become a net debtor. While trade numbers have been quite volatile, the United States has consistently been in trade deficit since 1976 and current account deficit since 1983. This has made the United States by far the world's largest net debtor nation. Despite real fears in the 1980s that U.S. current account surpluses might be unsustainable, however, U.S. external debt has continued to increase and foreigners have continued to be willing to finance it in dollars.[9]

Macroeconomic Interdependence

U.S.-Japan macroeconomic interdependence has been substantial yet asymmetric for the entire postwar period. In trade, Japanese, growth was dependent on U.S. demand for much of the period, especially in the 1950s and 1960s. Exports to the rest of the world, and particularly to the United States, have often played the role of buffer for excess production (both structural and cyclical) in the years since as well. Over time, imports have helped to keep domestic U.S. price levels stable in the face of excess demand. Nonetheless, America's relatively low level of dependence on world trade means that it is less dependent on the bilateral relationship than Japan, despite popular fears about the effects of bilateral trade deficits (figure 3-3).[10]

In terms of finance as well, the two countries' macroeconomic performances have helped to drive interdependence. This has been particularly true

Figure 3-3. *Total Trade by Partner, 1969–98*

Percent

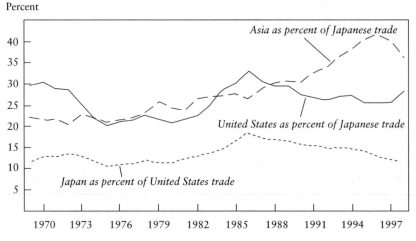

Asia as percent of Japanese trade

United States as percent of Japanese trade

Japan as percent of United States trade

40
35
30
25
20
15
10
5

1970   1973   1976   1979   1982   1985   1988   1991   1994   1997

Source: International Monetary Fund, *Direction of Trade Statistics*, various years.

since the late 1970s, as U.S. current accounts started moving into negative territory and Japan's began to move into persistent surplus. The result is that excess Japanese savings have flowed in large amounts to the United States, where they contributed to financing large budget deficits and excess demand.

These forms of interdependence have had political overtones as well. Both the bilateral trade imbalance and the large amount of Japanese investment and lending in the United States have raised fears at various times of hollowing out and of the possibility of economic dependence on Japan.[11] In Japan the denomination of U.S. debt in dollars has meant that depreciation of the dollar over time (and in specific instances) has led to losses in yen terms, which has stirred some Japanese resentment over perceived dependence on the United States.[12]

International Macroeconomic Issues

The combination of significant interdependence and often divergent macroeconomic performance between the two countries has brought macroeconomic issues to the negotiating table. These include not only exchange rates, but also each country's fiscal and monetary policies.

Exchange Rates

The yen-dollar exchange rate has seen a long-term appreciation of the yen in nominal terms since 1971, albeit with several prolonged reversals and large-scale volatility. (The appreciation has been much more modest in real terms due to consistently lower inflation in Japan.) The Japanese government has tended to be sensitive to movements in the nominal value of the yen, particularly resisting sharp appreciation. The government has often engaged in large-scale intervention in currency markets, and thus accumulated large amounts of foreign currency (mainly U.S. dollars) in official foreign exchange reserves—$357 billion as of August 31, 2001.

The United States has in general been far less active in trying to manipulate exchange rates. There have been several important exceptions, however, including the dollar rescue plan of 1978, the Plaza Agreement of 1985, the Louvre Accord of 1987, and other episodes of extreme misalignment in 1995 and 1998.[13] Also, it is widely agreed that the United States has talked down the dollar on occasion in order to put pressure on Japan, at least until well into 1995.

Exchange rate coordination (with the exceptions of 1978 and 1995) has usually meant that the United States and Japan acted together to increase the value of the yen in order to deal with the politically sensitive bilateral trade imbalance. While these efforts may have had some effects in the short term or medium term, they did not fundamentally alter either country's current account balance because they did not fundamentally change savings-investment balances in either economy. Thus Japan remained an overall creditor, and the United States remained an overall debtor. Due to trade structure and other factors, the bilateral imbalance also remained.

Macroeconomic Policy Coordination

In order to deal with the continuing payment imbalances without having a negative impact on world economic demand, Japan and the United States have also engaged in a number of negotiations over macroeconomic policy over the last quarter century. While several have involved other major economies—most notably, the London-Bonn Summit efforts of 1977–78 and the Plaza-Louvre efforts of 1985–87—bilateral negotiations about macroeconomics have been a frequent feature of U.S.-Japan relations.[14] The 1989–90 Structural Impediments Initiative (SII) specifically included U.S. and Japanese savings-investment balances as one of its four main pillars. Subsequently, the Clinton administration was often associated with calls for Japanese domestic demand expansion, particularly in 1993–94 and from 1997 onward.[15]

While the players and the specific situations may change, most negotiations have involved calls for greater Japanese demand growth in exchange for a reduction in excess U.S. demand.[16] Like exchange rate coordination, however, these agreements have not had long-term effects on the balance of payments. One reason is that—even where discussions of macroeconomic policy were presented to the world as mutual—there is virtually no evidence that such efforts ever had any effects on U.S. policy. On some occasions, however, they have had serious implications for the Japanese domestic economy.

The best example of this can be seen in the Japanese asset price bubble of the late 1980s, the bursting of which has been a major contributor to the financial problems and economic stagnation of the 1990s.[17] In the face of both a rapidly appreciating yen and internal and external pressure to stimulate domestic demand, Japanese monetary policy from 1986 to 1989 was highly expansionary. Easy money helped to fuel a rapid rise in stock and real estate loans. When policy shifted away from expansion, the asset prices crashed, laying the groundwork for a decade of severe financial problems. Certainly, the Japanese government's macroeconomic policy mix and financial regulation during both the bubble and its aftermath were the core of Japan's problems, but the bubble would likely not have occurred without the original international pressures for demand stimulation—or at least, without the pressures of a rapid rise in the value of the yen.

Ironically, despite the considerable political capital dedicated by U.S. administrations to encouraging Japanese demand in the 1980s and 1990s, the effects on the United States of both macroeconomic coordination efforts and changes in Japanese aggregate demand have been far more limited. Actually, the irony is only partial—most macroeconomic models have consistently predicted that changes in Japanese domestic demand should have little impact on the U.S. economy.[18] Despite the only marginal positive effects on bilateral imbalances (at least in dollar terms), macroeconomic policy coordination may well have reduced some of the contentiousness of other negotiations, especially in trade, by diverting attention from those specific issues toward more complex discussions.

Ironies for Macroeconomic Coordination since 1998

While a number of respected economists and policymakers continue to call for negotiations on macroeconomic policy, the close of the twentieth century has thrown a curveball. Both of the major intermediate goals of advocates of bilateral coordination came to pass with surprising swiftness and magnitude—U.S. budget deficits turned to surpluses, and Japan turned heavily toward fiscal stimulation—but the long-expected effects on savings-investment imbalances did not occur.

Japanese private saving has outstripped private investment by so much that even a central government deficit equal to 40 percent of total outlays did not mean an appreciable reduction in the country's current account surplus. Meanwhile, the massive improvement in the U.S. government's net fiscal position was leapfrogged by even more massive decreases in private savings relative to investment, and U.S. current account deficits actually increased.

Such household and corporate behavior probably reflects wealth effects (positive in the United States in the 1990s, negative in Japan) and precautionary saving by Japanese workers who feared losing their jobs or their future pension entitlements. So it is perhaps not surprising—at least in hindsight. Nevertheless, it appears to call into question much of the rationale for trying to coordinate macroeconomic policies. This assessment may be unfair, however, insofar as U.S. calls for Japanese monetary and fiscal stimulation since the mid-1990s have been far more focused on improving prospects for the Japanese economy than on reducing current account imbalances. This has been seen as important for both developed country growth and, especially after the onset of the Asian financial crisis in 1997, for the health and recovery of the developing and middle-income economies of East and Southeast Asia. In this sense the discourse on macroeconomic policy between the two governments should perhaps no longer be seen as being about "coordination" at all. Whether there remains a market in Japan for continued U.S. advice regarding how to manage the economy remains to be seen, but the discussion clearly appears to be a different ballgame from the tired, often disappointing rounds of attempts at coordination in the 1970s and 1980s. Interestingly, even in the face of prolonged bad economic performance, relatively few Japanese seemed to blame the more prosperous United States for their hardships, despite occasional frustrations with unsolicited advice from U.S. policymakers.

Perceptions versus Reality

The changing aims of macroeconomic policy negotiations point to another broad area of interest regarding macroeconomic performance—the problem of perception. Chapter 4 by Nitta looks closely at the various roles played by mutual images in the bilateral relationship, so this chapter will not discuss the general ways in which each country's image of itself and the other might contribute to or detract from the relationship. But it is important to note that perceptions have consistently lagged actual macroeconomic performance.

This statement is neither surprising nor remarkable: the economics profession has been much better at explaining marginal changes than major changes, and it has been major changes in the two economies that have consistently been missed by economists, economic actors, and policymakers. Four are most glaring: the rapid rise of Japan from developing economy in the 1950s to second-largest world economy in the 1970s; the rise of Japan as a creditor nation and the nearly simultaneous switch of the United States from world's largest creditor to world's largest debtor in the space of only a few years; Japan's economic chaos and stagnation in the 1990s; and the resurgence of the U.S. economy from the mid-1990s until 2001 (see table 3-1).

Perception lags can be serious when they lead to policies that fight the last war. In the case of the United States and Japan, the slowness of the United States to perceive Japan's rise as a major economic power may have contributed to a *laissez-faire* attitude toward Japan's continued violations of international trade and investment norms through the 1970s. Later, U.S. inability to see that Japan's economy really was in serious trouble by 1992 or 1993 and that its own economy was moving into an unprecedented period of productivity increases made it more confrontational in trade and security matters than it might otherwise have been in the early years of the Clinton administration.

Japanese leaders, similarly, were slow to recognize their own postwar rise in either income or current account surpluses, and thus were slow to realize the destabilizing economic and political effects that their continuing efforts at export promotion might have on other countries.[19] For several years in the early and mid-1990s, Japanese macroeconomic and financial policymakers were also unable to comprehend the stagnation of the 1990s as anything more than a cyclical downturn.

Thus misperception appears to have had several negative effects on both domestic and international economic policies over the last twenty to thirty years. Ironically, it may have had some beneficial effects as well. For example, Americans' inability to recognize the rapidity of Japan's rise may have allowed for smoother security relations in the 1970s and early 1980s. Also, had they been followed, the macroeconomic suggestions pressed on Japan

Table 3-1. *Real Growth Differentials, U.S.-Japan, 1980–2000*[a]
Percent

Year	Actual	Predicted same year	Predicted next year
1980	−3.0	−5.0	n.a.
1981	−0.7	−1.6	n.a.
1982	−5.1	−4.5	n.a.
1983	2.0	−0.4	n.a.
1984	3.4	2.3	−0.1
1985	−0.6	−0.9	−1.3
1986	0.5	−0.1	0.4
1987	−0.8	−0.4	−0.2
1988	−2.0	−1.2	−1.1
1989	−1.3	−1.4	−1.9
1990	−3.3	−2.7	−1.9
1991	−4.3	−3.4	−1.2
1992	2.0	−0.6	−0.4
1993	2.4	1.9	−0.3
1994	3.4	3.2	0.3
1995	1.2	1.4	−1.6
1996	−1.5	−0.9	−0.9
1997	2.8	0.8	−0.7
1998	6.9	2.9	0.9
1999	3.9	4.7	1.9
2000	n.a.	3.5	1.2

n.a. Not available.

Source: Expected figures are for GNP, and are from the IMF, *World Economic Outlook*, various years. The *Outlook* is published three times a year; the figures in this table come from the first issue of each year (April, May, or June, depending on the year), with the exception of 1984, which uses the September issue.

a. These differentials are obtained by subtracting Japanese real growth from U.S. real growth.

by the United States in the early years of the Clinton administration would probably have been appropriate for dealing with Japan's actual economic situation, even though the administration's motivation had far more to do with creating markets for U.S. exports. Even U.S. budget surpluses might never have materialized had policymakers recognized the domestic economy's actual growth potential—if they could have anticipated increased revenues, it is likely that those revenues would have been swallowed up in higher spending or tax cuts.

Explaining the Past

In looking back at the last half century, it is clear that the varying macroeconomic performances of the United States and Japan have had important effects on bilateral economic relations, as well as on the overall relationship. This chapter has not directly addressed the importance that U.S. administrations placed on making Japan a showcase of capitalism in East Asia, or the important historical role of the United States as a market for Japanese exports, significant though those were. Indeed it would be difficult to argue that the lessons of the relationship during the years of reconstruction can be directly applied to current or future bilateral relations, although indirectly the habits and institutions developed during those years may well have lasting significance.[20]

But over the last twenty to thirty years, several important trends have emerged in the effects of macroeconomic performance on the relationship that seem likely to continue to be salient into the future. The Japanese economy has become an important target of U.S. foreign economic policy, especially in terms of negotiations over trade and investment, in addition to episodic attempts at macroeconomic coordination. While bilateral tensions have taken many forms, however, differentials in macroeconomic performance have been a key driver of many of those tensions.

Changes in Relative Economic Power

Better macroeconomic performance in Japan than in the United States—both perceived and real—has been particularly important in creating tensions. As the magnitude of Japan's economy has grown from an insignificant fraction of American economic power in the early postwar era to close to 50 percent, U.S. expectations and attitudes toward Japan have changed dramatically (figure 3-4).[21]

A clear example of this can be seen in the "burden sharing" debate described in chapter 2 in this volume. That debate makes sense only insofar as Japan is seen as being economically strong enough to pay for its own defense, and perhaps even more able to do so than a fiscally strapped United States. In trade and investment as well, size matters: the damage caused to economic partners by exclusionary economic practices increases with the size of the market relative to other potential markets, while "predatory" trade practices are also more important the larger is the offending firm or country as a share of total supply. Finally, Japan's extraordinarily rapid growth also meant rapid technological transformation, and thus rapid inroads into product areas that had previously been comfortably dominated by its major trading partners in the West.

A broader political point seems to hold as well, particularly from the mid-1980s onward. U.S. policymakers and others began to see Japan's economic power as a threat to U.S. global power.[22] The logic proceeds directly from standard realist assumptions: that power and security are relative,

Figure 3-4. *Japanese Nominal GDP as a Share of*
U.S. Nominal GDP, 1955–99[a]

Percent

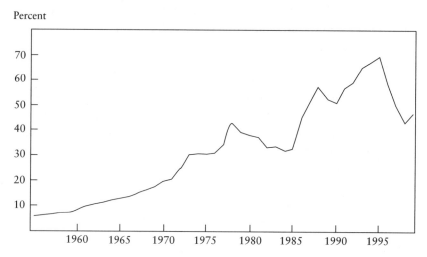

Source: U.S. Bureau of Economic Analysis; Japanese Economic Planning Agency.
a. Exchange rate basis.

and that economic power can be transformed into military or political power.[23] Thus the rise of Japan appeared to some to mean the relative decline of the United States, and the rate at which it was occurring made adjustment difficult. At the same time, Japan's increasing overall economic strength (in addition to its firms' dominance in certain product areas, as seen in chapter 9 of this volume) made Japan less dependent on U.S. markets and international political support, and thus less willing to give in to U.S. demands on it.

There are two ways of refining this general statement as hypotheses:

—Increases in the size of the Japanese economy relative to the U.S. economy (whether in real terms or at current exchange rates) created U.S. concern about America's position in the international political economy, and thus led to greater tensions.

—Japan's economic rise made it less willing to accede to U.S. demands. In combination with the other relative power hypothesis, this should have increased actual conflict in the relationship.

Insofar as perceptions have lagged economic reality, it also should be expected that perceptions of U.S. and Japanese macroeconomic strength will often be the better indicator of the threat felt by both U.S. and Japanese policymakers.

The evidence is consistent with these hypotheses. While it is probably impossible to come up with a rigorous measure of friction—and thus impossible to test quantitatively—we see clear evidence that Japan's economic rise contributed to greater friction. Looking at both real growth rates and the (economically ambiguous but politically important) measure of the relative size of the two economies at current exchange rates, the periods of most rapid Japanese relative growth are nearly the same as the troughs in relations described in the introduction to this volume (see figure 1-1 as well as table 3-1 and figures 3-2 and 3-4 in this chapter). In each of the tensest periods (at least until 1993), objective predictions saw Japanese growth as likely to continue to lead U.S. growth, which is consistent with the usual lag of expectations in catching up with actual conditions. This allows us to make sense of the continuing high level of U.S. governmental pressure into 1995, even as it was becoming apparent to many observers that the Japanese economy was subsiding as even a potential challenger to U.S. hegemony.

Scapegoating?

An alternative way of looking at U.S.-Japanese tensions created by differential macroeconomic performance is through the lens of domestic politics. While it is hard to see how domestic actors might be directly affected by another country's macroeconomic performance, it is a truism that economic conditions within a country have profound effects on domestic politics. Rising unemployment, rising inflation, and low growth all tend to create political dissatisfaction, and in turn a search for scapegoats.[24] Where there is another country (or region, class or ethnic group) that appears to be profiting during one's own misery, then that country may be an attractive target for blame (table 3-2).

In looking at U.S.-Japanese relations, then, we should consider the possibility that economic tensions have been more the result of dissatisfactions with growth or employment in the United States than of a clear causal link between Japanese success and U.S. downturns. In other words U.S.-Japan tensions should rise with slowdowns in the U.S. growth rate or rises in the U.S. unemployment rate, regardless of current Japanese macroeconomic performance or bilateral trade deficits.[25] Indeed, during periods of strong U.S. growth, tensions have been lower regardless of bilateral variables such as the trade balance or levels of direct investment. As in so many areas, scapegoating appears to occur asymmetrically: U.S. downturns since at least the early 1980s have inspired tensions in the relationship, while Japanese downturns have not caused much Japanese resentment toward the United States.

Table 3-2. *U.S. Economic Growth and Trade Deficits, 1969–99*

Year	U.S. growth (real GDP)	U.S. deficit (billions of U.S. dollars)		Japan (as percent)	Increase in U.S. trade deficit (percent)	
		With Japan	With world		With Japan	With world
1969	3.00	−1.398	1.963	−71.22	. . .	. . .
1970	0.20	−1.588	0.795	−199.75	13.59	−59.50
1971	3.30	−3.647	−4.212	86.59	129.66	−629.81
1972	5.40	−4.636	−9.104	50.92	27.12	116.14
1973	5.80	−1.934	−2.236	86.49	−58.28	−75.44
1974	−0.60	−2.646	−9.489	27.88	36.81	324.37
1975	−0.40	−2.773	4.203	−65.98	4.80	−144.29
1976	5.60	−6.778	−17.085	39.67	144.43	−506.50
1977	4.60	−9.674	−39.179	24.69	42.73	129.32
1978	5.50	−13.586	−42.279	32.13	40.44	7.91
1979	3.20	−10.576	−40.203	26.31	−22.16	−4.91
1980	−0.20	−12.183	−36.198	33.66	15.19	−9.96
1981	2.50	−18.081	−39.613	45.64	48.41	9.43
1982	−2.00	−18.965	−38.442	49.33	4.89	−2.96
1983	4.30	−21.665	−64.239	33.73	14.24	67.11
1984	7.30	−36.796	−122.388	30.07	69.84	90.52
1985	3.80	−49.749	−133.648	37.22	35.20	9.20
1986	3.40	−58.575	−154.988	37.79	17.74	15.97
1987	3.40	−59.825	−169.958	35.20	2.13	9.66
1988	4.20	−55.508	−137.515	40.37	−7.22	−19.09
1989	3.50	−52.526	−129.11	40.68	−5.37	−6.11
1990	1.80	−44.485	−123.395	36.05	−15.31	−4.43
1991	−0.50	−46.863	−86.633	54.09	5.35	−29.79
1992	3.00	−51.717	−105.759	48.90	10.36	22.08
1993	2.70	−62.468	−138.665	45.05	20.79	31.11
1994	4.00	−68.989	−176.694	39.04	10.44	27.43
1995	2.70	−62.897	−187.094	33.62	−8.83	5.89
1996	3.60	−50.427	−196.952	25.60	−19.83	5.27
1997	4.40	−58.593	−210.323	27.86	16.19	6.79
1998	4.40	−67.203	−262.215	25.63	14.69	24.67
1999	4.20	−76.276	−357.337	21.35	13.50	36.28

Source: Bureau of Economic Analysis; International Monetary Fund, *Direction of Trade Statistics Yearbook*, various years.

Asymmetry and the Dynamics of the Relationship

Meanwhile, power asymmetries clearly contribute strongly to the ways in which these forces actually play out in the bilateral relationship. At its core, the U.S.-Japan relationship is an asymmetric one, whether in terms of economics, security, or international rulemaking. In economics Japan has clearly been more dependent on the United States than vice versa, as seen in a variety of statistics. Most obviously, U.S.-Japanese bilateral trade has consistently been a larger percentage of Japan's total trade than of America's (over 25 percent for Japan for most of the 1980s and 1990s, versus under 15 percent for the United States), and that has been even more true for exports than for imports.[26] Asia as a whole has been a larger market for Japanese exports and supplier of Japanese imports than the United States for over a decade, but there is no one bilateral trading relationship that even comes close to that with the United States.

Japan's relatively higher dependence than the United States on bilateral trade links has made it much more sensitive to U.S. demands than the United States has been toward Japanese desires. (The asymmetry is, of course, even greater in the security sphere.) This may be seen in the fact that Japan has generally given in to U.S. demands for trade concessions such as market-opening measures and voluntary export restraints.[27] It is also seen in the sensitivity of the Japanese government to changes in the yen-dollar exchange rate, whereas the U.S. government has responded in a forceful manner to changes in alignment only intermittently, and generally only when they were very large.[28] Similarly, episodes of macroeconomic and exchange rate policy coordination have focused on increasing Japanese (and third country) demand rather than on supporting U.S. efforts to decrease budget or trade deficits.[29]

As asymmetry declined over time, however, this dynamic should have decreased. It is difficult to say to what extent that is true, since Japan's relative rise should have simultaneously created many more potential bilateral disputes. However, there is some evidence to be found in the 1990s of a new Japanese willingness to "say no," as seen in the disputes in 1993 over objective indicators, in 1994–95 over automobiles and auto parts, and in the refusal to even consider renewing the semiconductor agreement in 1996. It is difficult to make definitive statements about any of these high-profile episodes, given that the circumstances in any given bilateral dispute differ so much over time, but at the time they were considered harbingers of a new Japanese ability to express its opposition to U.S. pressures.

Another way in which this overall dynamic may be changing is that Japan's dependence on U.S. markets has declined significantly. Since 1988 a larger share of Japanese trade (and since 1991, a larger share of Japanese exports) has been with Asian countries than with the United States, a trend that accelerated rapidly in the 1990s. While there has by no means been a turning away from the United States toward Asia, the trend does suggest that Japan is no longer as dependent on U.S. markets as in previous decades.

Complementarity in Macroeconomic Performance

While many of the details of the relationship have been about tensions, the fact remains that trends in the two countries' macroeconomic performance have been beneficial to both in a broader sense and have contributed to long-term mutual gain. That has been particularly true on the Japanese side, where U.S. demand has been an important source of growth for producers, particularly in higher value-added products. More broadly, the bilateral relationship has been reinforced by the basic complementarity of the two economies at the macroeconomic level, both cyclically and long term.

Japanese and U.S. business cycles have often diverged over the years.[30] Although this pattern can create resentments when one partner (especially the United States) is slumping while the other is booming, it is also essentially beneficial to both. Increased demand in one economy can serve as a sort of shock absorber for producers in the other when it is suffering depressed demand. So although the relative growth gap at any given time can create frictions, the pains caused by business cycles would be far worse if those cycles were identical in the two economies.

Longer term as well, the macroeconomic patterns in the United States and Japan have complemented each other. This has been clearest in the balances of trade and payments over the last thirty years. Japanese savers have helped to subsidize the consumption and investment appetites of the U.S. economy, by protecting them from the dangers of crowding out. U.S. consumers have helped Japanese firms and labor to produce beyond the desires of their domestic economy. The long-term financing of U.S. current account deficits has been possible largely because of Japanese surpluses. Whether long-term U.S. deficits are a good thing is debatable, but the complementarity of the two economies and its positive results on U.S. and Japanese standards of living and wealth are clear.

Predictions

The preceding section identified enduring trends that help to explain behavior for extended periods of time. These trends accord not only with experience in the U.S.-Japan relationship, but also with widely held theories of political behavior. Thus they should also be useful in providing broad predictions of the future when juxtaposed with reasonable predictions of macroeconomic performance.

Effects of Growth Patterns

One of the most compelling conclusions about the past is that U.S.-Japan relations are smoothest when the U.S. economy is strong, both in absolute and relative terms. This reflects several possible causes, including U.S. fears of declining hegemony, scapegoating, and asymmetric interdependence. While Japan has experienced a variety of macroeconomic triumphs and tribulations, bilateral relations have been far more affected by changes in the United States. For most of the last thirty years or so, that pattern has meant continuing tension in the relationship, as Japanese growth outstripped U.S. growth, and the U.S. economy was beset by several key challenges, including stagflation in the 1970s and early 1980s, massive current account deficits in the 1980s and 1990s, and recession again in the early 1990s. Moreover, lagging perceptions meant that U.S. fears over relative decline continued to drive an aggressive official posture toward Japan at least into 1995.

This long-term irritant is now likely to abate, as expected growth patterns in the United States and Japan favor the United States over both the medium and long terms. While the U.S. productivity growth seen in 1997–2000 was clearly unsustainable, real increases appeared likely to resume following the difficult economic adjustments of 2001 and the short- to medium-term economic consequences of the horrendous terrorist attacks of September 11. Meanwhile, the natural rate of unemployment appears to have declined considerably, even though cyclical swings are sure to continue. The generally positive long-term outlook for the United States reflects high levels of labor mobility and of innovation and adoption of productivity-enhancing technologies.

In Japan on the other hand, long-term growth prospects no longer outstrip those of the United States, due to structural rigidities, large structural budget deficits, a financial system still suffering from a large stock of non-performing loans, and a rapidly aging society. For at least a decade and a half, Japan, as one of the world's most advanced economies, has no longer been able to increase productivity easily just by adopting the technologies and best practices of more advanced countries. Moreover, even high levels of gross investment will not create rapid growth in an economy that already has such a large capital stock, unless returns on capital increase sharply. In the medium term at least, structural rigidities such as regulation and the employment system will also retard structural adjustment into growth areas.[31]

Furthermore, an aging society, declining work force, and real fiscal constraints (not only the budget deficit, but also large unfunded national pension obligations) mean much lower potential growth for the longer term as well. Both Japan and the United States face the issue of low birth rates and rising life expectancy, but this will be a particular problem for Japan. The rapidity of the transformation of Japan into a society of senior citizens—currently about one-sixth of the population, but expected to rise to around a quarter in the next twenty years or so—is of a different order of magnitude than that being faced by the United States. This is largely due to different levels of immigration, which has kept the U.S. age profile relatively young and helped to continue the funding of national pension obligations. Organization for Economic Cooperation and Development (OECD) projections suggest that there will be only 2.2 workers for every senior citizen in Japan, which could put an untenable strain on society, politics, and the economy.[32] There are a number of options that remain for Japan, including increasing immigration, expanding female participation in the work force, and raising the retirement age, but none of these will be easy. Thus it is reasonable to expect that demographics will be a long-term drag on the Japanese economy.

This does not mean poverty for Japan or unending prosperity for the United States, but it does suggest that the kinds of large growth differentials in favor of Japan that once created discord are on their way out. Nor does it mean that tensions will disappear—business cycles (and the possibility that Japan will be cycling upward as the United States slows down) could again contribute to short-term tensions. The simultaneous downturns throughout most of the world in 2001, and particularly after the September 11 attacks, may provide one such example. But over the long term, tensions caused by differentials in macroeconomic performance are likely to be more muted, more occasional, and more temporary than the continuous refrain to which policymakers and publics on both sides of the Pacific grew accustomed in the 1970s, 1980s, and 1990s.

One possible new source of tension would be if Japanese people and leaders were to become resentful of the United States if the current decade-long stagnation continues indefinitely. At various points in the 1990s, some in Japan argued strongly that the country's economic problems were the result of U.S. actions, particularly the imposition of international capital-adequacy standards for banks at the end of the 1992 fiscal year and an alleged lack of U.S. concern over the Asian financial crisis in 1997–98. Although such complaints will likely always be around, it is hard to imagine them leading to really serious tensions in the bilateral relationship because of Japan's general isolation in the world political system and the continued importance to it of U.S. markets.

Effects of Savings-Investment Patterns

Likely patterns of savings-investment balances also suggest a turn of U.S. concern away from Japan. One of the major irritants in the relationship has long concerned the extent to which Japanese savings have been seen to finance U.S. spending and consumption.[33] At various points, Americans have expressed concern that assets owned by Japanese firms in the form of real assets, securities, or debt instruments threatened to place them in a dependent position. This was especially true in the late 1980s and early 1990s, when Japanese investment in and lending to U.S. private and public actors was increasing most sharply. The hysteria among some writers is exemplified by the breathless title of one 1989 book on the subject—*Selling Out: How We Are Letting Japan Buy Our Land, Our Industries, Our Financial Institutions, and Our Future.*[34]

While U.S. savings are extremely low relative to investment (resulting in immense current account deficits), the elimination of large federal budget deficits for the foreseeable future will reduce the need for the United States to force macroeconomic adjustment on its partners. Importantly, the United States need not worry about financing its own government operations from abroad, which should reduce some of the incentive for state action. (This point holds despite the abrupt disappearance of the U.S. fiscal surplus in 2001.) As for the private sector, consumption behavior should correlate more positively with growth than do government deficits. Thus if U.S. economic growth declines, so might current account deficits.[35] If that is the case, then scapegoating may also become less attractive.

In any event, trends in Japan are likely to turn any such attention away from it, and toward other emerging surplus nations, such as China. The aging of Japan's society should reduce net savings over time, and the continuing movement of production abroad will eliminate some of the pressures caused by bilateral trade imbalances. Together, these trends should make it a progressively less obvious target for U.S. pressure, even if the U.S. government does attempt to shift the costs of macroeconomic adjustment abroad.

Changes in Interdependence?

Even as relative gaps in macroeconomic variables such as growth and net savings in the two countries are likely to stabilize, patterns of interdependence are also shifting. In terms of trade and investment, the share of bilateral U.S.-Japan trade is declining from its late 1980s peaks in both countries, which reduces at least some of the most exploitable dependency.[36] At the same time, the globalization of production and services in many industries has made for more "deep integration" among economies—in other words, the development of multiple, multilateral, overlapping ties among firms and economies.

The form of interdependence is basically a microeconomic issue, but it shapes the ways in which macro variables pass through political systems. Two features of U.S.-Japanese interdependence stand out in this regard. First is the rising degree of intra-industry trade. Japan's trade profile has for many years been characterized by extremely low levels of intra-industry trade, suggesting low levels of interdependence within sectors. The extreme one-sidedness of Japanese trade in a variety of manufacturing sectors meant that damages to one U.S. producer in a given industry were unlikely to be offset by benefits to another within that sector—a clear recipe for political friction. Thus Japan's rising share of intra-industry trade in the 1990s suggests that even large movements in macro variables such as the U.S., Japanese, or bilateral trade balances may be less politically and socially inflammatory than in recent memory. Large movements should also be less likely in the first place, for reasons already addressed in this chapter.

Another important change is the apparent increase in cooperation between Japanese and U.S. firms, in terms of joint research and product development, joint production, and design-in vendor relationships. While U.S. and Japanese firms still compete vigorously with rivals on both sides of the Pacific, the number and magnitude of transnational corporate alliances appears to have increased considerably in the 1990s, especially the latter half of the decade. This is seen not only in the activities of troubled companies (such as Nissan, Mazda, and Mitsubishi Motors), but even in the activities of strong and confident manufacturers like Toyota and Intel. Thus we see a move from arm's-length interdependence as typified in interindustry trade and portfolio investment toward a deeper level of integration, raising the level of common interest and reducing the likelihood of rapid swings in trade and investment balances.

If these trends continue, there will be less leverage for the U.S. government to try to affect Japanese behavior because more U.S. producers in a given industry would be adversely affected by trade sanctions of any kind. There will also be less incentive to do so since there will be ever fewer "purely" Japanese or U.S. firms. This is indeed a hopeful sign as we begin the next fifty years of U.S.-Japan relations.

Perceptions

Finally, there seems to be no reason to expect that perceptions will not again lag or misrepresent reality. Perhaps even the "realities" presented here will soon prove to be misperceptions. However, the most likely source of misperceptions over the long term is shifts of economic paradigm rather than major shifts in the relative growth prospects of either economy. The maturation of both economies means that both should expect relatively moderate growth over the long term, with neither rapidly outstripping the other in terms of per capita income. (Population will be another story, of course, so the overall size of the U.S. economy is sure to grow relative to that of Japan.) Thus although there is always the danger of "fighting the last war" in any human endeavor, there seems to be reason to be cautiously optimistic that mistaken or lagged perceptions will not have a serious negative effect on long-term bilateral relations.

Conclusions

The U.S. and Japanese economies have been locked together in a tight embrace for the entire postwar period. Despite the mutual benefits of the relationship, macroeconomic performance has also been a source of tension. The rapid rise of Japanese economic strength over the period led in the United States to real (albeit exaggerated) fears of economic oblivion and to real annoyance with perceived Japanese free riding. For Japan the rapidity of the rise made it difficult to adjust to changed international expectations by changing its international profile, and later blinded many to the fragility of the post-bubble economy. By the 1980s scapegoating of Japan by influential political and economic actors in the United States had also become evident.

These long-term irritants contributed to concrete—and often sharp—bilateral conflict, including President Nixon's threat to use the Trading with the Enemy Act in 1971, the burden-sharing debates of the 1980s and 1990s, the passage of an Omnibus Trade Bill with enhanced ("Super") Section

301 in 1988, and the great automobile and auto parts confrontation of 1995, among others. Long-term issues were accompanied on occasion by the issue of divergent business cycles. Such divergence was especially politically inflammatory when U.S. growth was stagnant while Japanese growth was healthy.

Looking to the future, if these hypotheses concerning past relations are generally correct, and assumptions regarding future macroeconomic performance are also correct, we should expect less acrimonious bilateral relations over time. Despite the prospect of worldwide global economic downturn, the dawn of the twenty-first century still offers hope for an abatement of both long-term and cyclical tensions resulting from differential macroeconomic performance in the two countries, even while mutual economic benefits will remain important to both.

Notes

1. Macroeconomic performance in this chapter concentrates on GDP (level and growth), employment, government finances, and balance of payments. On these macroeconomic criteria, the U.S.-Japan relationship has been a fascinating study in contrasts and role reversals.

2. On public opinion, two data sets are used for this chapter. The longer and more consistent is the Yomiuri/Gallup poll conducted in both countries on an annual basis since 1978. Also referenced are the less complete Chicago Council on Foreign Relations quadrennial polls of U.S. public and "leaders" on foreign policy issues. It is somewhat difficult to present a fully consistent set of results, since questions in the polls vary either subtly or substantially from year to year—and even in the case of the Yomiuri/Gallup polls, there are some interesting questions that have appeared and reappeared in various years somewhat unpredictably. A data set on trade negotiations prepared by Amy Searight and Christopher Way (see Amy Searight and Christopher Way, "International Economic Disputes: A Report on Data for U.S.-Japan Disputes 1968–96," n.d., mimeo) also buttresses these judgments.

3. James Fallows, "Containing Japan," *Atlantic*, May 1989, pp. 40–54. Annual polling data from Yomiuri Shimbun show clear downturns around 1987 in both U.S. and Japanese public approval of the other, and the Chicago Council on Foreign Relations quadrennial polls of U.S. leaders found in 1990 that 63 percent felt that Japanese economic competition was a "threat" to the United States. The Omnibus Trade Act of 1988, with its strengthened (or "Super") Section 301, was a concrete manifestation of these beliefs.

4. The extremity of some statements may have been meant more for the negotiating table or for the consumption of specific domestic support groups than as serious plans, but the general point still holds.

5. Various books have applied growth theory to Japan, including: David Flath, *The Japanese Economy* (Oxford University Press, 1999); Takatoshi Itō, *The Japanese Economy* (MIT Press, 1993); and Hugh Patrick and Henry Rosovsky, *Asia's New Giant* (Brookings, 1976), among some of the standard textbooks.

6. Chalmers Johnson, *MITI and the Japanese Miracle* (Stanford University Press, 1982); Yasusuke Murakami, *An Anticlassical Political-Economic Analysis* (Stanford University Press, 1996); William Tabb, *The Postwar Japanese System* (Oxford University Press, 1995); and the World Bank, *The East Asian Miracle* (Oxford University Press, 1993).

7. See, *inter alia*, Richard Katz, *Japan: The System That Soured* (M.E. Sharpe, 1998); Adam Posen, *Restoring Japan's Economic Growth* (Institute for International Economics, 1998); Akiyoshi Horiuchi, *Kin'yū shisutemu no mirai (Future of the Financial System)* (Iwanami Shinsho, 1998); Adam Posen and Ryōichi Mikitani, *Japan's Financial Crisis and Its Parallels to U.S. Experience* (Institute for International Economics, 2000); and William W. Grimes, *Unmaking the Japanese Miracle: Macroeconomic Politics, 1985–2000* (Cornell University Press, 2001).

8. Katz, *Japan: The System That Soured*. See Kent Calder, *Crisis and Compensation* (Princeton University Press, 1988) on the tendency toward compensation politics. Other, perhaps more important, reasons for uniformity of income may have been the uniformly high skill level of the Japanese labor force and the Occupation-induced redistribution of wealth in the immediate postwar period.

9. On sustainability, see Paul Krugman, "Is the Strong Dollar Sustainable?" *The U.S. Dollar: Prospects and Policy Options* (Federal Reserve Bank of Kansas City, 1985), and Stephen Marris, *Deficits and the Dollar: The World Economy at Risk* (Institute for International Economics, 1985). For figures on denomination of U.S. international debt, see the Bank for International Settlements figures cited in Foreign Exchange Commission, *Internationalization of the Yen for the 21st Century: Japan's Response to Changes in Global Economic and Financial Environments* (Foreign Exchange Commission, April 20, 1999).

10. U.S. trade (exports plus imports) as a percentage of GDP was around 10 percent until 1971, then fluctuated between 15 and 20 percent until 1989, when it started trending into the mid-20 percent range. Japan's trade dependence is actually now lower than that of the United States (around 10–12 percent), but its bilateral dependence on U.S. markets is higher.

11. See, for example, Stephen Cohen and John Zysman, *Manufacturing Matters* (Basic Books, 1987); Laura D'Andrea Tyson, *Who's Bashing Whom? Trade Conflict in High-Technology Industries* (Institute for International Economics, 1992). The mercurial Shintarō Ishihara argued to his countrymen in the late 1980s that Japan should exploit this economic and technological edge over a supposedly dependent United States. Akio Morita and Shintarō Ishihara, *Nō to Ieru Nihon (The Japan That Can Say No)* (Kobunsha, 1989).

12. Mototada Kikkawa, *Manē Haisen (Defeat in the Money Wars)* (Bunshun Shinsho, 1998).

13. See Paul Volcker and Toyoo Gyohten, *Changing Fortunes: The World's Money and the Threat to American Leadership* (Times Books, 1992); I. M. Destler and C. Randall Henning, *Dollar Politics: Exchange Rate Policymaking in the United States* (Institute for International Economics, 1989); and Grimes, *Unmaking the Japanese Miracle*.

14. See Robert Putnam and C. Randall Henning, "The Bonn Summit of 1978: A Case Study in Coordination," in Richard Cooper and others, *Can Nations Agree? Issues in International Economic Cooperation* (Brookings, 1987); Robert Putnam and Nicholas Bayne, *Hanging Together: Cooperation and Conflict in the Seven-Power Summits*, revised edition (Harvard University Press, 1987); and Volcker and Gyohten, *Changing Fortunes*, among others.

15. See Leonard Schoppa, *Bargaining with Japan* (Columbia University Press, 1997), especially chaps. 1 and 5; and Edward Lincoln, *Troubled Times* (Brookings, 1999), chap. 4 on SII.

16. Several participants in this project's October 6, 2000, workshop in Washington argue that demand management has been the main focus of U.S. pressures on Japan since around 1994, and that this direction should have been followed much earlier. But the limited successes of earlier macroeconomic coordination efforts such as those in the Plaza-Louvre period and the Structural Impediments Initiative should cause skepticism about the likely efficacy of such efforts in making meaningful differences in either country's policies or in bilateral balances.

17. Grimes, *Unmaking the Japanese Miracle*.

18. See, for example, Masaru Yoshitomi, "Growth Gaps, Exchange Rates, and Asymmetry: Is It Possible to Unwind Current-Account Imbalances without Fiscal Expansion in Japan?"

in Hugh T. Patrick and Ryūichirō Tachi, eds., *Japan and the United States Today: Exchange Rates, Macroeconomic Policies, and Financial Market Innovations* (Center on Japanese Economy and Business, 1987); Warwick McKibbin and Jeffrey Sachs, *Global Linkages: Macroeconomic Interdependence and Cooperation in the World Economy* (Brookings, 1991); Naoko Ishii, *Seisaku Kyōchō no Keizaigaku (The Economics of Policy Coordination)* (Nihon Keizai Shimbunsha, 1990); Heizō Takenaka and others, *"Nichibei Seisaku Kyōchō to Kan-Taiheiyō Keizai: Sakkusu-kei Sekai Moderu ni Yoru Shimyurēshon Bunseki" (Japan-U.S. Policy Coordination and the Economy of the Pacific Basin: A Simulation Analysis Based on a Sachs-Type World Model), Fainansharu Rebyū*, no. 3 (December 1986), pp. 70–93; and Heizō Takenaka and others, *"Saiteki Seisaku Kyōchō no Keiryō Bunseki: Sakkusu-kei Sekai Moderu ni Yoru Gaisō Shimyureishon" (A Quantitative Analysis of Optimal Policy Coordination: Extrapolative Simulation Based on a Sachs-Type World Model), Fainansharu Rebyū*, no. 5 (June 1987): pp. 38–56. (Yoshitomi uses the Japanese Economic Planning Agency world model in addition to International Monetary Fund (IMF) and Federal Reserve Board models, while the others use variations on the Sachs-McKibbin-Ishii model.)

19. Japan's efforts to prevent appreciation of the yen at various points between the late 1960s and 1985 may have been at least partly due to a continued perception of Japan as a small and vulnerable economy. Robert Angel, *Explaining Economic Policy Failure* (Columbia University Press, 1993); Volcker and Gyohten, *Changing Fortunes;* Yoshiko Kojō, *Domestic Sources of International Payments Adjustment: Japan's Choices in the Postwar Period* (Ph.D. dissertation, Princeton University, 1993); and William W. Grimes, *From the Plaza to the Louvre* (Ph.D. dissertation, Princeton University, 1995).

20. In the United States, a variety of authors have pointed—often with frustration—to the subordination of economic relations to the political and security relationship, at least until the arrival of the Clinton administration. For example, see Clyde Prestowitz, *Trading Places* (Basic Books, 1988), and Lincoln, *Troubled Times.*

21. The magnitude of Japan's economy relative to that of the United States looks very different depending on whether one uses current exchange rates or purchasing power parity (PPP). PPP has the twin benefits of being much less volatile and of providing a more accurate picture of comparative standards of living. For those who have wanted to confirm their fears that Japan is a threat to the United States, however, there is no substitute for current exchange rates, which far overstate actual domestic purchasing power, although they may helpful in understanding international purchasing power. By current exchange rate measures, Japan's economy has shrunk considerably in comparison with the United States since its 1995 peak of over 69 percent. (The 1999 figure is 47 percent.)

22. Polling data from the Chicago Council on Foreign Relations found that 63 percent of U.S. leaders saw Japanese economic competition as a threat to the United States in 1990. More anecdotal evidence can be seen in Prestowitz, *Trading Places* and Tyson, *Who's Bashing Whom?*

23. See Robert Gilpin, *War and Change in World Politics* (Cambridge University Press, 1981), and Robert Gilpin, *The Political Economy of International Relations* (Princeton University Press, 1987), for the clearest expositions on hegemony and relative economic power.

24. Because of the close negative relationship between growth and unemployment, and the difficulty of quantifying the concept of bilateral friction, it is most sensible simply to look at changes in GDP to test these assertions.

25. Amy Searight and Christopher Way, "Electoral Incentives and International Bargaining: U.S.-Japan Economic Disputes and Elections, 1968–97" (n.d., mimeo), present evidence to support such effects on the initiation of trade disputes.

26. The latter point is not necessarily important in economic terms, but it does seem to have strong political overtones. At least in popular terms, exports are seen as a sign of strength, while imports are seen as a sign of weakness. Japan's extreme perception of its own vulnera-

bility in the postwar period has tended to make exports a particularly powerful symbol of economic health.

27. Although Japan has often nominally accepted U.S. demands, however, there is some question about the consistency of implementation. See, for example, American Chamber of Commerce in Japan, *Making Trade Talks Work: Lessons from Recent History* (American Chamber of Commerce in Japan, 1997).

28. On Japanese sensitivity to the yen-dollar rate, see Ryūtaro Komiya and Miyako Suda, *Japan's Foreign Exchange Policy 1971–82* (Sydney: Allen & Unwin, 1991); Volcker and Gyohten, *Changing Fortunes;* and Kojō, *Domestic Sources of International Payments Adjustment.* Volcker and Gyohten, *Changing Fortunes,* and Destler and Henning, *Dollar Politics,* describe U.S. proclivities toward inaction.

29. Nobuhiro Hiwatari, "The Domestic Sources of U.S.-Japan Economic Relations," presented at APSA 1996 annual meeting, and William Poole, "Exchange-Rate Management and Monetary-Policy Mismanagement: A Study of Germany, Japan, United Kingdom, and United States after Plaza," *Carnegie-Rochester Conference Series on Public Policy,* no. 30 (1992) pp. 57–92.

30. The correlation between GDP growth rates for 1956–99 was 0.186. Breaking this figure down by time period, correlation in the 1960s was –0.659; in the 1970s, 0.362; in the 1980s, 0.352; and in the 1990s, –0.55.

31. Michael Porter, Hirotaka Takeuchi, and Mariko Sakakibara, *Can Japan Compete?* (Perseus Publishing, 2000).

32. Hiromitsu Ishi, *Making Fiscal Policy in Japan: Economic Effects and Institutional Settings* (Oxford University Press, 2000), p. 231.

33. This is not actually a meaningful statement in macroeconomic terms, since if Japanese money avoided the United States there would almost undoubtedly still be other international sources of funds that would take its place. It has much more importance from a political, or even symbolic, point of view.

34. Douglas Frantz and Catherine Collins, *Selling Out: How We Are Letting Japan Buy Our Land, Our Industries, Our Financial Institutions, and Our Future* (Contemporary Books, 1989).

35. This chapter assumes that budget deficits are countercyclical due to changes in revenues and to a lesser extent entitlements. It also assumes that strict Ricardian equivalence does not hold in the United States (or anywhere) at this time, or any time soon. Finally, this chapter assumes that households make growth predictions based upon current growth rates and upon asset price values.

36. As trade with the United States becomes less important to Japan's economy, the threat of trade sanctions—for many years the most common and effective weapon used by the United States to change Japanese behavior—becomes less severe. Trends in intra-industry trade also make the threat of trade sanctions by the United States more difficult for political reasons.

CHAPTER FOUR

Paradigms

KEITH A. NITTA

O ver the past fifty years, given Japan's massive economic growth and corresponding shifts in the U.S.-Japan balance of trade, the dollar-yen exchange rate, technological leadership, and relative manufacturing productivity, one would expect significant tension or confrontation in the U.S.-Japan relationship. Such confrontation, however, was highly muted, and the nature of the bilateral relationship has remained largely unchanged.

To explain this puzzle, this chapter argues that the dominant American and Japanese foreign policy paradigms—containment and the Yoshida Doctrine, respectively—have locked in the roles of the two countries, harmonized their leaders' expectations, and thereby greatly enhanced the stability of the U.S.-Japan relationship. During a few key years after World War II, U.S. elites developed the idea of containment, the belief that unless Soviet communism was aggressively contained around the world it would spread and overcome capitalist democracies. In the wake of this change in U.S. policy thinking, and under the Allied Occupation, Japanese elites developed the Yoshida Doctrine, the idea that Japan should emphasize economic growth while assuming a subordinate role in the U.S. security system. Institutionalized into formal laws, such as the Japanese Constitution and the U.S.-Japan Security Treaty, as well as informal routines and beliefs, such as the Japanese reluctance to say no to U.S. demands, these twin paradigms locked the United States and Japan into roles of senior and junior partner. They also laid out a clear logic for how each country must approach the other and the world. The United States had to lead the free world, and accept the economic and security burdens associated with that leadership, to contain communism. Within this system, Japan was vulnerable and had to work for economic growth and stability by adapting Western practices and technology. By making causal logic and roles explicit, these paradigms harmonized expectations on both sides of the Pacific and laid the foundation for a highly predictable, even stylized, bilateral relationship.[1]

With the end of Japanese high economic growth and of the cold war, however, the United States and Japan have entered a period of "paradigm drift" in which the old ideas have begun to lose their salience but new dominant paradigms have yet to emerge.[2] The stability each country has enjoyed in the bilateral relationship can no longer be taken for granted. The old roles, United States as senior partner and Japan as junior partner, as well as the old logics underlying containment and the Yoshida Doctrine have become frayed and inconsistently applied, destabilizing expectations. Bilateral relations have become more unpredictable, as evidenced by the confusion on both sides during the Gulf war and the Framework Talks of the mid-1990s. Of course, that is not to say that bilateral relations are necessarily becoming worse, either in how harmoniously the process works or how cooperative the outcomes are. Relations, however, will become less stylized, less predictable, and more fluid.

This chapter is not suggesting that material concerns such as national security and economic prosperity do not affect the U.S.-Japan relationship. Of course they do. But material conditions leave a fairly wide range of possible choices and behavior. This implies that ideas matter.

Ideas can matter in two ways. First, people can use ideas as decision-making resources.[3] Political entrepreneurs use ideas as tools to formulate as well as gather support for policies. In this way ideas are an integral part of political struggle and policy conflict found in the foreground of policy debates. Ideas provide policymakers with ends-means logic to reach goals, acting as models or maps used to generate solutions to real world problems.[4] In this chapter, ideas used by policymakers as tools or resources are called "programs."[5]

In the long run, however, ideas can also constrain behavior. As programs become embedded into laws, are used as the basis for designing organizational structures, and sink into unexamined assumptions and routines, they limit what decisionmakers can legitimately do. As they endure, ideas move from the foreground of policy debate into the background of policy terrain. In an important sense, policymakers lose control of these ideas because the ideas define what is legitimate and reasonable. Thus, ideas also matter because they set the rules of the game and act as stabilizing constraints on decisionmaking and behavior. Ideas that work in the background of policy debates to constrain actors' behavior and choices are referred to as "paradigms" in this chapter.

Programs are most likely to become salient and enduring—become paradigms—during unsettled conditions in which preexisting ideas have been shaken, most typically through an external shock.[6] In this chapter the best examples are the Great Depression and World War II. If they generally fit with existing dominant ideas and prove to work in the real world, programs will survive during this unsettled period and can become formally and informally institutionalized. Formally, programs can be institutionalized in laws, treaties, and organizations such as government ministries. Informally, they can become institutionalized in routines, beliefs, and assumptions. Through these dual processes, policymakers lose control of ideas, and programs become paradigms that lock in roles, privilege certain causal logics, and harmonize expectations.

This chapter shows how ideas have affected the U.S.-Japan relationship in six specific cases. The first two cases show how ideas adopted during earlier periods acted as important precursors to postwar ideas, providing intellectual resources for debate and constraining what policies were legitimate options by privileging certain ends-means logic. The next two cases make up the core of the chapter. The third case describes how containment was championed as the proper response to the spread of communism in Eastern Europe and Asia. The fourth case shows how Shigeru Yoshida maneuvered through domestic political challenges as well as a dismal international situation in the aftermath of World War II to create a minimalist foreign policy predicated on the U.S.-Japan Security Treaty but emphasizing economic growth through mercantilist nationalism. Because Yoshida designed his doctrine in part as a response to the U.S. shift to containment, the two paradigms are almost perfectly complementary. Finally, the last two cases, the Gulf war crisis and the Framework Talks, show how the effects of Japanese economic catch-up and the end of the cold war have ushered in a new era of uncertainty and instability in U.S.-Japan relations. The Yoshida Doctrine and containment have begun to lose their salience because each has substantially succeeded in its goal—Japan has caught up economically and the Soviet Union has collapsed—calling each paradigm's basic assumptions and logic into question. If Japan has caught up economically, then it is not internationally fragile and its companies and products need not be given special treatment. If communism is not a threat and need not be maintained, the United States does not have to bear the trade and security burdens of leading the free world alone. Indeed, without the threat of communism to contain, the United States may not even have to lead. What will emerge out of this paradigm drift remains unclear, a topic to which this chapter returns later.

Late Tokugawa to Early Meiji: *Fukoku Kyōhei*

Fundamental postwar assumptions that would become embedded in the Yoshida Doctrine were rooted in the Japanese experience of the late nineteenth century. The United States' forced opening of the country marked the beginning of the national debate on how to respond to international Western threats, a debate that ended with the Meiji Restoration and the dominance of the idea of *fukoku kyōhei* (rich nation, strong army). The assumptions implicit in this early paradigm—Japan is vulnerable and the rest of the world is threatening—as well as its embedded causal logic—the means to protect Japan is to develop and catch up with the West by using their ways—later became central in the Yoshida Doctrine. In the language of this chapter, advocates of the *fukoku kyōhei* program emerged dominant from a crisis period and on the basis of these beliefs opened the country in a particular way. Always with the assumption that Japan was vulnerable and the West threatening, Meiji reformers aimed to gather Western technology and techniques to modernize and secure the nation. To do so, they created a centralized state bureaucracy modeled on those in Western Europe but even more directed toward economic development and military strength.

When Commodore Matthew Perry sailed into Tokyo Bay on July 8, 1853, with his four Black Ships and demanded an end to Japan's long isolation from the West, he created a powerful sense of insecurity among Japanese elites in the capital. Masahiro Abe, the effective head of the Tokugawa state, struggled with how to respond to the American demand and decided to accept suggestions from the feudal *daimyō* lords. Their responses were diverse and contradictory, and Abe's strategy ultimately threw the state's response into open debate.[7]

Two broad coalitions formed, one in favor of continued isolation and the other pressing for opening international trade. The isolationists, including the Shōgun Iesada and the Emperor Kōmei, emphasized the spiritual and cultural purity of Japan and pushed a program of domestic military buildup to enforce continued international isolation. The shōgun and emperor worried that the West presented a military threat as well as a more pervasive and dangerous spiritual threat that would result in political and cultural chaos. They drew on the theories of Seishisai Aizawa, who argued that Western rulers indoctrinated their own people as well as those in their colonies with the state cult of Christianity in order to achieve spiritual unity and allegiance, to support this belief that contact with the West would lead to contamination and ruin.[8]

The opposing group, led by the *daimyō* Naosuke Ii and Masayoshi Hotta, argued that Japan's isolation and technological weakness made it vulnerable to Western militaries. Accordingly, Western technology and the wealth necessary to turn that technology into military force were the only means of creating a strong and independent Japan. Hotta, for example, wrote that military power always springs from national wealth, and that such wealth could be found principally in trade and commerce.[9] *Fukoku kyōhei*—rich country, strong army—became a catchphrase of the coalition's policy ideas. Several intellectuals supported this logic that the key to national survival lay with developing national wealth through careful trade and a strong army through adopting Western technology. Takusui Ōkubo called *fukoku kyōhei* "the grand foundation, maintaining the world."[10]

Thus by the time of the Meiji Restoration, two coherent programs for responding to the Western threat existed. In 1868, riding a wave of dissatisfaction over the unequal treaties negotiated by the Tokugawa regime and emboldened by the regime's inability to control its *daimyō*, young samurai from the outlying domains of Satsuma and Chōshu seized control of the palace and had the boy emperor, Matsuhito (renamed Meiji), proclaim the end of the Tokugawa Shogunate and the restoration of imperial rule. The Meiji reformers, young and bold, rejected the shōgun's isolationist program and embraced the *fukoku kyōhei* program, along with its logic for how to overcome Japanese insecurity. *Fukoku kyōhei* became the national creed, and a clear national mission and path emerged. Forced by its late developer status to catch up economically, militarily, and technologically with the West, Japan must be guided by a centralized state to amass national wealth and create an army powerful enough to protect it from the Western powers. The influential liberal Yukichi Fukuzawa helped the Meiji reformers by openly advocating the *fukoku kyōhei* program. Fukuzawa argued that in order to achieve the ultimate goal of independence and autonomy,

Japan needed to strengthen both its economy and military by advancing the nation's knowledge and scientific competence.[11]

At a time when the old regime was breaking down, nationalist reformers used the programmatic idea of *fukoku kyōhei* to mobilize the nation to catch up with the West and ensure Japanese national security. *Fukoku kyōhei* became the Meiji oligarchs' rationale for instituting sweeping centralizing reforms to the educational system; the mining, munitions, and railroad industries; and the national army.[12] *Fukoku kyōhei* provided the foundation for Japanese policy thinking until defeat in World War II and the Allied Occupation forced a fundamental reexamination of the national purpose.

Great Depression: Reciprocal Tariff Reduction

The switch in U.S. policymakers' thinking away from protective quotas and toward more proactive reciprocal tariff reduction trade policies occurred in reaction to the Great Depression and the failure of the Smoot-Hawley Tariff. The idea emerged from hot debate within the Roosevelt administration to influence later U.S. policy in at least two ways. Most generally, reciprocal tariff reduction represents a turn away from inward-facing isolationism and toward outward-facing interventionism, perhaps best typified by containment. More specifically, although as a trade policy reciprocal tariff reduction was deemphasized in the two decades after World War II in favor of creating strong economic bulwarks against communism, the idea survived and became gradually more influential in the U.S.-Japan relationship. By the late 1970s, as the U.S. economy faltered and the trade deficit with Japan worsened, U.S. policymakers reacted not simply by threatening to impose tariffs and quotas on Japanese goods but by aggressively working to open up Japanese markets.

Through the 1920s, high tariffs and a protectionist orientation marked American trade policy. First embraced by the Republican Party in the antebellum years as a means of protecting business interests and keeping wages high, policy entrepreneurs institutionalized protectionist ideas over the following decades in Congressional trade acts and other regulations, culminating in the Smoot-Hawley Tariff of 1930, which set the highest tariffs in U.S. history.[13] As a response to the burgeoning Great Depression, however, Smoot-Hawley was a failure. The act did not reverse economic decline; it exacerbated it. The election of 1932 reinforced that message, as Democrats swept into control of the presidency and Congress. Smoot-Hawley's lesson was clear to the new freshman Democratic class: tariff politics and high tariffs breed economic and political decline. What type of trade liberalization the country should pursue, however, remained unclear.

When Franklin Roosevelt succeeded Herbert Hoover as president in January 1933, he solicited ideas for a trade policy that would aid economic recovery from members of his administration. Cordell Hull, the new secretary of state, quickly submitted a bill that would have unilaterally lowered American tariffs by 10 percent. Influential presidential advisors such as Rexford Tugwell and Raymond Moley criticized the proposed cuts as unrealistic and out of step with the existing international high tariff system. Assistant Secretary of State Francis Sayre summarized this dominant position by arguing if the United States pursued a unilateral strategy the country would not gain immediate reduction of foreign trade barriers, nor protect American goods from foreign discrimination.[14] While protectionist ideas had been discredited by the depression, they did not give way to textbook classical economic ideas. Policymakers still saw the world in zero-sum terms and were unwilling to throw the United States to the mercantilist wolves.

With protectionism discredited and unilateral tariff cuts out of the question, Hull and other free trade advocates pushed a program of reciprocal tariff cuts negotiated bilaterally with multilateral implications through most favored nation status. In advocating this program, Hull and his allies reconceptualized "reciprocity." Until the 1930s, the concept had been closely associated with Republican high tariffs. Reciprocity legislation in the nineteenth century gave the president the authority to punish nations that did not give American exporters "fair" access to their markets. Reciprocity was not a carrot to open trade but a stick to use if foreign nations discriminated against American products. Against this conceptualization, the free trade coalition forwarded a more proactive, incentive-oriented definition of reciprocity. The idea was to bilaterally negotiate trade concessions with countries. Countries that held unconditional most favored nation status would share in those concessions and enjoy the new lower tariff. In this way, trade barriers could be multilaterally lowered through bilateral negotiations. This reconceptualization originally met with skepticism. For example, George Peek, the special foreign trade advisor, argued that reciprocity and unconditional most favored nation principles were incompatible.[15]

Over time, however, Hull and his free trade coalition won the contest over the meaning of reciprocity, as well as the larger contest over the direction of U.S. trade policy, because they situated their program of reciprocal tariff reduction to be consonant with protectionist assumptions, yet still essentially oriented toward proactive free trade. At the same time, the free trade version of reciprocity began to gain acceptance as Hull and the State Department successfully negotiated reciprocal trade agreements and, more importantly, as the economy recovered. So for both ideational and material reasons, trade policy moved from the protectionist idea of reactively punishing unfair traders to the free trade idea of proactively negotiating trade concessions in the interests of free global trade.

Post–World War II: Containment

On the U.S. side, the bedrock idea underlying the U.S.-Japan relationship from World War II to the Gulf war was containment. In response to the spread of communism in Eastern Europe and Asia, George Kennan and key members of the U.S. State Department championed containment as the most logical response to an implacable communist expansion that threatened to topple countries like so many dominoes. Beginning with NSC 13/2 and culminating with the U.S.-Japan Security Treaty of 1951, containment became formally institutionalized into the U.S.-Japan relationship. Together with the Yoshida Doctrine, containment shaped role expectations and policy logic in both countries. The United States became the senior partner and Japan the junior partner in the relationship. The United States would provide military security but Japan would lack true foreign policy independence. Japan would concentrate on economic development while the United States would bear the economic burden of an unfavorable exchange rate and one-sided market access. By stabilizing and harmonizing behavioral and role expectations, containment and the Yoshida Doctrine provided the foundation for the highly predictable, stylized pattern that characterized U.S.-Japanese relations for so many years.

When he took over as Supreme Commander of the Allied Powers (SCAP) in Japan, General Douglas MacArthur and his administration initially pursued the twin goals of demilitarization and democratization. SCAP, staffed by idealistic New Dealers, instituted a sweeping series of reforms, including a land reform that reduced the incidence of tenancy from 50 to 5 percent of the population; family law reform that gave women equal rights as voters and property holders; labor law reform that allowed union organizing and collective bargaining; and aggressive dissolution of the military and industrial *zaibatsu* cartels.[16] These reforms were driven by the implicit assumption that the Japanese society, economy, and polity suffered from a pathology that led it to disastrous military expansionism. The cure was to reform the country root and branch in an idealized image of the United States.

This remaking of Japan was symbolized and institutionalized in the Japanese Constitution of 1946. Written by SCAP officials and only reluctantly authorized by the Japanese cabinet and Diet, the constitution recognized the Japanese emperor but reduced him to "the symbol of the state and of the unity of the people, deriving his position from the will of the people with whom resides sovereign power." It put political power in a popularly elected Diet and institutionalized a bill of rights more extensive than those guaranteed by the U.S. Constitution. Finally, and most importantly for U.S.-Japan relations, Article 9 of the constitution stated, "The Japanese people forever renounce war as a sovereign right of the nation and the threat or use of force as a means of settling international disputes. In order to accomplish the aim of the preceding paragraph, land, sea, and air forces, as well as other war potential, will never be maintained."

While the New Dealers in SCAP worked in Tokyo to remake Japan, however, a Soviet specialist named George Kennan was refining and popularizing a new program that questioned the basic nature of postwar international relations: containment. While working for the State Department in Moscow in 1946, Kennan began to worry about what he saw as American indecisiveness in the face of Soviet belligerence. He wrote a widely read report that urged the United States to abandon lingering illusions about cooperating with the Soviets. Familiar with the Soviet Union and its military capability, Kennan did not consider the Red Army the primary threat to U.S. security. The real threat was what he saw as internal economic and political weakness in Europe and Japan that made them ripe for communism. Communism would only spread in the wake of a Western collapse. Thus the economic rehabilitation and political stabilization of Europe and Asia became the core goals of the containment program as envisioned by Kennan.

Containment began to take hold in Washington in 1947. Newly appointed Secretary of State George Marshall was impressed enough with Kennan's ideas that he named him the head of the new Policy Planning Staff (PPS), which he created to devise long-term programs to achieve long-term foreign policy objectives. Marshall's appointment, his creation of the PPS, and Kennan's sponsorship of containment all took place in what appeared to be a rapidly deteriorating world situation. The Soviet Union had installed a series of puppet regimes in Eastern Europe, creating an "Iron Curtain." Mao Zedong's Chinese communists had begun to turn the tide against Chiang Kai-Shek's Nationalists and would eventually drive them off the mainland in 1949. In this atmosphere, containment offered a clear and direct course of action that would protect U.S. security. Communism could only be contained by stable political systems and prosperous economies, particularly in Europe and Asia. Applied to Asia, Undersecretary of State Dean Acheson envisioned a "great crescent," stretching from Japan through Southeast Asia, around India, and ending in the Persian Gulf, which would contain the Soviets and the Chinese if necessary.[17] As the anchor of the great crescent, Japan was the linchpin of the Asian containment program. As the linchpin, Japan's economic recovery was key to the stability and prosperity of the region—and the world.

Containment continued the activist turn in U.S. foreign policy thinking reflected in the transition from protectionism to reciprocal tariff reduction. Just as managing trade no longer implied simply restricting access to U.S. markets but actively reaching out to open foreign markets, U.S. policy-makers no longer considered an inward-facing security policy legitimate. Isolationism, like protectionism, had been discredited in the first half of the twentieth century. The United States must seek to actively manage its international environment. Containment provided a logical set of ideas to do exactly that.

With this new set of ideas emerging in Washington, the Allied Occupation suddenly came under fire. The containment program painted a new picture in which SCAP had destabilized Japan, making it vulnerable to communism and thereby threatening the security of the United States. MacArthur responded to the challenge by extolling SCAP's accomplishments, boasting that his administration had demilitarized Japan and nearly completed its democratization, leaving only the final challenge of economic recovery. In March of 1947, MacArthur described a "spiritual revolution" in Japan and rationalized Japanese military aggression as a mistake of a resource-poor country trying to acquire desperately needed natural resources. He hinted that the occupation had done its work and could soon end. Japan required neither an American military umbrella nor an expensive recovery program. From containment advocates' perspective, MacArthur seemed to dismiss both the security and economic bases of the containment program.

The State Department began to battle SCAP for control over the occupation for the rest of 1947 and into 1948. While Kennan, Marshall, Acheson, and the State Department's conception of containment fit the emerging security and economic context, as well as the activist turn in foreign policy thinking, SCAP's democratization was out of step with existing ideas about the world and the United States' place in it. Just as unilateral tariff reduction was unacceptable because it did not fit with policymakers' zero-sum ideas about a cut-throat world, the idealistic progressivism of the occupation, embodied by the many New Dealers within SCAP, proved unacceptable because the benefits to the United States were too vague. The case for containment fit the basically self- (or nation-) interested perspective of policymakers better than the promise of a diffusion of democracy and capitalism. SCAP's claim that Japan was transformed and therefore harmless also clashed with existing ideas about Japan and the Japanese. The war had only ended two years earlier, and most U.S. policymakers still viewed Japan with distrust and even loathing. In 1947 very few people had any expertise on Japan, and those who did viewed Japan as nationalist, unpredictable, and unstable. For example, in a 1946 textbook, Edwin Reischauer, later ambassador to Japan and strong pro-Japan advocate, described Japan as an isolated island nation, which "has made them painfully aware of their differences from other peoples and has filled them with an entirely irrational sense of superiority, which they are anxious to prove to themselves and others."[18] Writing at the Potsdam Conference in 1945, President Truman himself stated that Japanese were "savages, ruthless, merciless, and fanatics."[19] The containment program, which treated Japan as an ally under close U.S. supervision, fit these ideas better.

President Truman finally decided to adopt containment as official U.S. policy in late 1948. In October, the National Security Council approved and the president signed NSC 13/2, which codified Kennan's ideas on containment. Along with NSC 48/2, which focused more on China's role in Asian security, NSC 13/2 institutionalized the principles of Asian containment. NSC 13/2 made the economic recovery of Japan the prime objective of the occupation and urged a halt to the type of destabilizing reforms instituted by SCAP. Instead it called for industrial discipline and an emphasis on export production in order to rebuild and fortify the Japanese economy. Truman followed NSC 13/2 with a nine-point stabilization directive in December 1948. Using his authority to directly mandate policy for the first time since Japan surrendered, Truman removed much of SCAP's authority and dispatched a special emissary, Joseph Dodge, to oversee the Japanese economy. Arriving in February 1949, Dodge moved to balance the national budget and establish an official exchange rate to curb inflation and attract foreign investment. While the "Dodge line" required massive retrenchment by both government and business and set Japan into a recession that lasted until the Korean War boom, it also laid a foundation for the economic stability and prosperity that the containment program required. The "reverse course" of the Allied Occupation began, and containment, with its overt linkage between Japanese economic recovery and Asian regional security, became the official policy of the United States.

The containment paradigm encouraged U.S. policymakers to tolerate growing trade deficits with Japan in the interest of global security. In effect, through the 1960s containment superseded reciprocal trade reduction in the economic realm, as the United States allowed Japanese products open access to American markets while tolerating substantial barriers to Japanese domestic markets. In fact U.S. policymakers initially viewed Japanese economic growth with pride and even bemusement. In the early postwar years, it was unimaginable that Japan could threaten America's economy. For example, in 1952 John Foster Dulles commented, "suicide was not an illogical step for anyone concerned about Japan's economic future."[20] Most firms did not consider the Japanese market large enough to consider developing and instead sold technology rights to Japanese companies.[21] Thanks in part to a new set of ideas emerging in Japan in tandem with containment, however, these commentators and companies were proved fools.

After Defeat: Yoshida Doctrine

Together with containment, the Yoshida Doctrine provides the ideational foundation for the U.S.-Japan relationship from the late 1940s to the early 1990s. In the years following Japan's defeat in World War II, Shigeru Yoshida emerged to unify Japanese conservatives around a policy of diplomatic and security minimalism predicated on the U.S.-Japan Security Treaty coupled with emphasis on economic growth through mercantilist nationalism. The Yoshida Doctrine drew on assumptions of Japanese vulnerability as well as the belief, first developed in *fukoku kyōhei*, that the solution to this vulnerability was development through adoption of foreign practices and technology. Yoshida tailored these assumptions and beliefs to the reality of military defeat, the Allied Occupation, and the emerging cold war to create a winning paradigm, one that proved successful as the Japanese economy grew at incredible rates and political conservatives dominated Japanese domestic politics. Together with containment, the Yoshida Doctrine was formally institutionalized in the San Francisco Peace Treaty and U.S.-Japan Security Treaty. The Yoshida Doctrine worked in Japan to normalize behavioral and role expectations, while containment did the same in the United States. As these complementary ideas began to dominate and constrain behavior, bilateral relations took on their predictable and stable character.

After unconditional surrender to the Allies in August 1945, Japan was an international pariah and a completely devastated country. More than 2.5 million Japanese soldiers and civilians had died during the war.[22] One-quarter of the national wealth of the country was destroyed, the equivalent of national production since 1936. The destruction was concentrated in Japan's cities, completely ruining the country's industrial plant. Inflation spiraled out of control, and a large portion of the population was unemployed. The nation had also lost its moral and ideological direction. The war had discredited the old militarist, ultranationalist system. Wartime defeat struck at the heart and mind of the Japanese people, leading to a fundamental reexamination of the past decade, exemplified by Masao Maruyama's "Theory and Logic of Ultranationalism," published in one of the first issues of the influential journal *Sekai* in 1946.

In this profoundly unsettled cultural period, politician Shigeru Yoshida emerged at the center of the foreign policymaking sphere. A veteran diplomat with decades of service in the Ministry of Foreign Affairs, he entered politics in September 1945, becoming foreign minister when SCAP forced the acting foreign minister to resign. He served as prime minister from 1946 to 1947 and again from 1948 to 1954. A shrewd politician, Yoshida recognized the opportunities as well as the dangers that the new international order posed, observing that history provides examples of winning by diplomacy after losing in war. The prime danger was that Japan could be drawn into the burgeoning cold war, forcing it to divert limited resources from economic rebuilding to remilitarization. At the same time, however, the cold war made Japan strategically important to both the United States and the Soviet Union. As a conservative politician and former bureaucrat, allying Japan with Stalinist Russia was never a serious alternative. However, Yoshida could use Japan's strategic importance for bargaining leverage with the United States. He was convinced that the cold war would require the United States to maintain its presence in Japan, which alone would be sufficient to deter a Soviet attack. He would therefore give exclusive priority to pursuing Japanese economic recovery and maintaining political stability.

This bundle of ideas eventually provided the foundation for Japanese foreign policy. As laid out by Kenneth Pyle, the doctrine had three main tenets:

—Japan's economic rehabilitation must be the prime national goal. Political-economic cooperation with the United States was necessary for this purpose.

—Japan should remained lightly armed and avoid involvement in international political-strategic issues. Not only would this low posture free the energies of its people for productive industrial development, it would avoid divisive internal struggles—what Yoshida called a "thirty-eighth parallel" in the hearts of the Japanese people.

—To gain a long-term guarantee for its own security, Japan would provide bases for the U.S. Army, Navy, and Air Force.[23]

Thus the Yoshida Doctrine, like the U.S. containment program, had both a security and an economic aspect. While containment placed security concerns at the center and made economic policy subordinate, however, the Yoshida Doctrine put the emphasis on economic growth and accepted a minimalist security policy with a completely subordinate role within the American international security order as a consequence. In effect Yoshida worked to make a virtue out of necessity, as Japan was already under Allied Occupation and U.S. policymakers had already begun to implement its aggressive containment policies by early 1949. Japan was already subordinate to the United States. The question was how to work the context to Japan's advantage.

In addition to tailoring his program to the international material context, Yoshida framed it to be consistent with existing nationalist paradigms in Japan. The assumptions and logic behind *fukoku kyōhei* had not been discredited by the war. In fact World War II had only reinforced the basic Japanese insecurity born out of the forced opening of the country. Japan was still a small country in a hostile world that needed to catch up with the West. More specifically, while the *fukoku kyōhei* program's military aspect lost legitimacy during the Allied Occupation, its economic element did not come under attack. Unlike in Germany, the war experience in Japan did not discredit all forms of nationalism, only the military organization itself and military expansionism generally.[24] Yoshida's program thus appealed to *fukoku kyōhei* assumptions, while transforming Japanese nationalism into a purely economic strain. According to this new logic, first and foremost, Japan must grow economically in order to become secure and independent.

Yoshida faced two substantial domestic political challenges to his program. The first came from political liberals, who strongly opposed an alliance with the United States. These progressives wanted a new Japan, transformed by its experience of war, atomic bombings, and defeat and dedicated to showing the way to a new world without weapons and war. This was the ideology of the early occupation, before the reverse course. While Yoshida did draw on the antimilitarist sentiment behind this program to justify the minimalist security aspect of his program, he and his allies, including future prime ministers Hayato Ikeda and Eisaku Satō, successfully portrayed the larger progressive program as impractical and dangerous by drawing on *fukoku kyōhei* assumptions about Japan's insecure place in the world. In a Hobbesian world, one either needed to be strong or have strong protectors. Without a military, Japan needed the United States for protection. While drawing on old, traditional Japanese assumptions and paradigms, Yoshida and his coalition also portrayed the progressive program as un-Japanese, arguing that the values and institutions underlying it were Western imports, out of step with Japanese traditions and history. While liberal intellectuals such as Masao Maruyama, Jirō Kamishima, and Yoshikazu Sakamoto pointed to historical evidence that such values, beliefs, and institutions did exist in Japan, the anti-Japanese criticism resonated with the Japanese public.[25]

The more serious challenge to Yoshida's program came from conservative nationalists. Led by Hitoshi Ashida, who had served as prime minister for seven months in 1948, these nationalists opposed the exclusive emphasis on economic growth at the expense of security dependence. This coalition wanted Japan to become a "normal state," with an independent military and foreign policy.[26] Yoshida's more extreme conservative opponents, including future prime ministers Ichirō Hatoyama, Nobusuke Kishi, and Yasuhiro Nakasone, joined with Ashida in severely criticizing Yoshida's program for placing Japan in such a subservient position to the United States. They regarded security dependence on the United States as demeaning. Yoshida replied to these arguments by stressing the lessons of World War II. He echoed progressive arguments about the disastrous effects the military had on national policy in the 1930s and repeatedly cited strong public opinion against remilitarization. The strength of this Japanese anti-militarism was borne out in Kishi's disastrous renewal of the U.S-Japan Security Treaty in 1960 and Nakasone's unsuccessful attempt to revise the constitution and make Japan a "normal country" in the 1980s.

During the summer of 1950, still in power despite progressive and nationalist conservative challenges, Yoshida began to implement his doctrine during preliminary peace treaty talks with the special emissary of the secretary of state, John Foster Dulles. As he arrived in Tokyo on June 21, 1950, Dulles's attention, along with the rest of the State Department, was focused on twin crises in China and Korea. The United States had not yet decided how to respond to the communist victory and the Nationalist regime's retreat to Formosa-Taiwan. At the same time, tensions were rising on the Korean peninsula. In fact, on June 25, 1950, North Korean troops invaded over the thirty-eighth parallel and five days later the Korean War officially began. Against this background, the containment program seemed more pertinent than ever, as did Japan's strategic importance. Dulles considered it vital to maintain Japan's good will and feared that further delays in signing a treaty and ending the occupation might fatally undermine Tokyo's willingness and ability to ally with the United States. At the same time, he thought it reasonable that Japan take a more active role in the Asian security system. Dulles pushed Yoshida to rearm Japan and to join a regional defense alliance along the lines of NATO in Europe. He tried to use the Korean conflict as evidence that Japan was a desired prize for the communists, a natural target for the desire to dominate the Far East. Japan must rearm to be able to resist a Chinese, Soviet, or North Korean invasion. Yoshida responded to Dulles's arguments with a "puckish" performance, making light of Japan's security problems.[27] Parroting progressive arguments, he claimed that since Japan was democratic and peaceful, world opinion would protect Japan. In any case, Article 9 of the Constitution forbade any remilitarization, and public opinion was solidly against it.[28] Dulles left Tokyo flabbergasted and dissatisfied.

In later meetings with Dulles, Yoshida continued to resist rearmament and collective security commitments from this standpoint. He also began to appeal to containment ideas by arguing that rearmament would impoverish Japan and create the kind of social unrest that would make Japan ripe for communist takeover. Rearmament would also completely alienate Japan's neighbors, blocking off essential markets and resources. Yoshida even went so far as to enlist MacArthur's support in resisting rearmament. In order to get a peace treaty and bring an end to the occupation, however, Yoshida had to make minor concessions to Dulles. For example, in January 1951, Yoshida agreed to upgrade the new National Police Reserve from 75,000 men to 110,000 and rename it the National Security Force. This figure, however, was still far lower than the 500,000- to 750,000-man force Dulles and the State Department desired.

Yoshida's program was finally institutionalized in September 1951 with the signing of the San Francisco Peace Treaty and the U.S.-Japan Security Treaty. The peace treaty ended the occupation and returned national sovereignty to Japanese hands. The price for the treaty and Yoshida's refusal to rearm or participate in collective security arrangements, however, was the highly unequal security treaty. Preserving many of the occupation prerogatives of the U.S. military, the treaty in effect rendered Japan a military satellite of the United States, granting the United States military bases in Japan, the right to project military power from these bases without consulting Japan, extraterritorial legal rights for U.S. military personnel, and the right to quell domestic Japanese disorder. Dulles also forced Yoshida to recognize the Nationalist government in Taiwan over the communist mainland government.

In the short run, Yoshida's program survived because it was institutionalized in the security treaty and the constitution, making it extremely difficult for progressives and particularly conservative nationalists to dislodge the program. Yoshida's two immediate successors as prime minister, Hatoyama and Kishi, wanted to revise the constitution, rearm Japan, and renegotiate a more equal security treaty with the United States. Their policies proved bitterly divisive and unsuccessful, as the Japan Socialist Party had gained sufficient strength in the Diet to oppose the conservatives, and its hold on public opinion through the media, intellectuals, and the unions made constitutional revision impossible.

In the long run the Yoshida Doctrine survived continued progressive and conservative nationalist challenges for at least four reasons. First, and most fundamentally, it survived because it was successful in achieving its goal of economic growth. From 1950 to 1973, adjusted for inflation, the Japanese economy grew at an average of more than 10 percent a year, triple the U.S. economy's growth rate during the same period.[29] Second, the Yoshida Doctrine avoided divisive ideological struggles and provided a moderate policy line for the conservative Liberal Democratic Party (LDP), formed in 1955 just after Yoshida's resignation as prime minister, that allowed it to become a catch-all party and dominate Japanese politics since.[30] The Yoshida program thus acted as a rallying point for moderate conservatives to form a dominant coalition.[31] Under Yoshida school honor students Ikeda and Satō, the LDP concentrated on economic growth, epitomized by Ikeda's income doubling plan, while pursuing a minimalist foreign policy that avoided collective security agreements, exemplified by Satō's three nonnuclear principles and 1 percent cap on defense spending. Third, the program became institutionalized as economic ministries such as the Ministry of Finance, the Economic Planning Agency, and the Ministry of International Trade and Industry assumed substantial responsibility for foreign policy. Bureaucrats in these ministries supported the Yoshida Doctrine as the legitimate way of doing things, as well as the means by which they exerted major influence over foreign policymaking. The Yoshida Doctrine also meant that the development of the Japanese equivalent of the powerful U.S.

National Security Council and the Department of Defense was stunted, leaving no strong security advocates in the bureaucracy. Finally, the centrist Yoshida line of the LDP, along with the economic bureaucracy, actively promoted the Yoshida program's overriding goal of economic growth, working to give growth a sacred quality.[32] The economic press wryly named the three major postwar economic upswings the Jimmu Boom, Iwato Boom, and Izanagi Boom, implying the periods of prosperity were the most remarkable thing in Japanese history since the legendary first Japanese emperor Jimmu; the cave—Iwato—where the sun goddess Amaterasu rested before coming back into the world; and the even more ancient god Izanagi, who with his sister Izanami gave birth to the islands of Japan.[33] The state quickly picked up these labels, using the terms repeatedly in its Economic White Papers.[34] By associating economic growth with these sacred myths, the state seemed to recast the national Japanese purpose toward economic production and prosperity.

Containment and the Yoshida Doctrine together defined the core of the U.S.-Japan relationship in the fifty years after World War II. The paradigms still survive by being institutionalized in government organizations, such as the LDP, the Japanese Ministry of Finance, and the U.S. armed forces, and in deep-seated sentiments about hierarchical roles of U.S. superiority and Japanese subordinance. The two paradigms complement each other, as they were designed to, and they have served to smooth over fundamental differences in the economic approaches of the U.S. and Japan. Eventually, however, the two paradigms began to lose their saliency, first as Japan caught up with Europe and the United States, and more quickly as the Soviet Union collapsed in 1989 and the cold war ended. Without the bedrock paradigms and associated sentiments to serve as cognitive and normative guides, the U.S.-Japan relationship became much more unpredictable and confusing for officials in both the United States and Japan, as demonstrated by the cases of the Persian Gulf war and the 1993–94 Framework Talks.

Post–Catch-Up, Post–Cold War: Gulf War

By the 1970s, Japan had economically caught up with the West. By the 1980s, it had become clear to any observer that the Yoshida Doctrine had accomplished its goal: Japan had become one of the most industrialized, technologically advanced nations in the world. As Western scholars such as Ezra Vogel portrayed "Japan as Number One," U.S. economic policy changed from relative tolerance of the bilateral trade imbalance and of some closed Japanese market sectors to a close focus on both. By the mid-1980s, U.S. elites began publicly scapegoating Japan and Japanese companies for U.S. economic problems. Senator John Danforth publicly referred to Japanese as "leeches" as U.S. politicians began to publicly blame the Japanese for the $59 billion bilateral trade deficit.[35]

Roughly ten years after Japan had economically caught up, containment accomplished its mission when the Soviet Union disintegrated in 1989. In the United States, both elites and the larger public began debating how to spend the peace dividend from the end of the cold war. Without an evil empire to contain, the economic and security burdens of being the leader of the free world no longer appeared necessary to many U.S. policymakers.

In the language of this chapter, Japanese economic catch-up and the end of the cold war brought the basic assumptions and logic of the Yoshida Doctrine and containment into question. The specific problem or challenge each paradigm identified—economic backwardness and communist expansion, respectively—had disappeared, leaving no well-marked path to reaching larger goals of national security and prosperity. In other words, the means to achieving well-established ends came into question. Even more problematically, catch-up and the end of the cold war together eroded the basic role assumptions elites on both sides of the Pacific had of their own and of the other country, making both predicting reaction and acting in a predictable way increasingly difficult. In this way a new era of paradigm drift has begun, one in which the stylized interaction of the past no longer applies, roles have become unclear, and behavior can no longer be confidently predicted. In at least two cases, this led to conflict between the United States and Japan, one in the political-security realm and the other in the trade-economic realm.

On August 2, 1990, about 150,000 Iraqi troops invaded across the Kuwaiti border and easily overwhelmed the unprepared and inexperienced Kuwaiti military. By dawn Iraq had assumed control of Kuwait City and was soon in complete control of the country. Japan initially responded to the invasion by figuring out its domestic economic impact. Although Japan was dependent on the Middle East for 70 percent of its oil, it only depended on Iraq for 5.8 percent and Kuwait for 5.9 percent of its total oil.[36] Japan also had a 142-day reserve of oil as a result of the lessons from the 1970s oil shocks. The economic impact, then, was easily managed, and Japanese policymakers would have been relatively unconstrained by domestic economic requirements in responding to the crisis.

On the U.S. side, worried about instability in the key oil-producing region in the world, the Bush administration quickly began to assert U.S. leadership. President George H. W. Bush publicly declared that the Iraqi invasion would not stand and began building support for a coalition against Iraq. He personally called Japanese Prime Minister Toshiki Kaifu to encourage Japan to impose economic sanctions on Iraq. The Kaifu cabinet responded within the day, imposing sanctions that included the first oil embargo in Japanese history. The Bush administration also worked to build an anti-Iraq coalition in the United Nations, and four days after the invasion the UN Security Council imposed an economic embargo on Iraq that prohibited nearly all trade with Iraq. Working through the United Nations, the United States also took the lead in assembling a large international military coalition in Saudi Arabia. The United States sent more than 400,000 troops, and more than 200,000 additional troops came from countries including Saudi Arabia, the United Kingdom, France, Kuwait, Egypt, and Syria. Canada, Italy, Argentina, Australia, Belgium, Greece, Norway, Spain, Czechoslovakia, Poland, and South Korea contributed ships, air forces, and medical units. The United States continued to put heavy pressure on Japan to take an active role in the multinational effort. The U.S. Senate sent a formal message to Kaifu urging Japan to take "assertive action."[37] By mid-August Bush had called Kaifu several times, Secretary of Defense Dick Cheney had made a personal appeal to Self-Defense Agency Director General Yōzō Ishikawa, and U.S. Ambassador Michael Armacost made several requests to Vice Foreign Minister Takakazu Kuriyama. Through these conversations, Cheney and Armacost encouraged Japan to dispatch minesweepers, provide airlift support, transport food and supplies, and finally provide financial assistance.

On August 29, 1990, Japan announced its first official support package. It included unspecified loans and grants to Egypt, Turkey, and Jordan; providing 100 medical specialists; chartering two ships and two planes to provide supplies to the multinational coalition forces in Saudi Arabia and a pledge to supply refrigeration equipment, water, and other goods. Japan later valued the package at $1 billion.[38] Policymakers in both the Bush administration and Congress judged the contribution as insufficient and continued to press Japan for "active involvement," including minesweepers and logistical support. In an anti-Japanese fervor, the U.S. House of Representatives overwhelmingly voted to pull U.S. troops out of Japan unless the Japanese government funded the entire cost of stationing them in Japan.

Kaifu initially responded to U.S. demands by pledging an additional $3 billion in support. It was the only response Japanese actors were conditioned to offer. To that point, under the Yoshida Doctrine Japan's foreign policy had been predicated on avoiding such collective security ventures. Japanese foreign policy typically worked through direct aid and direct foreign investment and had been dominated by economic ministries such as the Finance Ministry and the Ministry of International Trade and Industry. As a legacy of the Yoshida Doctrine, the Japanese state was organizationally ill equipped to deal with the emerging crisis situation. The Self-Defense Agency did not have the stature and power of the U.S. Department of Defense or the National Security Agency. When it became clear that the United States wanted more than money, however, Kaifu began making plans to send uniformed, but unarmed, Self-Defense Forces (SDF) support personnel to the Persian Gulf. Kaifu introduced legislation into the Japanese Diet that would reinterpret the Japanese Constitution to allow SDF personnel outside Japan as part of UN peacekeeping forces. The proposed UN Peace Cooperation Law proved incredibly divisive, and debate over the measure stretched into October. By early November, when the Kōmeitō Party stiffened its resistance, it became clear that the measure would never pass the upper house of the Diet, and Kaifu withdrew the legislation.[39]

While policymakers did put pressure on Japan, they focused almost all of their attention on Iraq. In November the UN Security Council passed a resolution to allow member states to "use all necessary means" to force Iraq from Kuwait if Iraq remained in the country after January 15, 1991. The Iraqis rejected the ultimatum. Public opinion within the United States divided, with a large minority opposed military action. Bush, however, maintained that economic sanctions would not work and in January 1991, Congress narrowly passed a resolution authorizing him to use force against the Iraqis if troops did not withdraw from Kuwait by the United Nations deadline. On January 17 the multinational coalition began a massive air attack on Iraqi targets. Kaifu pledged an additional $9 billion to the war effort. The coalition launched its land offensive on February 24, and by February 28 the Iraqi army had been driven out of Kuwait and the coalition declared a cease-fire. A week later, the Japanese Diet finally approved a $9 billion aid and support package.

The Persian Gulf crisis revealed the extent of the paradigm drift in U.S.-Japan relations. Throughout the crisis, the United States pushed Japan for more active involvement but never clearly stated what that involvement should be. This vague but intense pressure generated considerable anxiety in Tokyo, and Japanese policymakers' behavior to U.S. pressure was chaotic and perceived as unresponsive. Not only was there no agreement on what Japan's role should be in the U.S.-led multinational effort, the crisis clearly showed that neither country held a clear idea of what role it envisioned for Japan in the post–cold war security order. If the United States was to be the first among equals in multilateral efforts, was Japan to be the banker, a full partner, or a free rider? The Gulf war began serious debate about Japan's role in the post–cold war world, both in Japan and the United States, a topic to which this chapter returns later.

Post–Catch-Up, Post–Cold War: Framework Talks

Having explored the security side of paradigm drift, it is time turn to the economic and trade consequences of the weakening hold of containment and the Yoshida Doctrine. The Framework Talks between the Clinton administration and the Hosokawa government showcased the end of stylized interaction, and the new role confusion, unanticipated behavior, and ultimately, bilateral conflict both in process and outcome that can occur as a result of paradigm drift.

In spite of facing twin oil shocks, the first of which signaled the end of the era of high Japanese economic growth, by the late 1970s the Japanese economy had caught up to the West, surpassing all countries but the United States in the size of its GNP. In fact, by 1978 Japan's GNP per capita surpassed that of the United States.[40] Japan had also developed into a world export power, with a $10 billion trade imbalance with the United States by 1978.[41] Against these developments, the containment paradigm of coddling Japan to ensure its economic stability in the face of communism made less sense, and the latent reciprocal free trade paradigm gained saliency.

As early as 1970, the United States exerted increasing bilateral pressure on Japan to open up sectors of its domestic market to American firms, as well as to slow exports of Japanese goods into American markets. Developed through repeated bilateral negotiations over textiles, automobiles, and semiconductors, a stable, even predictable, negotiating pattern emerged. The nature of this pattern took shape partly as the result of assumptions embedded in both containment and the Yoshida Doctrine that placed the United States in the role of leader and Japan in the role of subordinate.[42] In this negotiating pattern, the United States took the proactive role, identifying the problem and proposing solutions, while Japan took the reactive role, conceding to demands. More specifically, as described by John Creighton Campbell:

> The United States will castigate the Japanese behavior as unfair and as symbolic of Japan's overall neo-mercantilist policy. Japan will explain why things must be done that way and anyway it has done all it can, and complain about scapegoating, while dragging its feet through the negotiating sessions. Eventually, perhaps after a year, the Americans will seem to get angry and threaten dire consequences, usually a protectionist rampage in Congress. Japan will then give in and accept at least half of the American demands, pleading over-whelming pressure, *gaiatsu*.[43]

Thus despite Japanese economic catch-up, the bilateral negotiating pattern was distinctly unequal. Through the early 1990s, bilateral trade negotiations followed this basic pattern of American demands and Japanese concessions, peaking with negotiations over semiconductors in 1986, when for the first time U.S. officials successfully negotiated voluntary import expansions that specified a numerical import target for the Japanese semiconductor market—a 20 percent foreign market share.

As the Clinton administration took office in early 1993, his trade team seemed to agree that the semiconductor accords of 1986 and 1991 had worked. The new administration intended to pursue similar agreements with numerical targets on a broader range of issues during the U.S.-Japan Framework for a New Economic Partnership Talks (Framework Talks) set for summer of that year. This program represented a clear departure from the Bush administration's Structural Impediments Initiative (SII) negotiating strategy, which pushed for macro changes to the Japanese system instead of numerical, results-oriented deals.[44] With a domestic political coalition that was more supportive of tough trade tactics and, more importantly for this chapter, freed of the burdens of cold war leadership and the containment doctrine, Clinton had a freer hand to push hard to open up key Japanese markets.[45]

On the Japanese side, a similar set of circumstances developed that pushed new Japanese Prime Minister Morihiro Hosokawa's government to finally break the ritualized negotiating pattern of U.S. demands and Japanese concessions. Hosokawa became prime minister in July 1993, the first non-LDP prime minister to serve since 1955. The historic transfer of power from the LDP to Hosokawa's reform coalition helped to shake the Yoshida Doctrine's hold on policymaking. In addition, similar to the effect described earlier on U.S. policymakers, by 1993 the weakening hold of the Yoshida Doctrine resulting from Japanese economic catch-up had begun to take effect, making Japanese officials less apt to see Japan as subordinate to the United States. Accordingly, in response to the Clinton administration's stated desire for results-oriented trade agreements, Japanese officials pledged to never again make numerical targets in trade agreements.

Japanese officials were as good as their word and stubbornly resisted American demands to include quantitative criteria in agreements through 1993 and into 1994. Arguing that these numerical targets amounted to managed trade, Japanese officials attempted to frame the U.S. program as inconsistent with free trade ideas. By the summer of 1994, U.S. negotiators had officially given up on numerical targets but Japanese negotiators refused to even commit to annual progress in foreign access and sales. The first set of Framework Agreements reached in September 1994 did not commit Japan to any market share increase in any sector, and analysts in both the United States and Japan characterized the deal as a U.S. defeat.

The Framework Talks marked the end of the old bilateral negotiating pattern of American demands and Japanese concessions. For the first time, Japan said no. And Japanese negotiators continued to say no. In August 1996, during talks to renew the semiconductor accords, the United States had to concede not only to leaving out all references to market share targets but also to downgrading the agreement, which had been legally binding and subject to enforcement under Section 301 of U.S. trade law, to the status of a nonbinding joint statement. In contrast to developments in security issues, Japanese economic catch-up and the end of the cold war acted to dislodge sentiments associated with the Yoshida Doctrine and containment that assumed a hierarchical bilateral relationship with the United States as leader and Japan as subordinate. By the late 1990s, a new, more independent mind-set had taken root in Japanese trade circles, and Japan seemed to at last come out from under the United States' shadow, at times even working in concert with other nations against the United States.

Implications for the Future

While the Gulf war and the Framework Talks point toward a change in the U.S.-Japan relationship as a result of false assumptions and uncertain expectations about roles and causal logic, they do not reflect a definitive break in the bilateral relationship. In fact these two cases stand out for the very reason that they are unusual. Twenty years after Japanese economic catch-up and ten years after the end of the cold war, containment and the Yoshida Doctrine continue to shape bilateral interaction. They continue to be formally institutionalized in the U.S.-Japan Security Treaty as well as in the Japanese Constitution. Moreover, many of the assumptions and expectations embedded in the containment and the Yoshida Doctrines have not been challenged by historical events. For example, the collapse of the Soviet Union has not eroded the assumption in the United States that the country needs an internationalist, or interventionist, orientation in order to achieve national security and prosperity. Isolationism, either military or economic, has not entered the mainstream debate as a legitimate policy program in the United States. The lessons and memories of World War II and the cold war still resonate too strongly. Even without the threat of the Soviet Union, U.S. elites view a strong Japan, particularly a strong Japanese economy, as essential to global stability and prosperity.[46] On the Japanese side, economic catch-up has not spurred a debate about whether Japan should continue to play a role in the U.S. security and economic systems. At present, Japanese elites do not seriously question either the desirability of the U.S.-Japan relationship or U.S. global leadership in general. Instead, they debate how far to wander from U.S. leadership on specific issues, particularly within Asia. Thus the term "paradigm drift" best describes the current state of affairs in the U.S.-Japan relationship. Bilateral interaction has become less predictable and more fluid as economic and security reality has changed in the past twenty years. The old dominant ideas, however, continue to broadly constrain and shape action and thinking, just as established ideas constrained and shaped the creation of containment and the Yoshida Doctrine.

Reactions in both the United States and Japan to the September 11, 2001, terrorist attacks on the World Trade Center and Pentagon demonstrate how the old paradigms still matter. U.S. elites' immediate reaction to the attack was activist and interventionist. Even while mourning the dead, President George W. Bush promised to find and destroy the attackers and their supporters. The American public embraced this proactive response, with Bush's approval ratings soaring to 90 percent as he readied the nation for war.[47] Instead of recoiling from the world and reverting to isolationism, the U.S. public and elites seemed to take the attack as a reminder of the United States' role as world leader. In stark contrast to the slower and confused response to the Gulf war crisis, Japanese elites quickly and squarely put Japan in a supportive role behind U.S. leadership. Prime Minister Junichirō Koizumi quickly announced that the Japanese Self-Defense Forces would take rearguard action to support U.S. military retaliation. He also pushed legislation through the Diet to assist in intelligence gathering and delivery of supplies and medical services to U.S. forces.

At the same time, however, the September 11 attacks illustrate the discontinuities associated with paradigm drift. While generally activist, the direction of U.S. action and leadership remains unclear. No program has yet emerged a winner in laying out the specific steps for winning the war on terrorism in the same way that containment prescribed the United States' overall strategy during the cold war. Just as communist expansion immediately following World War II led to an unsettled period in which new programs could take root, the September 11 attacks have helped to accelerate debate about a new national foreign policy strategy in the United States.

Broadly speaking, two programs have emerged as the most promising successors to containment in the United States. The first program directly pursues national interests, usually through unilateral means. The United States should do what it takes to foster its interests, independent of world opinion. The program's implicit assumption is that national interests diverge, especially without a common enemy such as the Soviet Union. In practice this would mean fostering free trade through aggressively opening markets and ensuring global stability through a dominant military. This program is at the core of the Bush administration's foreign policy and can be seen in its rejection of the Kyoto Treaty on global warming and emphasis on the National Missile Defense initiative. As it applies to Japan, under the program the United States continues to participate in Asian security but would seek to increasingly share military burdens with Japan. Economically, the United States directly seeks more open Japanese markets through the reduction of trade barriers and domestic reform encouraging competition and privatization. This national interest-centered program resonates with old isolationist assumptions clearly dividing the United States from the rest of the world, while still embracing an internationalist, proactive approach. The risk with such a program is a backlash against the United States, leaving it internationally isolated and creating problems coordinating multinational responses to issues such as global warming, the AIDS epidemic, and even terrorism.

While the first program in many ways represents a continuation of containment methods tailored to a new environment, the second program represents a clear break from containment by framing the United States as a member of the international community, albeit a dominant member. It makes the opposite assumption about interests by assuming that U.S. interests will tend to converge with those of other nations. In this view, the best way to achieve national goals of security and prosperity is to work with friends and allies to create a community of nations. Accordingly, the United States would work primarily through international organizations, such as the World Trade Organization (WTO) and the United Nations, to cooperatively identify and solve regional and global problems. This program informed the Clinton administration's approach to foreign policy. The program deemphasizes the U.S.-Japan relationship in favor of working through international organizations. In practice Japan would not be expected to subordinate its foreign policy to the United States' foreign policy but to serve in international debates as a valued ally. Ideational resources also exist for this program, as Amy Searight shows in chapter 7 of this volume in her account of U.S. leadership during the creation of international organizations such as the International Monetary Fund (IMF) and the General Agreement on Tariffs and Trade–World Trade Organization (GATT-WTO). The question will be how amenable the United States will be to multilateralism when other nations frustrate U.S. policies and initiatives.

On the Japanese side, two existing programs seem most likely to emerge as paradigms. First, Japan could continue to defer to the United States on most issues, particularly security issues. This would not, however, represent a simple continuation of the Yoshida Doctrine. Under this program, Japan would continue to expand its multilateral activities, working through international organizations with the United States and Europe to pursue independent policy aims, particularly in the economic arena. This program generally assumes that what is in the best interests for the United States is in the best interests of Japan. In cases where this assumption proves untrue, Japan can work through established institutions. This modified Yoshida Doctrine resonates with existing ideas for many of the same reasons as the original one. It fits with the idea that Japan benefits as an adaptive follower but fails through bold independent action.

Second, a more openly nationalist program could emerge in Japan. This program would embrace an independent foreign policy and unconstrained military, making Japan what Ichirō Ozawa called a "normal country." Japan would remain within the U.S. security system while bearing a greater security burden. Economically, the mercantilist policies of the Yoshida Doctrine would continue. While open nationalism has remained outside of mainstream policymaking since World War II for cultural, legal, and ideational reasons, in the past decade it has become influential in popular literature and art. Revisionist interpretations of World War II, aided by the

Japanese government's refusal or failure to explicitly recognize Japan's wartime atrocities and tactical mistakes, have proliferated. A nationalist program brings the implicit nationalism of the Yoshida Doctrine to the forefront and would resonate with the nationalist ideas of the pre–World War II era.

The most likely combination of programs emerging to become paradigms would be the U.S. international community-based program combined with modified Japanese subordination. The September 11 attacks softened the Bush administration's unilateralist tendencies and underscored the importance of securing international approval. In Japan the attacks both demonstrated Japanese support for U.S. leadership and perhaps started the process of rearming the nation. However, given the continuing Japanese economic malaise that has caused Japanese elites to question the nation's banking system, protected "pork" sectors, and even its neomercantilist trade policies, modified Japanese subordination appears more likely than a nationalist paradigm to emerge. Together, the two would-be paradigms of U.S. multilateralism and modified Japanese subordination would not fit as well as the Yoshida Doctrine and containment did, but they would lead to complementary roles and common expectations. Both the United States and Japan would be members of a larger international community, in which Japan would typically defer to U.S. leadership. Under this scenario, the U.S.-Japan relationship would be deemphasized in favor of a friendship within larger institutions.

The biggest risk to the U.S.-Japan relationship would come from a self-interested unilateralist U.S. paradigm. If the United States contests increased Japanese assertiveness in international organizations, expecting a continued Japanese subservient role on every issue, Japan may turn to regional organizations as arenas for action, moving from a foreign policy of open regionalism to closed regionalism. The solid assumption that Japan should primarily work within a U.S.-led system could come into question, potentially giving rise to a closed Asian economic organization, one more similar to the European Union than to Asia Pacific Economic Cooperation (APEC). This scenario would threaten U.S. economic interests in Asia by restricting U.S. access, at least relative to Japanese access, to key markets in China and Southeast Asia. The outlook for U.S.-Japan relations would be even gloomier if Japan pursued a closed regional security system as well. The core institutional feature of the bilateral relationship, the U.S.-Japan Security Treaty, would come under attack, substantially weakening the bilateral relationship. Given such potential dangers, U.S. elites would be wise to pay attention to international organizations and respect Japanese initiatives within them.

Notes

1. These ritualized games are described in John Creighton Campbell, "Japan and the United States: Games That Work," in Gerald L. Curtis, ed., *Japan's Foreign Policy after the Cold War: Coping with Change* (M. E. Sharpe, 1993).

2. Thomas Rohlen contributed the term "paradigm drift" during early workshops on this chapter.

3. This conception of ideas as resources comes from sociologists such as Mary Douglas, with her concept of bricolage, and Ann Swidler, with her conception of culture as a tool kit from which people construct strategies of action. Mary Douglas, *How Institutions Think* (Syracuse University Press, 1986), pp. 66–67; and Ann Swidler, "Culture in Action: Symbols and Strategies," *American Sociological Review*, vol. 51 (1986), pp. 273–86.

4. See Judith Goldstein and Robert O. Keohane, "Ideas and Foreign Policy: An Analytical Framework," in Judith Goldstein and Robert O. Keohane, eds., *Ideas and Foreign Policy: Beliefs, Institutions, and Political Change* (Cornell University Press, 1993), pp. 13–17.

5. The concepts of programs and paradigms come from John L. Campbell, "Institutional Analysis and the Role of Ideas in Political Economy," *Theory and Society*, vol. 27 (1998), p. 385.

6. The concepts of settled versus unsettled cultural periods come from Swidler, "*Culture in Action.*" Kowert and Legro make a similar point when they argue that conditions of ambiguity and external shock, hallmarks of unsettled cultural periods, facilitate normative change. Paul Kowert and Jeffrey Legro, "Norms, Identity, and Their Limits: A Theoretical Reprise," in Peter J. Katzenstein, ed., *The Culture of National Security: Norms and Identity in World Politics* (Columbia University Press, 1996), pp. 469–83.

7. See Harold Bolitho, "Abe Masahiro and the New Japan," in Jeffrey P. Maas and William B. Hauser, eds., *The Bakufu in Japanese History* (Stanford University Press, 1985).

8. Bob Tadashi Wakabayashi, *Anti-Foreignism and Western Learning in Early Modern Japan: The New Theses of 1825* (Harvard University Press, 1986).

9. See Walter LaFeber, *The Clash: A History of U.S.-Japan Relations* (W.W. Norton & Company, 1997), p. 20.

10. Sadayoshi Fujii, "*Bakumatsu no Fukoku Kyōhei Ron (The Late Tokugawa's Rich Nation, Strong Army Debate)*" in Sadayoshi Fujii, ed., *Shakai Keizaishi no Shomondai (Problems Related to Social and Economic History)* (Gennando Shoten, 1973), pp. 192–96.

11. Yukichi Fukuzawa, *An Outline of a Theory of Civilization*, translated by David A. Dilworth and G. Cameron Hurst (Sophia University Press, 1973).

12. For more on the role of *fukoku kyōhei* in Meiji reforms, see Richard J. Samuels, *Rich Nation, Strong Army: National Security and the Technological Transformation of Japan* (Cornell University Press, 1994).

13. For this history, see Judith Goldstein, *Ideas, Interests, and American Trade Policy* (Cornell University Press, 1993), pp. 23–136.

14. Ibid., p. 146.

15. Ibid., p. 152.

16. For a detailed account of this process see Michael Schaller, *The American Occupation of Japan: The Origins of the Cold War in Asia* (Oxford University Press, 1985), pp. 20–51.

17. After Acheson became secretary of state in 1949, he used the "great crescent" metaphor several times to describe the Asian containment policy. See William S. Borden, *The Pacific*

Alliance: United States Foreign Economic Policy and Japanese Trade Recovery 1947–55 (University of Wisconsin Press, 1984).

18. Quoted in Nathan Glazer, "From Ruth Benedict to Herman Kahn: The Postwar Japanese Image in the American Mind," in Akira Iriye, ed., *Mutual Images: Essays in American-Japanese Relations* (Harvard University Press, 1975), p. 153.

19. Quoted in Michael Hunt, *Ideology and U.S. Foreign Policy* (Yale University Press, 1987), p. 163.

20. Quoted in Kenneth B. Pyle, *The Making of Modern Japan* (D.C. Heath and Company, 1996), p. 244.

21. Yutaka Kōsai, "The Postwar Japanese Economy, 1945–73," in Peter Duus, ed., *The Cambridge History of Japan, Vol. 6: The Twentieth Century* (Cambridge University Press, 1988), pp. 520–21.

22. These statistics come from John W. Dower, *Empire and Aftermath: Yoshida Shigeru and the Japanese Experience, 1878–54* (Harvard University Council on East Asian Studies, 1979).

23. Kenneth B. Pyle, *The Japanese Question: Power and Purpose in a New Era* (AEI Press, 1996), p. 25.

24. Thomas U. Berger, "From Sword to Chrysanthemum: Japan's Culture of Anti-Militarism," *International Security*, vol. 17, no. 4 (1993), p. 134.

25. See Pyle, *The Japanese Question*, pp. 48–49.

26. While chairman of the Diet committee that reviewed the SCAP draft of the Japanese Constitution, Ashida had inserted two phrases into Article 9, one at the very beginning, "Aspiring sincerely to an international peace based on justice and order" and the other at the beginning of the second paragraph, "In order to accomplish the aim of the preceding paragraph." Ashida later argued that these two amendments made defensive wars and self-defense forces constitutional. See Pyle, *The Japanese Question*, pp. 9–10.

27. Dower, *Empire and Aftermath*, p. 383.

28. Pyle quotes Yoshida in admitting that he used the Constitution as a pretext to avoid rearmament. Pyle, *The Japanese Question*, pp. 26–28.

29. Pyle, *The Making of Modern Japan*, p. 244.

30. Muramatsu and Krauss distinguish between a highly successful "policy line," represented by Yoshida, Ikeda, and Satō, and a less successful "politics line," represented by Kishi and Nakasone. See Michio Muramatsu and Ellis S. Krauss, "The Conservative Line and the Development of Patterned Pluralism," in Kōzō Yamamura and Yasukichi Yasuba, eds., *The Political Economy of Japan* (Stanford University Press, 1987), pp. 516–54.

31. The notion of ideas serving as rallying points, or in their language "focal points," for domestic coalition building comes from Goldstein and Keohane, *"Ideas and Foreign Policy."*

32. Laura Hein explores this "economic growthism" in Japan. Laura E. Hein, "Growth versus Success: Japan's Economic Policy in Historical Perspective," in Andrew Gordon, ed., *Postwar Japan as History* (University of California Press, 1993).

33. Takafusa Nakamura, *Nihon Keizai: Sono Seichō to Kōzō (Japanese Economy: Its Development and Structure)* (University of Tokyo Press, 1993), p. 108.

34. See Japan Economic Planning Agency, *White Papers on Economy 1956–68.*

35. LaFeber, *The Clash*, p. 376.

36. Michael Blaker, "Evaluating Japan's Diplomatic Performance," in Gerald Curtis, ed., *Japan's Foreign Policy after the Cold War: Coping with Change* (M. E. Sharpe, 1993), p. 18.

37. Blaker, *"Evaluating Japan's Diplomatic Performance,"* p. 19.

38. In the end Japan only sent seventeen medical personnel and the supplies were delayed until late September.

39. The Japanese Diet did pass a revised UN Peacekeeping Operations Law in June 1992 and sent almost 700 nonmilitary SDF personnel to join the UN peacekeeping mission in Cambodia in September 1992.

40. Ezra F. Vogel, *Japan as Number One: Lessons for America* (Harvard University Press, 1979), p. 21.

41. Ibid., p. 12.

42. Leonard Schoppa has made a similar point, arguing that the "social context," loosely similar to what this chapter refers to as paradigms, was a key factor in both the stability of the U.S.-Japan negotiating pattern, as well as for the timing of its breakdown. Leonard J. Schoppa, "The Social Context in Coercive International Bargaining," *International Organization,* vol. 53, no. 2 (1999), pp. 307–42.

43. Campbell, *"Japan and the United States: Games That Work,"* p. 49.

44. Leonard Schoppa shows how a combination of domestic politics supporting free trade ideas developed during the Great Depression in addition to lingering cold war containment ideas shaped Bush's policy decision. Leonard J. Schoppa, *Bargaining with Japan: What American Pressure Can and Cannot Do* (Columbia University Press, 1997).

45. Ibid., pp. 260–62.

46. See two policy papers perceived as guides for future U.S. policy toward Japan: Council on Foreign Relations, *"Task Force Report: Future Direction for U.S. Economic Policy toward Japan,"* October 2000 (the Tyson Report); and National Defense University, *"The United States and Japan: Advancing toward a Mature Partnership,"* Institute for National Strategic Studies Special Report, October 2000 (the Armitage-Nye Report).

47. "A Snapshot Gives Bush 90 Percent Approval," *New York Times*, September 24, 2001, p. A1.

CHAPTER FIVE

Domestic Politics

LEONARD J. SCHOPPA

W̶hen looking back at how domestic politics in the United States and Japan has affected relations between the two countries over the past fifty years, what stands out is the mismatch between the by-and-large harmonious and cooperative relations between the two and the almost constant conflict over the terms of the relationship within each country. In the first two decades after the war, Japanese attitudes toward U.S.-Japan security cooperation were so polarized that they sometimes escalated into violence. Similarly, during the 1980s the U.S. debate over Japan policy was so intense that members of Congress once took out their anger on Japanese electronic products on the steps of the Capitol. Yet through it all the two governments steadily increased cooperation. Japan made bases on its territory available to the United States despite the protests, and slowly expanded its contribution to the alliance. The two nations prevented their bilateral disputes from setting off trade wars, and they made deals that allowed bilateral trade and investment to steadily expand over time.

Given this mismatch between high and persistent levels of cooperation between the two countries and recurrent conflict at home, it is tempting to conclude that domestic politics does not matter. The two governments managed to work together despite internal conflict, so this must mean that their national interests in maintaining security and economic cooperation triumphed over domestic squabbles. Many analysts of international relations make precisely this assumption, that domestic politics can be pushed into the background.

This chapter, however, argues that domestic politics has had major consequences for U.S.-Japan relations. Specifically, it contends that domestic divisions within the two countries have not impeded bilateral cooperation, but greatly facilitated it. If domestic political actors were arguing about whether or not to cooperate with the other nation, the implication is that some of them highly valued the bilateral relationship. International developments turned some Japanese or Americans against cooperation, but the same developments often made others value the relationship even more. When bilateral disputes threatened to get out of hand, the doves on one side or the other would prevail over the objections of others and push through concessions. This dynamic also shaped the terms of bilateral cooperation: that is, which side ended up yielding more ground in order to preserve or expand cooperation. The following chapter develops the argument in three parts. An outline of some prevalent hypotheses about how domestic conflict affects international cooperation is presented, followed by a demonstration of how these insights can help explain some of the twists and turns in U.S.-Japan security and economic relations.

Domestic Politics and International Cooperation

Domestic politics matter because internal actors rarely value a cooperative deal in exactly the same way. When the United States agreed in 1988 to keep its market open to Japanese exports in exchange for Japanese liberalization of beef and orange markets, for example, this deal looked attractive to Toyota and Sony but not to Japanese farmers. Similarly, when Japan agreed in 1951 to reestablish military forces in exchange for a peace treaty, this was seen as less of a concession by nationalist advocates of rearmament than it was by members of the progressive camp who thought these troops might be used against them. Domestic differences of this type naturally complicate efforts by national leaders to strike cooperative deals with their international counterparts.

Variations in the preferences of domestic actors have effects on the level and terms of international cooperation because such deals require the approval of more than one person in each nation. Deals must be struck by a negotiator representing each country and then ratified by domestic actors who have the ability to veto the deal. In democratic countries, these actors are likely to include first and foremost the members of the legislature. In most countries, however, bureaucratic agencies and interest groups such as unions and business federations hold veto power as well. International negotiations therefore can be seen as two-level games where deals must be approved at both the international level and at the domestic level in each country.[1]

Theorizing in this two-level game tradition has led to a variety of predictions about how domestic conflict is likely to affect the level and terms of international cooperation. The first type of domestic politics that scholars have emphasized is conflict between chief executives and legislatures. Since both of these generally have to sign off on international bargains, disagreements between them naturally affect whether cooperation is possible. Scholars focusing on this type of domestic conflict, most notably Helen Milner, have argued that any level of conflict between these two actors reduces the likelihood that a cooperative deal can be negotiated and ratified. This follows from the fact that the more hawkish of the two actors—the one further from the terms the foreign counterpart is willing to offer—can veto any unacceptable deal.[2] If a deal can be struck despite divisions in domestic politics, however, the terms are likely to be closer to the position of the divided side.[3] This second prediction follows from the fact that the more hawkish player in a divided polity can force the unified side to make most of the concessions if it strongly desires a negotiated settlement.

While executive-legislative conflict is an important element of domestic politics, an exclusive focus on this kind of conflict misses a great deal of what is interesting about internal politics by using the median legislator to represent what that body is willing to approve. A legislature polarized between almost equal numbers of extreme hawks and doves can nevertheless produce a median legislator who is quite close to the position of the chief executive. To get a more complete understanding of how domestic conflict relates to international cooperation, therefore, the distribution of preferences within the domestic arena needs to be examined.

Robert Putnam, the architect of the two-level game approach, proposed that there are essentially two ways in which domestic preferences can be distributed.[4] The distribution is homogeneous if all or most domestic actors agree that the best deal for their country lies at one end of a continuum, disagreeing only about how much to compromise away from this ideal. This would be the appropriate characterization, for example, if all Israelis agreed that an ideal peace settlement would be one under which the Palestinians agreed to end their violence without asking Israel to cede any control over

Jerusalem. In many cases, however, domestic actors cannot agree on any single ideal set of terms. In trade negotiations, for example, producers threatened by low-cost foreign competition often fight for deals that preserve high tariffs even as exporters and consumers argue for deals that provide for substantial trade liberalization. Putnam calls this second type of preference distribution heterogeneous.

In earlier work, I picked up this distinction and argued that domestic conflict generated by heterogeneous preferences is often quite compatible with high levels of international cooperation. Pointing to the pattern of results from a series of U.S.-Japan economic negotiations during the late 1980s and early 1990s, I argued that domestic divisions sometimes increase opportunities for cooperation. Domestic divisions in Japan that have involved a substantial segment of opinion supportive of the U.S. government's position have created opportunities for the United States to strike cooperative deals with an initially resistant Japanese government. At the same time, I argued, divisions of this kind have actually helped shift the terms of bilateral deals in favor of the United States.[5] While my earlier work focused exclusively on economic bargaining, I argue in this paper that heterogeneous preferences have also shaped the level and terms of U.S.-Japan security cooperation.

Understanding how domestic politics have affected U.S.-Japan relations over the postwar period requires appreciation of how the two types of domestic conflict discussed above have combined to shape bargaining outcomes. The two-by-two matrix in figure 5-1 shows the patterns that are expected to be associated with varying types and levels of domestic conflict. Cooperation is most likely and a country is likely to make the most concessions when its preferences are heterogeneous and the government is united. This prediction follows because a country with heterogeneous politics is likely to have a significant faction of doves who favor policies close to those demanded by the other government. If the chief executive shares this dovish position (a united government), she should be able to push through the compromises necessary to sustain cooperation.

In contrast figure 5-1 shows that cooperation is least likely and a country is likely to make the fewest concessions when preferences are homogeneous and the government is divided. It is possible, of course, that one might find a situation where domestic preferences are uniformly dovish and the chief executive is even more dovish, but in this case the nation would probably not even be involved in international negotiations. It would simply do what the other nation wanted for its own reasons. More

Figure 5-1. *Preference Heterogeneity and Government Unity*

	Homogeneous preferences	Heterogeneous preferences
United government	Moderate cooperation and concessions	Cooperation and concessions most likely
Divided government	Cooperation and concessions least likely	Moderate cooperation and concessions

frequently, homogeneous preferences radiate from a position removed from the policies demanded by the foreign partner. Think of Israel. A more dovish chief executive (Barak) then simply complicates the task of negotiating a deal since he may miscalculate and bring home a deal that requires concessions the legislature-domestic politics will not approve. Figure 5-1 shows that the other two combinations yield predictions of moderate cooperation and concessions.

Note that figure 5-1 assumes that domestic politics on only one side is relevant. Since politics on the other side will also affect cooperation, what is actually needed is something like a two-by-two-by-two-by-two matrix. To spare readers from that, however, this chapter focuses on the empirical analysis that follows on paired cases where the politics on one side is relatively constant. This chapter is not trying to argue that domestic politics is all that matters. The international context also has a significant effect on how far apart two nations' preferences lie. If their interests are fundamentally opposed, cooperation is unlikely even if there is some heterogeneity in domestic politics. As their interests converge, however, levels of heterogeneity and unity of government are likely to have a significant effect on whether cooperation is possible and the terms under which such deals are struck.

Japanese Domestic Conflict and U.S.-Japan Security Relations

This chapter began with the puzzling juxtaposition of domestic conflict and international cooperation that has characterized much of postwar bilateral relations. Nowhere has that jarring contrast been clearer than in U.S.-Japan security relations during the decade of the 1950s. The issue of whether their nation should be involved at all in a security relationship with the United States, much less providing bases and rearming, was so polarizing in Japan that it pushed tens of thousands of protesters into the streets. In 1960 when the Security Treaty was revised, parties other than the ruling Liberal Democrats refused even to participate in the debate, boycotting Diet proceedings and participating in extraparliamentary rallies instead.

Nevertheless, the United States and Japan did reach an accord on security cooperation during this same decade that has now lasted for fifty years. Judged by the results, fifty years of peace and stability in the Northeast Asian region and victory in the cold war, there can be no doubt the deal the two parties worked out provided immense collective benefits that would not have been available had they failed to work together. Why did not polarized politics derail security cooperation during this period? How did divisions in Japan shape the terms of the relationship? In the following section, some of the concepts developed earlier in this chapter are employed to address these questions.

Japanese politics surrounding security policy during this period were conducive to the establishment of a cooperative relationship because some elements within Japan were sympathetic to the demands being made by the United States. This heterogeneity made possible the close alignment between the two countries starting in 1951 and early steps toward Japanese rearmament that were sought by the United States. Although this opinion gap became more pronounced over the decade as geopolitical developments drove the positions of the two Japanese camps further apart, it did not undermine cooperation because the majority remained supportive of U.S. demands. The analysis of variations in domestic preferences and positions taken by chief negotiators, furthermore, helps account for differences across issues and over time in the degree to which Japan was able to accommodate U.S. demands.

The foregoing analysis suggests a need to proceed as follows in order to determine how Japanese politics shaped U.S.-Japan security cooperation. First, there is a need to figure out who the relevant domestic actors were, along with the basic rules of the domestic ratification game; then, to identify the most important issues; finally, to determine where the various actors stood and how this shaped the outcomes.

The most important domestic actors affecting security policy during the postwar period have been political parties. Much more so than in the area of economic policy, where bureaucratic agencies and interest groups played important roles, parties have been the dominant actors in the area of security. Since Japan has a parliamentary system where parties usually vote in unison, the main players to focus on are the parties as blocs. However, since parties have frequently split and merged, sometimes over security issues, and since some members of parties voted against their parties on key security policy votes, it is appropriate to break some of them down into groups based on their security policy views.

The domestic ratification game in 1951 was also somewhat more complicated than the majority rule provided for in the constitution. According to official rules, Shigeru Yoshida needed just a majority vote in the Diet in order to win approval of the Peace and Security Treaties, something that should have been easy for him to arrange since his Liberal Party controlled 284 of the 466 seats in the lower house in 1951. Nevertheless, on a set of treaties of this importance—restoring the nation's independence, establishing terms for peace with the United States and other Western allies, and providing for the United States to continue using bases in Japan for a variety of purposes—Yoshida needed to win more than a simple majority. He needed the support of a super-majority of Diet members, including parties other than his own, if he was to convince the public that the outcome was legitimate.

The other major parties at the time included the Democrats with sixty-six votes, led by Hitoshi Ashida and including a young Yasuhiro Nakasone as well as a few relatively progressive types like Takeo Miki; the Socialists, split over how to cast their treaty ratification votes into a "right" group with twenty-nine seats and a "left" group with sixteen seats; a Communist Party with twenty-two votes; and assorted independents and minor party members.[6]

There were two important, but distinct, issues over which the United States and Japan were negotiating. In exchange for granting Japan independence, restoring peace, and providing for the nation's security, the United States wanted Japan to sign a security treaty that would effectively make it an American ally in the emerging cold war. Japan would in the process give up the opportunity to sign a comprehensive peace that would formally end its war with China and the Soviet Union. Japan was also being asked to provide the Americans with virtually unconstrained use of bases on its territory, bases that were likely to involve Japan in any future wars that broke out in the region—the first one of which was already under way in Korea.[7] Japanese, not surprisingly, differed in the degree to which they were willing to align their nation so closely to the United States. Some felt strongly that Japan should remain neutral in the cold war. Others felt that it should at least aim to preserve more of its autonomy by avoiding a deal that closed off the possibility of peace with China and the Soviets.[8]

The second American demand called for Japan to reestablish a military force that would assist the United States in protecting Japan and maintaining stability in the region. Yoshida had already agreed to establish a 75,000-man police force to take over much of the work of maintaining order inside Japan after the outbreak of the Korean war. Now he was facing demands from Dulles for the nation to establish a 300,000-man military force that might be asked to fight alongside Americans in regional conflicts, demands that would effectively emasculate Article 9 of the 1947 Constitution. Again, Japanese were sharply divided. Some were eager for the nation to reestablish military forces and get rid of the limits on the nation's ability to use force in its own defense, but others felt that such a course would simply involve the nation in another disastrous war.

Tables 5-1 and 5-2 show how the preferences of leading groups within the Diet in 1951 are placed. Placement of the parties and party fragments is based on how legislators actually voted as well as the statements of party leaders and members during the Diet debate.[9] Nevertheless, the documentary record cannot tell precisely how far parties would have been willing to go had they been presented with alternative deals. Neither can it tell exactly how many Liberals and Democrats disagreed with their official party line and would have preferred another set of terms. The information here should therefore be treated as an estimate representing the overall contours of domestic preferences.

On both issues, there was no agreement on what would constitute the best deal for Japan. Unlike the hypothetical Israeli case discussed earlier in this chapter, where all Israelis agreed that they would prefer a peace settlement allowing them to hold onto all of Jerusalem, Japanese approached the questions of alignment and rearmament from opposite poles. On the question of how closely to align with the United States, the communists and the left wing of the Socialist Party felt strongly that Japan should remain neutral in the emerging cold war, and they were not willing to compromise even if this meant the nation would remain under Allied Occupation. The depth

Table 5-1. *Domestic Views on Alignment with the United States in 1951—How Closely Aligned in Order to Achieve a Settlement?*

Number of votes	Relevant information about values and preferences
Japanese Communist Party (22)	Opposed bases and separate peace
Japanese Socialist Party-Left (16)	Opposed bases and separate peace
Neutralist Democrats (17)	Opposed bases and separate peace
Mainstream Democrats (49)	Willing to support bases/separate peace for end of occupation
Japanese Socialist Party-Right (29)	Willing to support bases/separate peace for end of occupation
Moderate Liberals (100)	Willing to support bases/separate peace for end of occupation
Yoshida Liberals (180)	Preferred alignment with the United States (including bases)

Sources: All tables and figures in this chapter are compiled by the author based on sources listed in note 9.

of their feeling is shown by the fact that they voted against the Peace Treaty as well as the Security Treaty. The Democrats too included a sizable contingent of members who opposed the way Yoshida was agreeing to close the door on rapprochement with the Soviet Union and the People's Republic of China. This would isolate Japan in the region, they argued, and leave it perpetually dependent on the United States.[10] Seventeen members felt strongly enough about this that they voted against the Peace Treaty or absented themselves from the vote, contradicting the party's official position.

Yoshida and many members of his Liberal Party, in contrast, approached the issue from the opposite pole. When officials in the Treaty Bureau of the Ministry of Foreign Affairs (MOFA) presented Yoshida with a draft of Japan's opening position insisting that the Peace Treaty be signed by the

Table 5-2. *Domestic Views on Rearmament in 1951—What Size Military in Order to Achieve a Settlement?*

Number of votes	Relevant information about values	Willing to support military of
Japanese Communist Party (22)	Opposed rearmament linked to United States	0
Japanese Socialist Party (16)	Opposed any rearmament	0
Small Military Liberals (220)	Willing to support limited rearmament	0 to 100,000
Japanese Socialist Party-Right (29)	Supported some rearmament	50,000 to 200,000
Moderate Liberals (60)	Supported some rearmament	50,000 to 200,000
Moderate Democrats (44)	Supported moderate rearmament	75,000 to 300,000
Armament Democrats (22)	Supported rapid rearmament	200,000 to 300,000

Soviet Union and China, "his face turned bright red." As one of the officials recalled, "Yoshida raked me over the coals for supporting the bankrupt position of the opposition parties."[11] Instead, Yoshida insisted that MOFA draft an opening position that accepted one of the United States' primary demands: that Japan agree to a treaty that aligned it clearly on the American side of the emerging cold war.[12] On American bases, Yoshida also began from a position close to that of the United States. As early as 1946, when he was foreign minister, Yoshida had commissioned a study that recognized that even after independence Japan would have to rely on the American military, operating out of bases in Japan, to provide for the nation's security.[13] Such bases were necessary, Yoshida felt, not merely because the United States needed them to defend Japan but also because they would link the two countries together and cement America's defense commitment. Consequently, Yoshida began negotiations with John Foster Dulles in 1951 with an offer to allow the Americans to continue using bases.[14]

Clearly Japan's need to win American assent in order to regain independence affected Yoshida's position, shaping his initial bargaining position and pulling him even further toward alignment with the Americans than he would have preferred. For example, Yoshida fought and schemed to avoid being boxed into signing a peace treaty with the Nationalist regime on Taiwan, a step that promised to isolate Japan economically and militarily in the region by aggravating the People's Republic of China (PRC). He also endeavored to secure more balance in basing rights in the administrative agreement that went with the Security Treaty. In both areas, however, he was forced to give in to American demands when it became clear this was the price he would have to pay to win ratification by the U.S. Senate.

If Yoshida was pulled in this direction by his realization that compromise was necessary if Japan was going to secure an end to the Occupation, this was all the more true of the politicians who occupied the vast middle of the spectrum of opinion in the Diet. Moderate Democrats and members of the Liberal Party critical of Yoshida's policy both approached the question of alignment from a position that sought greater autonomy from the United States. During Diet deliberations on the treaties, for example, Democratic Party leader Hitoshi Ashida strongly criticized Yoshida for agreeing to allow the Americans to continue occupying Okinawa and the Ogasawara Islands and for agreeing to a clause inviting the American military to help preserve domestic order inside Japan.[15] While Ashida himself was enough of a realist to realize early on that Japan would need to side with the United States in the emerging cold war, his party remained officially committed to a total

Figure 5-2. *Votes Available in Support of Terms Providing Various Degrees of Alignment with the United States*

Votes available (of 466)

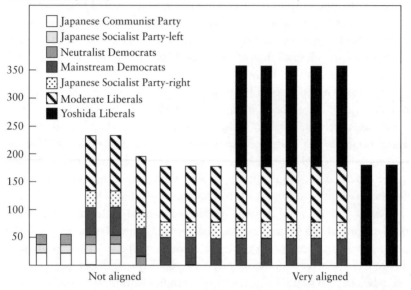

peace until after the start of the Korean War.[16] That the bulk of this party and Liberals with similar views ended up going along with the treaties is evidence of how far they were pulled from their ideal position by their desire to secure independence for Japan.

Figure 5-2 takes the information about the terms the various parties and party fragments were willing to accept (presented in table 5-1 and summarized above), and plots the basic contours of domestic opinion. It suggests that there was a potential majority in the Diet in support of a much more neutralist position, in the area where the views of the progressive parties and the autonomy-seeking moderates overlapped, but shows the even greater majority available in support of the final deal Yoshida negotiated. Yoshida won 307 votes in favor of the Peace Treaty, versus forty-seven opposed, achieving the super-majority he needed to legitimate the settlement.

The argument here is not that Japanese domestic politics alone dictated the final terms, but that the heterogeneity of Japanese views on the question of alignment—with Yoshida starting from a position that saw close alignment as preferable to neutrality—helped make possible the compromises that were necessary for the bargaining to result in a cooperative deal. With Yoshida, the chief negotiator, taking a position at the leading edge of what a median voter in the Diet could support, this also meant Japan had a "unified government" in Milner's terms. The case therefore fits comfortably with the prediction contained in the upper right box of the two-by-two matrix in figure 5-1, which predicted that domestic politics with these characteristics would be conducive to cooperation and to concessions.

Turn then to the other issue at stake in the 1951 negotiations: rearmament. Once again, as shown in table 5-2, the various parties in the Diet approached this question from opposite poles. Faced with demands from Dulles that Japan increase its troop strength to 300,000, a substantial segment of opinion was strongly opposed. The left wing of the Japan Socialist Party (JSP) was firmly committed to unarmed neutrality, while the Japan Communist Party (JCP) opposed rearmament linked to the United States. Both felt strongly enough that they voted against the Security Treaty.[17]

This time, however, Yoshida was sympathetic with the pacifists' position. When drawing up Japan's initial negotiating position in late 1950, he insisted that Japan start from a position proposing no rearmament at all, and he stuck stubbornly to this position through the early months of 1951 even when rebuffed by Dulles at their initial meeting.[18] Yoshida believed that Japan could best provide for its security by relying on the U.S. military, saving its scarce resources for economic reconstruction and industrial growth, a policy later known as the Yoshida Doctrine.[19] To help convince the Americans, Yoshida used every strategy at his disposal, using his contacts in the pacifist camp to arrange a protest demonstration timed to coincide with one of Dulles' visits and soliciting support from the Supreme Commander of the Allied Powers, General Douglas MacArthur.

Other members of the conservative camp, however, were not as eager as Yoshida to avoid rearmament. Recognizing that Japan's failure to provide for its own defensive capabilities would leave it perpetually dependent on the United States, Democrats such as Ashida urged revision of Article 9 so that Japan could undertake rapid rearmament.[20] Japan could then negotiate with the United States from a position of greater equality and avoid a one-sided security pact on American terms. Consequently, Ashida and most other members of the Democratic Party, as well as some members of the Liberal Party, approached this issue from a position close to the American one.[21] Some, including twenty-two Democrats and some Liberals, felt strongly enough that they resisted pressure from party leaders to fall in line behind the Security Treaty and abstained or voted against it.[22]

Figure 5-3. *Votes Available in Support of Terms Providing Varying Levels of Rearmament*

Votes available (of 466)

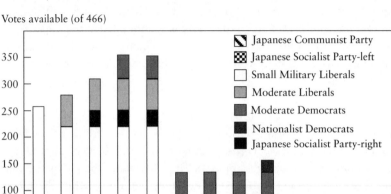

Size of military (thousands of troops)

While this indicates that there were elements of heterogeneity in Japanese domestic politics surrounding this issue already in 1951, the bubble of support in favor of the American position was much smaller than the one on alignment. As shown in figure 5-3, an estimated 150 votes may have been available in support of rearmament at or near the level Dulles requested, but this number of votes fell short of a simple majority, much less the supermajority Yoshida needed. As a result, Japan's ability to compromise on this issue was more constrained. The fact that Yoshida sought an even lower level of troop strength than the median voter would have approved further limited movement in the American direction.

In the end, although the United States and Japan reached a cooperative settlement in the form of a Security Treaty, Japan did not concede as much ground as it did on alignment. Nor was the agreement as cooperative as it could have been. The treaty preamble included a reference to the expectation that Japan would "increasingly assume responsibility for its own defense," but did not represent a specific commitment. Yoshida agreed to establish a security force, separate from the National Police Reserve, of 50,000 troops, but this was well short of the level where it could make a functional contribution to its own defense.[23] In 1951 he capped Japan's total troop strength at 110,000 and continued to refuse American requests, accompanied by offers of aid, for a larger contribution to the joint security effort.[24] Partly because of Yoshida's refusal to concede more in this area, the Security Treaty also did not contain an explicit pledge by the United States to defend Japan against attack. Instead, the treaty language merely stated that American forces operating out of bases in Japan "may be utilized to contribute to the maintenance of international peace and security in the Far East and to the security of Japan." This tenuous form of cooperation reflected domestic political conditions (less heterogeneity and more division of government) that were less conducive to cooperation and concessions.

While these events transpired fifty years ago, the basic contours of domestic politics surrounding the security relationship have remained strikingly constant over the succeeding decades. While the intervening years (especially the 1950s) were to see some growth in the segment of opinion opposed to alignment and rearmament, the segment in support of the close geopolitical relationship and greater contributions to the joint security effort grew even faster. This increase in heterogeneity and the resulting internal conflict, however, did not undermine cooperation. A brief description of two episodes that marked turning points in U.S.-Japan security relations follows to show how the framework advanced here can help understand how cooperation has continued despite domestic conflict.

Security Treaty Revision of 1960

The 1950s saw a sharp polarization of opinion on security issues. The camp supporting unarmed neutrality grew in size and in the vehemence of its views, but so did the side supporting rearmament and the relationship with the United States. The tensions between these two camps climaxed in May and June 1960 as the Diet debated, and then ratified, revisions in the Security Treaty—over the vehement protests of the opposition parties and amidst demonstrations by thousands of unionists, students, and intellectuals in the streets.

The negotiations over revisions to the treaty began with relatively high hopes in 1958. The Japanese economy had grown rapidly during the 1950s, and Japan had begun to assume a larger role in international affairs with its admission to the United Nations in 1956. These developments led a wide range of Japanese to support the idea of reopening talks on a Security Treaty that the United States had essentially imposed on Japan as a condition for ending its military occupation. At a minimum, it was widely felt, revisions should aim at addressing inequalities in the security relationship. In the United States too there was a growing recognition of the need to adjust relations in the direction of greater equality, with a 1957 National Security Council study recommending revision of the Security Treaty to firm up the ground on which bilateral security relations rested.[25]

Once the negotiations on treaty revision commenced in September 1958, however, they quickly became caught up in the intense Japanese domestic conflict that had been building all decade between the progressive and conservative camps. Since the original treaty had no expiration date, the Americans once again enjoyed a strong bargaining position. If no agreement were reached on revision, the original treaty would remain in effect. Comfortable with this fallback position, the Americans were in no hurry to accept major revisions—and yet this is exactly what the progressive forces, as well as some members of the conservative camp, demanded.

As treaty negotiations got underway, the progressive forces were even more committed to the position of unarmed neutrality they had advocated in 1951. The Socialist Secretary-General, Inejirō Asanuma, had gone so far as to make common cause with the PRC on a visit there in 1959, declaring "the United States is the common enemy of the Japanese and Chinese peoples."[26] The progressive camp was also a larger bloc within the Diet, with the Socialist Party (reunited in 1955) having won 166 seats in 1958 and with the Communists holding one more. Though the Socialists remained split into the left and right blocs over security issues, and split again in 1959 as the treaty debate exposed their differences, defections left the Socialist Party with 128 seats—a substantial increase over the seventeen seats the left wing of the Socialists had held in 1951.

International developments in the late 1950s simply hardened this camp's resolve. The launch of Sputnik in 1958 and the failure of the U.S. attempt to launch a satellite at about the same time led many progressives to become more convinced than ever that the Security Treaty was a net negative for the security of the nation. George Packard put it this way: "The feeling was, in essence, that it would be like holding onto a lightning rod in the middle of a thunderstorm: Wouldn't the U.S. bases simply attract a rain of Soviet missiles without in themselves being able to prevent the total destruction of these four islands?"[27]

The Chinese shelling of Quemoy and Matsu in the Taiwan Straits similarly aggravated worries among many in this camp that Japan might be caught up in a war between the PRC and the Nationalist regime on Taiwan if the Americans used bases in Japan as a staging area for their intervention in such a conflict. The Americans promised during the negotiations on revision to engage in prior consultations with Japan on such matters, but Diet debate on what this meant revealed that Japan would essentially have to trust the Americans to respect their wishes if Japan refused to approve a specific use of U.S. bases during prior consultations. The Americans were not willing to offer Japan a veto. The progressives, in particular, were not predisposed to trust the Americans. The Americans had given them the Peace Constitution but had since that time been pressuring Japan to rearm anyway. They had approved the Red Purge and repressive labor laws in 1949 and were channeling Central Intelligence Agency funds to the Liberal Democratic Party (LDP). An appeal to trust in such an atmosphere held little meaning to the progressives.

These concerns were simply magnified many times over with the U-2 incident of May 1, 1960, right in the middle of the treaty debate in the Japanese Diet. The breakdown in what had been warming relations between the United States and the Soviets over the intrusion of American spy planes over Soviet territory aggravated Japanese worries about getting caught in a rain of missiles between the two powers, especially after it was revealed that U-2 planes also operated out of the American airbase at Atsugi, near Tokyo. The American attempts to assure the Japanese that these planes had only flown "along the frontiers of the free world" and were used only for "legitimate scientific purposes" also served to aggravate left-wing distrust of the U.S. military.[28] If the Americans could not admit the truth after they had been caught red-handed, how could Japan count on them to own up to controversial uses of the bases before the fact? These events, combined with the way the government of Prime Minister Nobusuke Kishi handled the process of treaty ratification in the Diet, led to the biggest outpouring of anti-American demonstrations ever seen in Tokyo, forcing the cancellation of President Eisenhower's visit at a moment when the United States and Japan had supposedly renewed their security bond.

These events affected all Japanese, of course, and are commonly seen as shaping the nation's interests, making Japan more worried about the dangers of "entrapment" through the alliance (see chapter 2 in this volume). These events, however, affected the left wing of the political spectrum most strongly. The progressives were predisposed to distrust Americans, so the events of 1958 to 1960 simply fed that distrust and pushed them further to the left and made them more determined to block treaty revision. They were also ideologically predisposed to see neutralism, and improved relations with China and the Soviet Union, as a realistic alternative to the security alliance with the Americans. So events that seemed to make the alliance strategy more risky simply reinforced their preference for the alternative neutralist path.

The conservatives, on the other hand, were more trusting of the Americans and were ideologically disinclined to see neutralism as an attractive option. As a result, when the Americans offered prior consultations, Kishi and his supporters in the mainstream of the LDP were willing to take on faith the American promises that their views would be respected. Even after Sputnik and the Taiwan Straits crisis, and even after the U-2 incident, they saw no realistic alternative to a continuation of the security alliance. If anything, rising East-West tension, along with the ideologically polarized riots at home, led conservatives to cling more closely to the alliance, even if the Americans were willing to offer few revisions. Despite the events that pushed the progressives further toward the left, therefore, mainstream conservatives remained close to the American position, willing to support a treaty with only limited modifications on the questions of consultation, geographical specificity, and time limit.[29]

What this analysis shows is that security policy in Japan, at least during this period, operated in an environment where the major blocs saw policy not in terms of a single rationale based on national interests but in starkly distributional terms. The revised treaty presented to the Diet in 1960 promised the conservatives international security without much risk, but it promised the progressives international insecurity. International developments did not shift the entire spectrum away from the United States' position but instead pushed one faction (the JCP and JSP) further away while leaving another large faction (mainstream conservatives) firmly committed to the U.S. alliance. Divided politics did not undermine, but instead helped make possible, the continuation of U.S.-Japan security relations.

Nakasone's Enhancement of Japan's Security Contribution

After the tumultuous events of 1960, the contours of domestic politics surrounding U.S.-Japan security cooperation remained largely frozen in place for thirty years. The JSP, the largest opposition party throughout this period, continued to support unarmed neutrality. The LDP, meanwhile, continued to support close alignment with the United States with a limited defense role for Japan. The one exception to this pattern came during the mid-1980s when Prime Minister Yasuhiro Nakasone pushed to enhance Japan's security contribution to the alliance. A brief look at domestic politics during this episode will update the story of how domestic politics surrounding the rearmament dimension developed after 1951.

Starting way back in 1950, as noted earlier in this chapter, the American government began pushing the Japanese to contribute more to their own defense and to the maintenance of peace and stability in the region. This pressure continued over the succeeding decades, with particularly strong demands in the mid-1950s with the drawdown of U.S. forces after the Korean War; again in the late 1960s with the drawdown in Vietnam; and again after the Soviet invasion of Afghanistan in 1979. In each of these periods, there were segments within the LDP supportive of expanding Japan's security role, just as in 1951, but in each case the Japanese resisted significant expansion. While this resistance reflected in part the pacifism of the median legislator in the Diet, it also reflected the fact that the prime ministers during these periods came from the limited-defense-role segment of the LDP: Yoshida in the early to mid-1950s; Eisaku Satō in the late 1960s; and Masayoshi Ōhira and Zenkō Suzuki after Afghanistan. Just as during the episode in 1951, divided government (the commitment of the chief executive to a more limited defense role than the median legislator was willing to support) constrained this dimension of cooperation and limited Japanese concessions in the face of U.S. pressure.

This situation changed when Nakasone became prime minister in late 1982. For many years Nakasone had been one of the leading supporters of rearmament within the conservative camp, backing faster rearmament in his days as a young legislator at the time of the San Francisco settlement in 1951, working for revision of Article 9 in the late 1950s, and pushing for an expanded defense role as head of the Defense Agency in the early 1970s. In each case, however, he had been stymied by a lack of support from top levels of the party. He came to power in 1982 not because the party had embraced his views on defense but due to factional machinations within the LDP: Nakasone had made a deal with Kakuei Tanaka, then on trial on corruption charges, under which Tanaka agreed to lend Nakasone the support of his large faction.[30]

This shift tipped Japanese policy markedly in the direction of a larger security role. This time, the change had little to do with shifts in the preferences of domestic political actors. Before and after Nakasone's assumption of the prime minister's post, the JSP and JCP were committed to abolishing the Self-Defense Forces if they ever came to power; the Kōmeitō Party was committed to a pacifist platform; and the Democratic Socialists supported a moderately larger defense role. The LDP itself was made up of a majority group committed to revision of the constitution and a larger defense role and a minority group committed to the limited defense posture of the status quo Yoshida Doctrine.[31] Because the pro-rearmament group was larger than the pacifist camp within the LDP, there was room for policy movement in this direction in response to U.S. pressure, even before Nakasone came to power.

The shift in the top spot was critical because how far Japan moved toward playing a larger security role depended not just on the preferences of the legislature but on what the chief executive was willing to support. Yoshida and other prime ministers from his school had been unwilling to move very far. Japan in effect had a divided government on this issue, and this restrained Japanese concessions and the amount of cooperation possible. Once Nakasone came to power eager to push policy in the American direction as far as the median legislator was willing to go, however, Japan had a united government and the nation's security contribution was enhanced. Nakasone pushed defense spending above the previously sacrosanct level of 1 percent of GNP, committed the government to defending the sea lanes around Japan up to 1,000 miles, and directed the Defense Agency to begin acquiring the defense weaponry required to carry out this mission in cooperation with the United States.[32]

American Domestic Conflict and Economic Cooperation

Although this chapter has focused exclusively on Japanese politics up to this point, patterns of U.S.-Japan cooperation have been influenced as well by the contours of American domestic politics. In the area of security relations, during the cold war, those politics were relatively constant through Republican and Democratic administrations from the 1950s through the 1980s. The U.S. government was united in pressuring Japan to align itself closely to the United States, and it was also united in its desire to see Japan moderately increase its defense contribution. Because politics on the American side were so united, the ability of the two sides to reach a cooperative security arrangement depended largely on the willingness of Japan to accept these American demands—something that was facilitated, as described above, by heterogeneity within Japanese politics, especially when accompanied by unified government.

With economic relations, in contrast, the two countries reversed roles for most of the postwar period. This time, Japanese politics were homogeneous, with all parties and key bureaucratic agencies agreeing that the best deal for Japan would be one where Japan opened its markets as little as possible while maintaining access to U.S. markets. The ability of the two countries to continue carrying out a large volume of trade and avoiding any tit-for-tat trade war therefore depended on the ability of American politics to accept limited liberalization. This it did in large part because U.S. politics were heterogeneous. Although a growing segment of American opinion was concerned about unfair Japanese trade policies and practices—concerns that sometimes boiled over to produce stark anti-Japanese rhetoric and theatrics, another segment remained willing to overlook these transgressions in the interest of maintaining smooth security relations.

This pattern was disrupted in the 1980s, however, by geopolitical developments that unified American opinion in favor of more aggressive demands on economic issues. The dimming of the cold war led those most concerned about the security relationship to relax their objections even as the rise of Japan's economic power to near parity with the United States led some of the same individuals to support more aggressive economic demands, especially when they involved products with security implications. Fortuitously for the relationship, Japanese domestic politics related to trade policy became more heterogeneous just as American politics were becoming more unified. The Ministry of International Trade and Industry (MITI), export-oriented firms, and some members of the Diet came to recognize that economic liberalization might actually be good for Japan. In the 1990s, therefore, the pattern of domestic politics on trade has come to resemble the pattern found in the security area: the United States makes demands, and Japan's responses are facilitated by the existence of a segment of opinion that supports the U.S. position—at least when these demands are consistent with the principles of multilateral trade liberalization. Divisions in Japanese politics have thus come to substitute for divisions in U.S. politics in facilitating the compromises that have allowed economic cooperation to continue.

This section reviews the highlights in the story just summarized, focusing on the American and Japanese politics that surrounded key market-opening negotiations.[33] Given space constraints, separate tables and figures mapping out the politics in detail have not been generated, as was done for the security cases above. The section concentrates on the impact of the overall contours of politics, neglecting the role of divided-unified government. Consider first two disputes that generated domestic politics that were typical of the pre-1985 pattern: foreign investment (1968–71), and beef and citrus (1977–78). In the foreign investment case, large American multinationals such as Texas Instruments (TI) wanted Japan to speed the pace at which it was implementing its 1964 pledge to open the nation up to foreign investment, a condition for its membership in the Organization for Economic Cooperation and Development (OECD). Japan had opened up some sectors such as soy sauce, but was delaying the removal of licensing rules that protected priority sectors such as semiconductors and computers. These licensing rules forced companies like TI to negotiate with MITI, which insisted they enter joint ventures with Japanese partners and share valuable patents with Japanese firms as a condition for market entry.[34]

Despite the fact that these rules hurt American firms that were important to the nation's economic strength, the United States did not press hard. In the late 1960s, Commerce Secretary John Connor intervened on TI's behalf and asked MITI to give positive consideration to the terms the firm was seeking.[35] In addition President Nixon raised the broader issue of capital liberalization in high technology sectors in negotiations with Prime Minister Eisaku Satō between 1969 and 1971—talks that also dealt with higher profile issues involving the reversion of Okinawa and Japanese exports of textiles to the United States.[36] With the Japanese unwilling to bend in the TI case or on the timetable for capital liberalization in high technology sectors, however, the American government decided not to press the issue. TI was forced to accept terms close to those MITI had originally suggested, requiring it to license its valuable Kilby patents to Japanese competitors and forcing it to make its initial investments in the form of a joint venture with Sony Corporation.[37] The broader timetable for liberalization in high technology sectors, moreover, ended up delaying liberalization in computers until the end of 1975, by which time TI and other American firms had already licensed away their most valuable patents to Japanese competitors. Seeking to explain why the American government had failed to press more vigorously for investment liberalization in this case, Mark Mason points to the divisions within the American government where a large segment of the political elite was preoccupied with maintaining the security relationship.[38]

In another early case involving pressure to open Japanese markets, the beef and citrus dispute of 1977–78, the Americans pressed harder.[39] Seeking an end to quota systems that kept Japanese markets for these products closed in violation of GATT rules, American negotiators steadily ratcheted up the pressure during these two years. U.S. Trade Representative Robert Strauss was heavily involved, and President Jimmy Carter personally raised the issue in contacts with Prime Minister Takeo Fukuda. In the initial round of 1977, the Japanese made some concessions, agreeing to expand the quotas in ways that favored American producers, but when the Americans pressed for a scheduled end to the quota system, Japanese negotiators refused to budge. Unwilling to let this issue upset the broader relationship, the Americans ended up dropping their key demand and accepting another small increase in quotas and a commitment to talk about the future of quotas again in 1983. Japan did not actually agree to end its quota regime in these sectors until 1988, by which time the Americans had become much more aggressive in seeking market-opening concessions.

In the years since these early market-opening encounters, Americans have become much more homogeneous in their demands for market access. The semiconductor dispute of 1986 represented a turning point. Japanese semiconductor producers had advanced tremendously since the days when they had relied on licensed patents. By 1986 they had taken a lead in the production of leading edge memory chips (64K and 256K), and Japanese firms had driven seven out of nine American firms out of the dynamic random access memory chip business.[40] Worried that this trend could leave the American military, not to mention the civilian economy, dependent on Japanese firms for a vital component in the new high tech economy, American officials from the political and security side of the government joined those from the economic agencies in backing aggressive demands, seeking to force the Japanese to stop dumping memory chips and asking them to accept a minimum market access quota of 20 percent for American chips.[41]

Initially, the Japanese government resisted strongly, and even after accepting the American demands in 1986, MITI had difficulty forcing Japanese chipmakers to comply with the terms of the deal they had struck. As a result, the Reagan administration imposed sanctions on Japanese electronics firms in April 1987. Japanese firms eventually came into line with the terms of the antidumping agreement, allowing the U.S. to reduce sanctions later in 1987 and avoid escalating the dispute into a tit-for-tat trade war.[42] After another agreement in 1991 confirmed the 20 percent market target, the Japanese also came into compliance with that provision of the semiconductor accords.

This dispute helped crystallize new patterns of domestic politics surrounding market access disputes on both sides of the Pacific. On the American side, the nation's success in opening a valuable and growing market helped cement homogeneous support for a more aggressive market-opening policy in dealing with Japan. Numerous Congressional votes in the 1980s confirmed that this strategy enjoyed broad support in the legislature.[43] Within the administration, the strategy also enjoyed strong support from the Commerce Department, the Office of the U.S. Trade Representative, and (within limits) from the other agencies involved: Treasury, State,

Defense, and the Council of Economic Advisers. In the opening months of the George H. W. Bush administration, a brief battle was fought over the specific demands the United States should pursue with the help of the new Super 301 provision of U.S. trade law. One side called for more sectoral market access targets, along the lines of the semiconductor deal, while the other argued for broad structural changes designed to open markets in many sectors at once. Those advocating the latter course prevailed, but once the administration committed to this strategy, all agencies worked in unison to press these demands on Japan.[44]

The Clinton administration that came into office in 1993 was even more unified in its support for an aggressive Japan policy. Unlike the Bush team that had emphasized structural barriers, the Clinton administration initially emphasized numerical targets, based on the model of the semiconductor accords. Once again, Congress strongly supported this even more aggressive agenda, typified by the Americans' insistence that the Japanese agree to a set of objective criteria for evaluating the results of market-opening efforts in autos and auto parts during talks that continued for two acrimonious years.[45] The Clinton administration, however, eventually pursued a more diverse set of demands. For example, the administration: called on the Japanese to liberalize the cellular phone market (1994); called on them to liberalize financial regulations that prevented pension assetholders from turning to foreign asset managers (1996); demanded compensation for past policies that discriminated in favor of Fuji and against Kodak in the photographic film business (1995–98); and called on Nippon Telegraph and Telephone (NTT) to lower local telephone access charges (1998–2000). All of these demands were made through lower-profile negotiations than in the case of autos, but these too enjoyed broad support within the administration and Congress.

While the semiconductor accords thus marked a shift toward much greater unity behind America's demands for Japanese market liberalization, they also represented a turning point for the Japanese side. Export-oriented industries, MITI officials, and senior LDP politicians responsible for managing the bilateral relationship all learned from the experience that American economic demands now needed to be taken more seriously. The self-examination that this induced, through exercises such as the Maekawa Reports in the mid-1980s and the Hiraiwa Commission activities in 1993, also led more economic elites to realize that Japan could benefit from liberalization and a shift toward heavier reliance on domestic demand. MITI, for example, published a vision report for the retail industry in 1989 that supported relaxation of Large Store Law regulations as a means of accelerating the modernization of one of Japan's most inefficient sectors.[46] Business organizations such as Keidanren and Keizai Dōyūkai similarly published a string of reports calling for regulatory reforms designed to lower their costs of production. While this conversion remained somewhat superficial during the bubble years of the late 1980s, the share of elite opinion supportive of liberalization grew as the recession-wracked decade of the 1990s wore on.

This did not mean that the nation was willing to accept each and every one of the United States' market-opening demands. A substantial segment of Japanese society remained supportive of protection. The new heterogeneity in preferences on economic issues created opportunities for the Americans to win concessions, but only when their demands enjoyed strong support from economic interest groups, government officials, and senior politicians who were willing to broker deals. The record of Japan's responsiveness to U.S. pressure since 1985 thus shows an uneven, issue-specific pattern.

In some cases, American demands received particularly strong support from actors inside Japan. In the Large Store Law case from 1990, for example, liberalization was supported not only by MITI but also by some chain stores inside Japan that hoped to take advantage of a relaxation of rules governing the establishment and hours of large stores. Prime Minister Toshiki Kaifu, moreover, saw that by brokering a deal on this issue, he could increase his opinion poll ratings by showing that he was willing to resist protectionist demands from a traditional LDP client group. Consequently, the United States was able to convince Japan to adopt far-reaching changes in the Large Store Law that allowed a sharp increase in the number of large store openings, including openings by American chains such as Toys-R-Us.[47] Similar support for the U.S. position from certain Japanese makers of cell phones and telecommunications equipment helped the United States win concessions on cell phone issues in 1994, ushering in a rapid increase in cell phone use that is recognized as one of Japan's few economic success stories of the 1990s.[48] Subsequent cases of significant liberalization in the area of pension asset management (1996) and interconnection charges for local phone access (2000) have also been linked to substantial support inside Japan for the policies demanded by the United States.

In contrast the United States has run into much greater difficulty when it has attempted to press demands that faced homogeneous opposition inside Japan. This was the pattern, for example, in the case of the U.S.

demand for objective criteria in the auto talks (1995) and its call for concessions in the Fuji-Kodak case (1995–98). Both of these demands were strongly opposed by MITI officials, business interest groups, and senior LDP politicians, none of whom could see any advantages for Japanese industry from making concessions in these areas. In the former case, despite the pressure of $6 billion in luxury auto sanctions hanging over final negotiations, the Japanese refused to accept any responsibility for numerical targets, leaving the United States to claim that a deal on other issues nevertheless represented enough of a victory to cancel the sanctions. In the latter the United States won no concessions at all after the Japanese forced the United States to take the issue to the World Trade Organization and prevailed in the process there.[49]

Despite the Americans' failure to win concessions in these latter cases, cooperation did not break down. The United States did not impose sanctions, and U.S.-Japan trade continued to expand. What has been seen in the period since the Semiconductor Accords is a more complex pattern than characterized the earlier era. Though the great homogeneity in preferences on the American side has made it necessary for Japan to make some concessions in order for cooperation to continue, the Japanese have not had to concede on all issues. Fortunately for the relationship, heterogeneous preferences—where a significant segment of Japanese opinion sees advantages in accepting American demands—have characterized the internal politics of Japan on enough issues that the Americans' increased appetite for concessions has been satisfied.

Conclusions and Implications

This review of U.S.-Japan security and economic relations over the past fifty years has made it clear that periods of stark domestic conflict over the terms of bilateral ties have not prevented significant and persistent cooperation. On the contrary, it has shown how domestic conflict—defined as heterogeneous preferences dividing those supporting concessions to the other side from those rejecting moves in this direction—has actually facilitated the compromises necessary to sustain cooperation.

In the area of bilateral security relations, most of those compromises have come from a Japan that has been persistently divided over the questions of how closely to align with the United States and how much to contribute to its own defense. At the time the peace and security treaties were ratified and repeatedly since that time, Japanese have disagreed strongly with each other about whether moving in the directions sought by the Americans was in Japan's national interest. Sharply differing levels of trust in the United States and competing ideological views led progressive and conservative elements within Japan to opposite conclusions about the direction in which the nation should move. Divided politics meant that when international events pushed the progressives further away from the American position, as they did in 1960, there still remained a large segment willing to support the compromises necessary to accommodate U.S. demands.

In economic relations, the pattern for most of the postwar period was a mirror image of the one characterizing security ties. Faced with uniform opposition to liberalization on the part of the Japanese, Americans were able to accept limited liberalization because they were sharply divided over how hard to press economic demands at possible expense to bilateral security relations. Later, after the Americans became more homogeneous in insisting on genuine market opening, the emergence of political actors on the Japanese side that supported liberalization for their own reasons reversed the pattern one more time: conflict in Japan helped produce concessions the Americans needed.

This analysis has important implications for continuing efforts on both sides to sustain cooperative security and economic relations. Turning first to security relations, it identifies what questions to ask to determine how far the Japanese will be willing to go as they face pressure from the United States to align their security policy to face the rise of Chinese military power and to further increase their contribution to the common defense effort. Identifying the latest security threats facing Japan and determining how these affect Japan's national interest is not enough. Policy needs to be based on knowledge of who the principal domestic actors are and how their ideologies will refract the way they view Japan's security situation and alternative security options.

Today, the size of the progressive faction that opposed the alliance with the United States and rejected any military contribution is much smaller than it was in 1960. The Socialists, much reduced in size, accepted the alliance and the Self-Defense Forces when they joined the LDP in a coalition government in 1994. Even the Communists are now debating whether to make similar changes in their platform. Nevertheless, most of those who remain in these parties, together with a substantial number of legislators in the Democratic Party and Kōmeitō, as well as a diehard group of Yoshida Doctrine supporters within the LDP, continue to believe that Japan cannot improve its security by aligning itself against China or by expanding the size of the nation's military.[50] This means that constitutional reinterpretation to authorize Japan's exercise of the right of collective self-defense, much less actual revision of the constitution, remains controversial.

While the domestic politics surrounding security issues thus remains heterogeneous, it continues to leave room for a gradual expansion in Japan's security role. Today most Diet members in the LDP and many Democrats and Liberals support an expanded security role for Japan, including constitutional reinterpretation or revision. Moreover, the prime ministership of Japan has for some time now been in the hands of men publicly committed to such an expansion. In combination these developments mean domestic politics in Japan today resembles the situation seen under Nakasone, when Japan was able to significantly expand its security contribution to the bilateral alliance.

Indeed, under Ryūtarō Hashimoto (1996–98) and Keizō Obuchi (1998–2000), the Japanese were able to implement new guidelines for U.S.-Japan security cooperation that have expanded the range of contributions Japan will be able to provide in various security contingencies. The current prime minister, Junichirō Koizumi, backs further moves in this direction and has publicly stated that he believes Japan should reinterpret its constitution so that it can exercise its right of collective self-defense. This next step is delayed today not so much by opposition as by the distraction of Japan's economic problems. Koizumi realizes that the public support he currently enjoys derives from his commitment to implement painful structural reforms in the economy, including cuts in pork barrel spending and a push to force banks to write off their bad loans. His efforts to live up to those expectations have put him into conflict with members of his own party who oppose these changes in economic policy, creating a rift within the conservative camp that has not been conducive to bold moves toward an expanded security role.

The above discussion of how divisions within domestic politics are likely to shape bilateral security cooperation in the near future focused entirely on politics inside Japan. This emphasis reflects the fact that politics on the American side have remained unified in pressuring Japan to do more in this area, just as they have over the entire fifty-year period dating back to the 1951 San Francisco treaties. In contrast, when one turns to economic relations, one finds that emerging cleavages in American politics are once again playing an important role in sustaining cooperation—just as they did in the period before the Semiconductor Accords. With the Japanese economy much weaker than it was in the 1980s, opinion in Washington has diverged once again on the question of how hard to push Japan. Some argue that pressing too hard for liberalization when the Japanese economy is weak risks pushing the nation into a deeper macroeconomic crisis that risks aggravating economic weakness abroad (the Asian Financial Crisis in 1997–98; the slowdown in the U.S. economy since 2000). Others insist that liberalizing, structural reforms in the economy are necessary before Japan can emerge from its decade-long economic stagnation. One result of this split opinion on the U.S. side is a dramatic drop in the number and salience of trade disputes since 1997—a trend that is likely to continue as long as economic weakness in Japan persists.

Domestic divisions on the Japanese side, meanwhile, have also continued to contribute to the cooperative resolution of bilateral economic disputes. Indeed, with the stubborn recession convincing Japanese that liberalization is necessary to regain economic vitality, the United States has had more sympathetic allies than ever when it has urged Japan to adopt regulatory reforms that promise to increase competition and cut costs.

On this dimension too, however, internal divisions within the LDP have slowed the pace of change. Although Koizumi has come down firmly in favor of liberalization, many members of his own party oppose abrupt moves in this direction. As Steven Vogel has argued, similar internal divisions over economic policy characterize other political parties and interest groups in Japan.[51] The ability of Japanese domestic politics to accommodate faster and more far-reaching policy change in response to future pressures therefore depends heavily on whether Koizumi, or another political leader, succeeds in bringing about a political realignment that simplifies the process of coalition building required to push through reforms.

One fascinating scenario, glimpses of which could be seen in Koizumi's posturing during the 2001 upper house election, would involve efforts to convince opponents of the prime minister's economic reform agenda within his own party to accept movement in the neoliberal direction in exchange for a bolder security policy. Koizumi's willingness to risk offending Asian neighbors by promising to visit Yasukuni Shrine may have reflected his hope that moves of this kind (nationalist rhetoric, perhaps followed by an expanded security role) would consolidate his support among conservative voters, regardless of the economic pain some of them are having to bear as the nation cuts back on public spending in rural areas. If such a strategy were successful in redefining the LDP as a neoliberal, hawkish party in the mold of Reagan and Thatcher, it would create a force within Japanese politics that was committed to increasing cooperation with the United States on both the security and economic dimensions.

Of course, such a consolidation of conservative support would likely prompt realignment on the left as well, with opponents of an expanded security role from various parties joining those opposed to harsh economic reforms. Even if Koizumi or another leader is successful in bringing about a political realignment, therefore, Japan is likely to be characterized by divided politics on issues related to U.S.-Japan cooperation. Domestic politics, in summary, will continue to define both the possibilities and limits of U.S.-Japan cooperation just as it has for the past fifty years.

Notes

1. Robert D. Putnam, "Diplomacy and Domestic Politics: The Logic of Two-Level Games," *International Organization*, vol. 42, no. 3 (Summer 1988), pp. 427–60; Peter B. Evans, Harold K. Jacobson, and Robert D. Putnam, eds., *Double-Edged Diplomacy: International Bargaining and Domestic Politics* (University of California Press, 1993); and Leonard J. Schoppa, *Bargaining with Japan: What American Pressure Can and Cannot Do* (Columbia University Press, 1997).

2. Helen V. Milner, *Interests, Institutions, and Information: Domestic Politics and International Relations* (Princeton University Press, 1997), p. 98.

3. This is a restatement of what is known as the Schelling Conjecture. See Thomas Schelling, *The Strategy of Conflict* (Harvard University Press, 1960), pp. 28–29.

4. Putnam, *"Diplomacy and Domestic Politics,"* pp. 427–60.

5. Leonard J. Schoppa, "Two-Level Games and Bargaining Outcomes: Why *Gaiatsu* Succeeds in Japan in Some Cases but Not Others," *International Organization*, vol. 47, no. 3 (Summer 1993), pp. 353-386; and Schoppa, *Bargaining with Japan*.

6. Twenty-four Diet members were independent or belonged to minor parties, bringing the total number in the Diet in 1951 to 441. The total was short of 466 due to twenty-five vacancies, thirteen of which had been created when some Communist Party Diet members were purged in 1950.

7. On America's demands, see John W. Dower, *Empire and Aftermath: Yoshida Shigeru and the Japanese Experience, 1878-1954* (Harvard University Press, 1979); Michael M. Yoshitsu, *Japan and the San Francisco Peace Settlement* (Columbia University Press, 1983); and Michael Schaller, *Altered States: The United States and Japan since the Occupation* (Oxford University Press, 1997).

8. On Japanese responses, see Dower, *Empire and Aftermath*; Takatsugu Miyazaki, "Sengo hoshuseiryoku no keisei," in *Sengo nihon senryō to sengo kaikaku*, vol. 2 (Iwanami Shoten, 1995), pp. 219–23; Kikuo Nakamura and others, *Sengo nihon seijishi* (Yūshindō Press, 1973), pp.136–38; Hiroshi Masuda, "Kōwa jōyaku to anzen hoshō ronsō," in Kenzō Uchida and others, eds., *Nihon gikai shiroku*, vol. 4 (Daiichi Hōki Press, 1990), pp. 229–30.

9. Sources consulted include Dower, *Empire and Aftermath*; Frederick S. Dunn, *Peace-Making and the Settlement with Japan* (Princeton University Press, 1963); Hideo Ōtake, ed., *Sengo nihon bōei mondai shiryōshū*, vol. 2 (Sanichi Press); Kazuto Ishimaru, *Sengo nihon gaikōshi I* (Sanseidō, 1983), p. 292; Shigeru Yoshida, *Kaisō jūnen*, vol. 3 (Shinchōsha, 1957), p. 59; and Kiyoaki Tsuji, *Shiryō sengo nijūnenshi 1 Seiji* (Nihon Hyōronsha, 1970), p. 92.

10. The group of Democrats strongly in favor of total peace included the young officer group led by Tokutarō Kitamura—see Miyazaki, "Sengo hoshuseiryoku," pp. 218–19.

11. Kumao Nishimura, *Anzen hoshō jōyakuron* (Jiji Tsūshinsha, 1959), p. 27, cited in Yoshitsu, *Japan and the San Francisco Peace Settlement*, p. 43.

12. Yoshitsu, *Japan and the San Francisco Peace Settlement*, p. 44.

13. Dower, *Empire and Aftermath*, p. 373.

14. Yoshida's initial position called for Japan to lease bases in the Bonin and Ryūkyū Islands, but not on the mainland, to the United States. Faced with American insistence that Japan allow the United States to continue using bases on the Japanese main islands, however, Yoshida quickly acceded. See Yoshitsu, *Japan and the San Francisco Peace Settlement*; and Schaller, *Altered States*.

15. Ishimaru, *Sengo nihon gaikōshi I*, pp. 294–96.

16. Miyazaki, "Sengo hoshuseiryoku," pp. 218–19.

17. The JSP-Right voted against the Security Treaty as well, but these votes are best interpreted as votes against the extensive basing privileges provided to the Americans (on the alignment dimension) rather than as votes against the limited rearmament agreed to by Yoshida. Members of the JSP-Right were on record advocating rearmament as "a matter of course"—Miyazaki, "Sengo hoshuseiryoku," p. 222.

18. Yoshitsu, *Japan and the San Francisco Peace Settlement*, pp. 49–52; and Ōtake, *Sengo nihon bōei*, pp. 36–47.

19. Kenneth B. Pyle, *The Japanese Question: Power and Purpose in a New Era* (AEI Press, 1992), pp. 21–23.

20. Dower, *Empire and Aftermath*, p. 391; and Ōtake, *Sengo nihon bōei*, p. 68.

21. Ashida advocated more rapid rearmament during Diet deliberations on the treaties—see Ishimaru, *Sengo nihon gaikōshi I*, p. 297.

22. Democratic abstentions and votes against the Security Treaty reflected dissatisfaction on both of the dimensions discussed here. Some voted against the treaty or abstained because it allowed the Americans extensive basing rights and thus aligned Japan too closely to the United States. Others voted against the treaty because it was unbalanced due to Yoshida's decision to limit Japan's rearmament. This ambiguity means it is difficult to draw inferences based on voting records about the proportion of Democratic (and other party) Diet members subscribing to the various views summarized here.

23. Yoshitsu, *Japan and the San Francisco Peace Settlement*, p. 61.

24. Schaller, *Altered States*, p. 64.

25. "Progress Report on U.S. Policy toward Japan" (NSC 5516/1), February 6, 1957, cited in Schaller, *Altered States*, p. 130.

26. George R. Packard, *Protest in Tokyo: The Security Treaty Crisis of 1960* (Princeton University Press, 1966), p. 85.

27. Ibid., p. 60.

28. Schaller, *Altered States*, pp. 149–50.

29. These were the three most contentious issues. Critics of the treaty wanted explicit veto rights but had to settle for "consult together from time to time" in the text of the treaty and "prior consultations" in an exchange of notes. They sought a five-year time limit, after which either party could terminate the treaty with a year's notice, but had to settle for a ten-year wait. They also sought greater clarification of what the treaty meant when it provided for U.S. forces based in Japan to maintain peace and security "in the Far East," but had to live with this vague language.

30. Jacob Schlesinger, *Shadow Shoguns* (Simon and Schuster, 1997), pp. 120–23.

31. One measure of the balance of preferences within the LDP is membership in the Diet Member's League for the Realization of an Independent Constitution, a group closely associated with Nobusuke Kishi, who remained a member of the Diet for two decades after he stepped down as prime minister. In February 1980, 163 Lower House members (60 percent of the LDP delegation) belonged to this group, signaling their support for revision of Article 9—*Kempō*, April 15, 1983.

32. On the changes in defense policy implemented under Nakasone, see Aurelia George, "Japan and the United States: Dependent Ally or Equal Partner?" in J. A. A. Stockwin and others, eds., *Dynamic and Immobilist Politics in Japan* (University of Hawaii Press, 1988), pp. 260–72.

33. In choosing to focus on this class of market-opening cases, this section neglects two other common types of economic negotiations: cases where the United States has asked Japan to restrain its exports and where the United States and Japan have bargained over macroeconomic adjustment.

34. For background on the Foreign Investment Law of 1950 and the restrictions it placed on foreign investment, see Mark Mason, *American Multinationals and Japan: The Political Economy of Japanese Capital Controls, 1899-1980* (Harvard University Press, 1992), pp. 155–59.

35. Ibid.

36. Marie Anchordoguy, *Computers Inc: Japan's Challenge to IBM* (Harvard University Press, 1989), pp. 95–96.

37. Mason, *American Multinationals*, pp. 181–87.

38. Ibid., pp. 246–47.

39. This account is based on Hideo Satō and Timothy Curran, "Agricultural Trade: The Case of Beef and Citrus," in I. M. Destler and Hideo Satō, eds. *Coping with U.S.-Japanese Economic Conflicts* (Lexington Books, 1982).

40. Laura D'Andrea Tyson, *Who's Bashing Whom? Trade Conflict in High-Technology Industries* (Institute for International Economics, 1993), p. 101.

41. Kenneth Flamm, *Mismanaged Trade? Strategic Policy and the Semiconductor Industry* (Brookings, 1996), pp. 168–74; and Ellis S. Krauss, "U.S.-Japan Negotiations on Construction and Semiconductors, 1985–88," in Evans, Jacobson, and Putnam, *Double-Edged Diplomacy*, pp. 267–71.

42. Sanctions were completely eliminated only in 1991 when a new semiconductor agreement was reached—I. M. Destler, *American Trade Politics*, third edition (Institute for International Economics, 1995), p. 130.

43. Destler, *American Trade Politics*, pp. 89–96.

44. Schoppa, *Bargaining with Japan*, pp. 69–76.

45. Ibid., pp. 257–63; Lincoln, *Troubled Times: U.S.-Japan Trade Relations in the 1990s* (Brookings, 1999), pp. 131–33.

46. MITI, *Kyūjū-nendai no ryūtsū bijon* (1989).

47. Schoppa, *Bargaining with Japan*, pp. 146–80.

48. Ibid., pp. 274–75.

49. Leonard J. Schoppa, "The Social Context in Coercive International Bargaining," *International Organization*, vol. 53, no. 2 (Spring 1999), pp. 328–30; Lincoln, *Troubled Times*.

50. Berger attributes these attitudes to the lingering effects of a "culture of antimilitarism." See Thomas U. Berger, "Alliance Politics and Japan's Postwar Culture of Antimilitarism," in Michael Green and Patrick M. Cronin, eds., *The U.S.-Japan Alliance: Past, Present, and Future* (Council on Foreign Relations Press, 1999), p. 191.

51. Steven K. Vogel, "Can Japan Disengage? Winners and Losers in Japan's Political Economy, and the Ties That Bind Them," *Social Science Japan Journal*, vol. 2, no. 1 (April 1999), pp. 3–21.

CHAPTER SIX

Media

LAURIE A. FREEMAN

Throughout much of the postwar period, the U.S. and Japanese governments were able to limit the damage that their differences of opinion had on the bilateral relationship. Then, in the mid- to late 1980s, tensions escalated dramatically as Americans engaged in Japan bashing and Japanese countered by condemning the United States. American workers smashed Japanese-made products in Detroit and members of Congress followed suit on Capitol Hill. Prominent Japanese such as the novelist and politician Shintarō Ishihara and Sony Chairman Akio Morita began arguing that Japan should say no to U.S. demands. For the first time since the early postwar period, feelings of mutual mistrust moved out of the realm of public posturing over specific trade and other issues to the public at large. American newspapers and television began to fuel anti-Japanese sentiments, and the Japanese media popularized new terms such as *kenbei* (dislike of Americans).

In the United States, scholars such as Chalmers Johnson and novelists such as Michael Crichton joined the popular media in disseminating critical portrayals of Japan. An overcited, and somewhat misleading, opinion poll taken in 1989 found that the American public thought Japan a greater threat than the Soviet Union.[1] By the early 1990s, the implosion of the Soviet Union and the bursting of the Japanese economic bubble meant that America no longer faced a threat—real or illusory—from either nation. Yet it would be a number of years before the reality of the Japanese recession fully set in (see chapter 3 by Grimes in this volume), and the American media turned their interest to other nations, most notably China. Japan bashing then turned to Japan passing for the media and, partially as a result, for the general public.

In Japan meanwhile, the popular response was less to engage this challenge than to celebrate Japan's cultural distinctiveness. This was done through the explosion of a genre of articles and books known as *nihonjin-ron* (theories of Japaneseness). In 1992 historian John Dower referred to this literature as the "seemingly interminable discussions of being Japanese that has dominated pop culture discourse for a decade or so."[2] He also noted that some Japanese used these evocations of uniqueness to justify the less-than-nimble Japanese response to American trade demands. In this way they used *nihonjinron* as a rationalization for Japanese restrictions on imports of such items as skis and beef, and even for the exclusion of foreign contractors on domestic construction projects.[3]

In evaluating the impact of the media on the U.S.-Japan relationship, this chapter addresses several issues. First, a variety of quantitative and qualitative data are used to analyze the reporting on the relationship in each country over the past fifty years. This impact is shown to be substantial, but it is also closely intertwined with the state of the relationship itself. That is, the media both shape and are in turn shaped by contemporaneous conditions between the two countries in ways that make it difficult to disentangle independent and dependent effects. The chapter also evaluates the impact of specific media institutions and practices on reporting, emphasizing ways that country-specific considerations affect the quantity and the quality of media coverage in both countries. The chapter concludes by speculating about how the rise of the new media, such as the Internet, will affect the relationship in the future.

Why and How Media Matter

Why should the media be examined? The most important reason is that the media and media institutions are the primary conduit through which most people in the two countries—from policymakers to citizens—understand one another. Survey evidence has found that no institution has a greater impact on how the public and elites view significant domestic, bilateral, and international issues than the mass media. When groups of nongovernmental elites in the United States and Japan were asked, as part of a comparative study of elites conducted by Sidney Verba and his colleagues, to situate themselves within a power hierarchy composed of other elites, they placed the media at the apex of that hierarchy.[4] In Japan all groups except the media (who put bureaucrats slightly ahead of themselves) chose the media as the most powerful elite actor in society—in some cases by a wide margin. In the United States all groups except the media rated them among the top two. Moreover, the media's importance may be increasing over time, as the complex and split-second demands of contemporary diplomacy become more dependent on news reports over other types of information, such as in-depth internal analyses.

Clearly key elites recognize the power of the media, but what about the general public? The Japanese are among the most literate and active newspaper readers and television viewers in the world. In fact in a recent work Pippa Norris notes that the Japanese are distinctive in the extent to which they consume large quantities of information from both of these media. The public in most other OECD nations are either television-centric (for example, the United States and Italy) or newspaper-centric (for example, Norway, Sweden, and Finland), but rarely both. Only the United Kingdom comes even remotely close to Japan.[5] Though they are somewhat less likely to subscribe to daily newspapers or watch television than their Japanese counterparts, Americans still say that they get most of their images of Japan from these two media. Extensive focus group sessions were held in 1995 as part of a larger study to ascertain American images of Japan, conducted by EBR Consulting in collaboration with the Japan Economic Institute and with support from the Japanese Foreign Ministry. In these sessions participants were asked how they obtained their images of and information about Japan.[6] Most replied that, "it was on the news, or I saw it in a documentary." The report on these focus group sessions noted that although sometimes respondents could remember the specific story, more often their references were vague statements that they had either read it in the newspaper or seen it on TV.

Still, while recognizing their power and influence, critics on both sides of the Pacific have at times suggested that the media in each country distort and exaggerate their news reporting in order to maximize their bottom line. American critics of the Japanese media have argued that they provide the Japanese public with a misleading and misguided portrayal of issues related to poverty, racism, and crime in this country. Japanese (and some American) critics of the U.S. press have claimed that it depicts the Japanese as xenophobic nationalists, or, alternatively, as inscrutable mercantilists seeking to expand national wealth at the expense of the Japanese consumer and the rest of the world.[7]

Some charge that the media tend to define news in negative terms—a happy bilateral relationship is not worthy of media attention, whereas a friction-filled one is—but clearly, there is more to it than this. The media in both countries are subject to a variety of institutional, structural, and situational constraints that limit the control they have over the news they transmit and provide the framework within which news stories are written. Any comparative analysis of Japanese and American news reports about the bilateral relationship and their impact on the relationship as a whole must: first, be based on a thorough understanding of the nature of these institutional arrangements and situational imperatives; second, pay considerable attention to how they differ cross-nationally; and third, acknowledge ongoing changes in them. The media, therefore, are not simply neutral conduits, but active in channeling and shaping news and opinion.

Still, many would agree that the media have the potential to shape public opinion and influence the policymaking process by telling people what to think about. Yet most recent studies also recognize that the power of the media to do so varies under different circumstances. Zucker, for example, suggests that one of the factors affecting the ability of the media to influence political agendas and public opinion is the existence of alternative sources of information or personal experience about the topic at hand.[8] In the case of unobtrusive issues such as foreign affairs, where the public has to rely heavily on the mass media for details of important policies and events, the media have a much greater opportunity to shape public and elite perceptions and to set the agenda of discourse than they do in other instances.

This demonstrates that there is a strong role to be played by the media in determining public and elite views and understanding of the U.S.-Japan relationship, especially given the limited real world experience that most people from either nation have of the other. It does not, however, tell us when media coverage will affect the relationship and when it will not, or whether the impact of media coverage will be positive or negative, long-term or ephemeral. Each of these potential outcomes is itself affected by a number of factors. As suggested later in this chapter, at a minimum the following features of media coverage matter when considering the overall potential impact of the media on the U.S.-Japan relationship: the quantity of coverage; the quality of coverage (measured in terms of objectivity and balance); and finally, the tone of the coverage.

Another factor complicating the ability to reach meaningful conclusions about how media coverage affects the U.S.-Japan relationship in the abstract is the fact that the relationship itself is also a key determinant of media coverage. Even more than the other factors examined in this volume, media coverage not only affects the relationship but is itself a product of the relationship. That is, it is both an independent and dependent variable and it is difficult, if not impossible, to specify the primary direction of causality. Later in this chapter this point is emphasized by showing how much the level and substance of media coverage itself reflects the state of the relationship. With respect to the 1983–93 interlude in U.S.-Japan relations, for example, it is difficult to sort out to what extent bilateral friction generated biased media coverage and negative images of the other country, and to what extent this coverage created or exacerbated the friction.

Despite the difficulties disentangling causality, there are strong reasons to believe that media coverage in both countries does have a direct impact on the relationship itself. At times this impact is positive and at other times negative. That is, while on the one hand helping Americans and Japanese understand each other better, it can also fuel misconceptions and misunderstanding. It gives Americans and Japanese positive images of each other but it projects negative images as well. It is known, however, that accurate coverage is more conducive to mutual understanding than distorted coverage, and that positive coverage is more conducive to harmonious relations than negative coverage. Moreover, the relationship is affected not only by these qualitative differences in reporting, but by quantitative differences as well. Insufficient coverage or imbalances in the amount of reporting in each country (primarily the vastly greater coverage of the relationship in Japan) can also potentially worsen relations.

Balanced against these effects is the fact that the media are themselves also sensitive to the state of the relationship. That is, causal influences flow in the opposite direction as well. In the case of the U.S.-Japan relationship, for example, the evidence presented here suggests that shifts in the balance of power between the two nations may also have an impact on the agenda-setting role of the mass media. For this reason, scholars have come to the realization that they cannot talk intelligently about the impact of media coverage without also considering how the media agenda gets set in the first place. This is particularly important when comparing media effects cross culturally, as different media institutions can potentially lead to quite different media effects. Thus, this chapter has been careful to consider not only media effects but media agenda formation as well, keeping in mind that various institutions, behaviors, and practices may play an important role in shaping the news agenda in each country.[9]

In sum, the following predictions are made. First, the media in each country do have an important effect on the U.S.-Japan relationship. Second, this effect itself varies over time depending on the state of the relationship. That is, causality flows in both directions. Finally, the media's impact on the relationship in the two countries also varies as a result of different news gathering practices and institutions in each country as well as different assumptions about what constitutes the news. In other words, domestic institutions are also key determinants of media effect.

These predictions are evaluated below using two different data types. First, this chapter considers quantitative differences in media coverage in the two nations, including different levels of public and elite interest and media attention over time, and changes in the relative position of power each nation holds vis-à-vis the other in both military and economic terms. Second, this chapter evaluates important qualitative differences, both in terms of media content and the kind of information that gets relayed by the mass and popular media, and bilateral differences in media institutions and industry structure. While it is more difficult to evaluate and measure qualitative differences, this can be done through careful triangulation of a number of comparative methodologies, including the interpretation of content analyses, "thick description" (to borrow from Geertz's famous phrase), and placing media coverage in historical and comparative perspective.

Bilateral Relations and Media Coverage

An analysis of changes in news volume over time suggests that one of the key factors driving media reporting on both sides of the Pacific is the state of the relationship itself. It is important to remember, occasional protests notwithstanding, that the bilateral relationship has never been a true marriage of equals: Americans have been in a dominant position throughout the postwar period. As historian John Dower has noted, "No reasonable observer can deny that the U.S.-Japan relationship since 1945 has rested on the assumption of inequality—whether phrased as teacher and pupil, parent and child, leader and follower, or simply superior and subordinate."[10] While American dominance over Japan was most striking during the six and a half years of Occupation tutelage, the assumption of inequality of which Dower speaks did not disappear once Japan regained its sovereignty. Indeed, it was institutionalized in 1951 with the signing of the Peace Treaty and the

Figure 6-1. *Coverage of Japan by the* New York Times, *1950–2000*

Number of articles

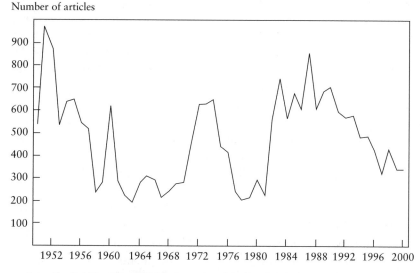

Source: New York Times Index, 1950–81, current series: vol. 38-69, *New York Times*, 1951–82. Newspaper Articles Database. Information Access Company, 1982–2000, available from California Digital Library (www.dbs.cdlib.org/ ?CSdb=news).

formal establishment of the bilateral military relationship. It remains today, although the degree of inequality has varied over time. Most notable in this respect is the relatively short-lived period of Japanese economic ascendancy in the 1980s, which occurred around the same time that the U.S. economy was experiencing a period of apparent decline. The impact of this shift not only on the U.S.-Japan relationship but also on media coverage of the relationship is revealed most dramatically in figure 6-1.

Information and Knowledge Divide

Before detailing more fully the impact of the state of the U.S.-Japan relationship on the tenor and volume of news reporting, it is useful to consider bilateral differences in levels of interest and attention, real knowledge, and information flows more generally. Mike Mochizuki notes in a recent article that "there has long been a fundamental asymmetry between the attention given the U.S.-Japan security alliance in Japan, and the lack of attention given the issue in the United States."[11] Likewise, a Japanese scholar has suggested that many Japanese can identify the American Civil War, the state of Florida, and former president Clinton, but most Americans cannot identify the Meiji Restoration, Kagoshima, or the Japanese prime minister.[12]

This suggests the existence of a genuine information divide between Japanese and Americans. By just about any measure, the Japanese public is more interested and more knowledgeable about Americans than Americans are about Japan. The number of books translated from English into Japanese in 1995, for example, was 2,466 (most from the United States) while the number of translations from Japanese to English was 32.[13] Japanese enrollments in American universities are increasing, but American enrollments in Japan are in decline. Many scholars who teach about Japan are finding that fewer students seem interested in taking courses on Japanese business, economics, politics, culture, or history. Additionally, enrollments in Japanese-language courses are down, and the number of dissertations on Japan-related topics has also fallen when compared to a decade ago.[14]

The same is true about media coverage. A study conducted in the 1980s by the Research Institute of the Japanese Newspaper Publishers and Editors Association found that in a one-week period, 112 news items about the United States were reported in the *Asahi Shimbun,* while its counterpart in the United States, the *New York Times,* published only twenty-four stories about Japan.[15] These numbers are particularly revealing given that they come from the period of heightened American interest in Japan. Similarly, a joint international project to study Japanese and American television news content conducted by the Mansfield Center for Pacific Affairs in 1992–93, found that Japanese television coverage of the United States was considerably greater than U.S. television coverage of Japan. In fact it was approximately twelve times greater in Japan.[16] When overall international coverage was compared, the Mansfield Center analysis found that news about the United States accounted for 33 percent of all international news covered on Japanese television, while news about Japan accounted for only 3.4 percent of all international news on U.S. programs.[17] The list goes on.

It is not always clear how these facts should be interpreted. Does America's broader involvement in the world mean, as some have suggested, that the American media have a limited capacity to cover any single country in detail, and thus the limited coverage of Japan makes sense?[18] Or is it that the Japanese media, for historical and other reasons, are particularly fixated on the United States, and therefore in some real sense tend to "over cover" it?[19] Most likely there is truth in both views. Admittedly, quantitative measurements are not always very good indicators of reportorial quality or depth, or of balance measured in terms of the world of topics and themes that might potentially be covered. The Mansfield survey of U.S. and Japanese television news coverage found, for example, that although both sides tended to have an equal number of human interest stories about one another, the emphasis given to other categories of news differed markedly. Although American television coverage was more limited overall in terms of time spent covering Japan, when it did report on Japan it was more likely to focus on such issues as business, economics, domestic politics, or the U.S.-Japan relationship and other international issues. In contrast, while Japanese television programs covered the United States more frequently, the programs were more likely to address domestic troubles such as crime, violence, corruption, social disorder, and disasters, and less likely than their American counterparts to focus on economic or business issues.[20] This suggests, again, the wisdom in taking both qualitative and quantitative factors into consideration when evaluating bilateral news coverage of the relationship over time. Clearly, it is not just an issue of how much information flows in one direction or the other, but of what kind of information is being disseminated.

It should not be surprising that the Japanese know more about the United States than Americans know about Japan, or that Japan's mass media cover the United States more frequently than the American media cover Japan. Similarly, the Japanese public and elites take a greater interest in the United States than vice versa. As historian Carol Gluck has noted, power imbalances "always ha[ve] the consequence of an imbalance of knowledge."[21] In the nineteenth century, the imbalance in military and economic power between Japan and the Western world was painfully obvious to Japanese leaders. Intent on catching up rather than being carved up, they began seeking knowledge from all corners of the globe, especially from Europe and the United States. This pursuit of knowledge was enshrined in the Charter Oath proclaimed by the Meiji emperor in 1868 and quickly became a national preoccupation, though it was hardly anomalous in comparative terms. Gluck suggests, for example, that "India and Java were also similarly obsessed with their imperialist rulers," and that while these rulers also had an interest in and some knowledge of their colonies, that interest "tended to be voluntary, intermittent, and immersed in the exotic."[22]

While not suggesting that Americans view their relationship with Japan in colonial or imperialistic terms (though some would not rule this out), the reality is that Japan's long-running adoration from afar and accumulation of knowledge about the United States remains largely unrequited. The American public and elite knowledge of and interest in Japan pales in comparison with the Japanese. A recent report published by the Henry Luce Foundation in honor of the twenty-fifth anniversary of the establishment of the Luce Scholars Program shows just how little attention Americans pay not only to Japan, but to most of the rest of the world. This study found that not only were global events not followed closely by most Americans, but that news coming from and about Asia was especially low on the nation's public agenda.[23] The Luce report cites a recent survey carried out by the Pew Research Center for the People and the Press which found that since 1986, the year this index started, not a single Asia-related story has been "watched very closely" by a majority of Americans.[24] Among the Asian stories of the 1990s that were watched very closely by at least one American in five, the top story about Japan involved a speech by a prominent Japanese politician in which he claimed that American workers were lazy (34 percent of respondents said that they had followed this story). In order of diminishing interest: 31 percent of those surveyed claimed to have followed the fiftieth anniversary of the bombing of Pearl Harbor (1991); 26 percent noted the gas attack in a Tokyo subway (1995); and 25 percent mentioned having followed reports about the earthquake in Kobe (1995).[25]

It is evident from this and similar surveys that American economic and military hegemony has not had a correspondingly positive or enlightening impact on the public's interest in the rest of the world. If anything, it has afforded them the perverse luxury of remaining largely parochial in their interests and created a genuine information divide between themselves and the nations with which they have otherwise close ties, including Japan. As suggested below, however, there are times when American public, elite, and media interest in Japan is piqued, largely as a result of either a dramatic event occurring within Japan or between the two nations, or as a consequence of real or perceived shifts in the economic balance of power.

Trends and Patterns in American Media Coverage, 1950–2000

This chapter relies on two of the most common types of media-based data: measurements of media volume and events counts.[26] The data are used to get a better picture of critical moments in the relationship between the two countries as suggested by media focus over time, and to ascertain major trends and patterns in media coverage as well as the factors driving the coverage. Analysis of *New York Times* coverage of Japan shows considerable variability in the volume of news stories over time, revealing four major peaks or peak periods in coverage for the period 1950–2000 (see figure 6-1).[27] What causes this variability and what factors drive media coverage? On closer inspection, the data reveal two broad patterns in American media coverage of Japan during the last half century. In the first pattern, sudden short-term jumps in the number of articles result from some crisis or dramatic event either in Japan or within the relationship itself. These events often occur within the context of a relatively stable (albeit unequal) bilateral framework in which the United States is the dominant partner, and may be economic, political, or social-cultural. Under this category are the first three peaks in volume: the peace settlement, 1950–52; the Security Treaty revision, 1960; and the Nixon shocks and return of Okinawa, 1972–74. In the second pattern, a much longer and sustained period of increased coverage is found, especially in the case of the period 1982–93. This second pattern suggests that increases in the volume of media coverage may be driven by real or perceived changes in the relationship itself, as exemplified by shifts in the relative economic strength of one of the partners vis-à-vis the other. An example of each of these patterns of media coverage is provided below.

PATTERN ONE: EVENTS DRIVE COVERAGE. The most common cause of increased media attention is, unsurprisingly, the occurrence of a dramatic event either within Japan itself or between the two nations. Japan-related and bilateral events that have been widely reported by the *New York Times* in recent years include the Gulf war (1990), the Kobe earthquake (1995), the Tokyo subway gassing (1995), the rape of a young girl by American servicemen (1995), and the Asian financial crisis and Nagano Olympics (1998). Given that this volume is being published in acknowledgment of the fiftieth anniversary of the signing of the San Francisco Peace Treaty, it is worth examining media coverage of that treaty in more detail here. Figure 6-1 reveals that the number of articles about Japan in the *New York Times* almost doubled from 1950 to 1951, the period during which the signing and ratification of the peace and security treaties occurred. Moreover, the negotiation, signing, and subsequent ratification of these treaties appears to have been the most important bilateral event in the U.S.-Japan relationship covered by the *New York Times* in the last half century, at least when measured in terms of article volume. Still, in 1957 when Bernard Cohen contemporaneously analyzed and compared newspaper coverage by the *New York Times* and the *San Francisco Chronicle* for the twelve months preceding Senate ratification of these treaties, he concluded that "the coverage accorded the settlement was hardly of a kind to arouse and sustain more than a casual interest in the subject even among attentive newspaper reading Americans."[28] Cohen argued that if the treaty coverage was measured in terms of actual column inches, the volume of coverage on this issue was in fact quite low, especially when compared to the coverage of other key treaties concluded at around the same time.[29] He noted that the Japanese peace settlement received only half as much attention as the North Atlantic Treaty in 1949, about a quarter of the attention the recognition of Israel in 1948 received, and considerably less attention than Greek-Turkish aid and aid to China in 1948. However, when compared to coverage of other events in the U.S.-Japan relationship over the full half century under review here, only 1987 comes close to 1951–52 in terms of the volume of annual coverage.

PATTERN TWO: PERCEIVED POWER SHIFTS DRIVE COVERAGE. While the U.S.-Japan relationship has largely been an asymmetrical and unequal one, there is one brief exception to this rule worth considering in more detail. This would be the approximate ten-year period from the early 1980s to the early 1990s when influential leaders on both sides of the Pacific increasingly viewed Japan as an economic power capable of challenging American industrial supremacy. The impact of this shift in power between the two nations on American media coverage of Japan is revealed in figure 6-1 as a sudden, and then sustained, increase in the volume of coverage beginning in 1982. The higher levels of coverage continued until approximately 1993 and represented a second type of media coverage of the relationship—coverage driven not so much by an individual event, but by the perception that there had been a realignment in the balance of economic power between the two countries, and it was tipped in Japan's favor.

Events data are more helpful in revealing and chronicling qualitative shifts in the U.S.-Japan relationship over time, particularly in the economic realm. These data—which differ from media volume counts in that a single international event is counted only once, irrespective of the number of stories that are written about it—suggest that as social, economic, and diplomatic intercourse between the two nations increased over time and ties between them became denser, there was a concomitant increase in the annual volume of events between the two nations, especially economic events.[30] Indeed, looking at events volume from the period 1948–97, it becomes clear that while the total volume of events between the two countries remained fairly consistent during the first three and a half decades of that period, there was an abrupt rise in the number of economic and political events beginning in 1983. The events data show that: in terms of sheer numbers, the bilateral relationship had come to be dominated by economic developments in the 1980s; the annual total of such events was positively related to U.S. imports from Japan; over time there was a cooling of relations (evaluated in terms of a decrease in the number of events considered

Figure 6-2. *Coverage of Japan by U.S. Newspapers, 1982–2000*

Number of articles

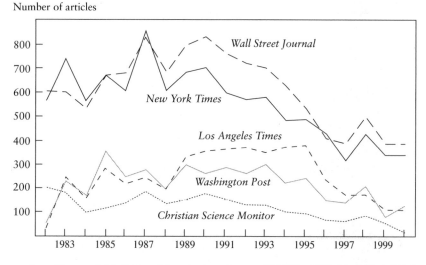

Source: Newspaper Articles Database. Information Access Company, 1982–2000, available from California Digital Library (www.dbs.cdlib.org/?CSdb=news).

cooperative) as this occurred.[31] The high number of economic events continued until 1995, after which it dropped by almost 75 percent.

As can be seen in figures 6-1 and 6-2, American media coverage of Japan largely parallels this rise and decline in the number of economic events.[32] Beginning in 1982, there is a precipitous increase in the overall number of stories on Japan in the *New York Times* and other major newspapers. Once the Japanese economy was no longer seen as a threat, however, the number of articles on Japan in five elite newspapers as well as several popular weekly newsmagazines (see figure 6-3) gradually decreased, though admittedly in some cases there was a two- to three-year lag before this occurred.

The data on *New York Times* coverage over the last half century show that the period from approximately 1983 to 1993 was distinctive in terms of the volume of articles written about Japan. What this and other data do not (and cannot) reveal is the tone and framing of these articles, as well as that of other popular, academic, and nonspecialist literature about the U.S.-Japan relationship written around the same time. By all accounts, however, this literature was fairly distinctive when compared to prior writing on Japan. While on the one hand offering suggestions for how Americans might learn from Japan, it was at the same time frequently critical of the Japanese economic system and Japan's commitment to democracy, and

Figure 6-3. *Coverage of Japan by Popular U.S. Magazines, 1988–2000*

Number of articles

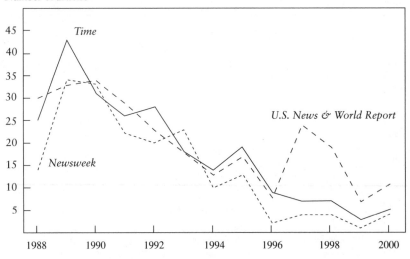

Source: Magazine and Journal Articles Database. Information Access Company, 1988–2000, available from California Digital Library (www.dbs.cdlib.org/?CSdb=mags).

generally included calls for a reappraisal of the bilateral relationship over-all. Its distinctiveness in the context of the relationship was captured by *BusinessWeek*'s Robert Neff in 1989 when he coined the term "revisionists" to describe those most active in pushing for this reappraisal. While the term was never intended to describe elite journalists and editors from such news-papers as the *New York Times*, the increase in the volume of reporting about Japan in these newspapers suggests that they were very much caught up in the debate about how to understand Japan's economic miracle, espe-cially in the face of an apparent American industrial decline. Moreover, though one of the major intellectual sources of this literature was the clas-sic work by Chalmers Johnson (sometimes referred to as the godfather of revisionism), *MITI and the Japanese Miracle*, most of the revisionist liter-ature was not written by academics. Andrew Horvat notes, in fact, that "since much of the debate about Japan was in the hands of nonspecialists, many of whom were journalists, revisionist arguments were more likely to be found in newspapers, on television, or even in movies, than on the pages of academic journals."[33]

It can be said with some certainty that Japan's rise as an economic power in its own right and America's relative decline at about the same time were among the factors driving both the revisionist movement and increased coverage of bilateral affairs. But what can be said about the impact of this on the U.S.-Japan relationship itself? Although a few retrospective examinations of revisionism have recently appeared, including those by the Cato Institute and a conference sponsored by the Asia Foundation, to date there has been no systematic analysis of the literature (news accounts as well as popular magazines and film) of this period or of its impact on the bilateral relationship as a whole.[34] Perhaps unsurprisingly, those who have talked about its legacy and impact offer divergent appraisals. Some, such as journalist Charles Burress from the *San Francisco Chronicle*, are inclined to argue that "revisionism had opened a Pandora's Box from which unflattering images of Japan continue to flow." Others, such as professor Richard Samuels from the Massachusetts Institute of Technology (MIT), take a more optimistic view of its impact, noting that while it may have exacerbated tensions at the time, "revisionism also served to popularize discussion of Japan and drew into Japanese studies a new generation of Americans many of whom went on to engage in policy-relevant research."[35]

This generation of scholars is at least partially responsible for the increase in the number of books published about Japan in the last decade. A search of *Books in Print* shows that there were almost twice as many books about Japan in print in the more recent, postrevisionist decade from 1991 to 2000, than in the period 1981–90.[36] Additionally, two books about Japan (by John Dower and Herbert Bix, respectively) have recently received Pulitzer Prizes for nonfiction and have become popular sellers. This suggests at the very least that there remains an enduring interest among some Americans in learning about Japan. Moreover, even if the more negative images and stereotypes of the revisionist period remain in the public consciousness and in the mass media as Burress suggests, the results of recent opinion polls imply that they have not induced an enduring or widespread mistrust or dislike of Japan and of the Japanese by Americans. In fact Americans' assessment of U.S.-Japan relations was better (as measured by the percentage of Americans who responded that they thought relations were good) during the height of revisionism than it was in the period between 1991 and 1995, and is higher now than it has been at any point since 1987. These results suggest an altogether different scenario than the rather pessimistic one posited by Burress.

Japanese Coverage of the United States: A Brief Assessment

How does American media coverage of the relationship over time compare with that of Japan? Due to the limited nature of existing computerized data, Japanese data (see figure 6-4) are limited to a single newspaper, the *Asahi Shimbun,* and are of a shorter duration than the American data, covering only fifteen years (1985–2000) instead of the fifty years covered by the American data. These data reveal a somewhat different pattern than the American one: Japanese media coverage of the United States during the key period examined here is fairly flat over time and shows limited variability. This is especially the case when looking at the number of articles in the *Asahi Shimbun* in which the words "United States" appeared in the heading during this period. When the search is narrowed to account only for those articles in which the words "U.S.-Japan" (*nichibei*) appear (figure 6-4), there is more variation, but it is still considerably less than that of American media coverage of the same period. Moreover, the peaks in Japanese media coverage generally come after the period of admittedly intense economic friction between the two nations in the mid- to late 1980s, and after Japan had entered the post-bubble period and was no longer seen as a potential economic rival to the United States. This suggests that changes in the relative power balance between the United States and Japan, especially Japan's rise as an economic power in its own right in the 1980s, may have had a less prominent impact on Japanese reporting on the relationship than on American reporting. One reason may be the already extremely high level of coverage of the United States by the Japanese media. In an average year there may be as many as 5,000 articles in a Japanese newspaper containing the words "United States" in the headline, whereas the number of articles having "Japan" as the subject in the *New York Times* currently hovers in the 300 to 400 range in an average year, and has never exceeded 1,000 in a year in the last half century.

From Japan Bashing to Japan Passing?

In a 1984 *New York Times Magazine* cover article entitled "The Danger from Japan," Theodore White wrote the following retrospectively alarmist comment: "Today, forty years after the end of World War II, the Japanese are on the move again in one of history's most brilliant commercial offensives, as they go about dismantling American industry. Whether they are still only smart, or have finally learned to be wiser than we, will be tested in the next ten years. Only then will we know who finally won the war."[37] Where White was most prescient was in his suggestion that the test would last around a decade. By the early 1990s, once it was apparent that not only was Japan no longer threatening U.S. competitiveness but that there would be no immediate renascence in Japanese economic prowess, Japan seems to

Figure 6-4. *Number of* Asahi *Headlines That Include "U.S.-Japan,"* *1985–2000*

Number of articles

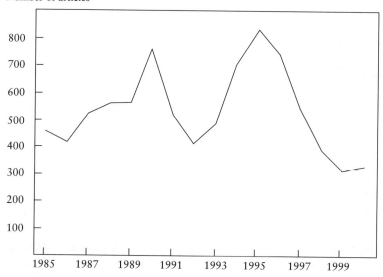

Source: Asahi.com Newspaper Articles Database (http://asahisearch.cab.infoweb.ne.jp/cgi-bin/common.cgi).

have largely disappeared from American newspapers' front pages, and partially as a result, from American public consciousness.[38] An examination of the number of articles written about Japan by the American media having a noticeable presence in Japan—namely the *New York Times, Washington Post, Christian Science Monitor,* and *Wall Street Journal*—reveals that regardless of which was being read, between 1995 and 2000 the total number of articles about Japan in these newspapers dropped substantially. Comparing the period of heightened media interest from 1985 to 1995 with the more recent five-year period from 1996 to 2000, there is a 37 percent decline overall in the number of articles about Japan in the *New York Times* (see figure 6-2). The dramatic decline in the level of Japan coverage by both the print and broadcast media has also been noted by others. The 1996 report by EBR Consulting and the Japan Economic Institute for the Ministry of Foreign Affairs cited earlier found that the "frequency of network news stories about Japan has fallen to less than one-third of the 1989 figure."[39] Similarly, a recent report released by the Japanese Consulate General in New York, which was based on a survey of three major East Coast newspapers (including the *New York Times*), the three major TV networks, and the Public Broadcasting System, concluded that the level of American coverage of Japan in 2000 was the lowest in seven years.[40]

The decline is even more dramatic in the case of popular weekly news-magazines like *Time, Newsweek,* and *U.S. News & World Report.* The number of articles in *Time,* for example, dropped from more than forty in 1989, to five in 2000 (see figure 6-3). Among these three magazines, only *U.S. News & World Report* experienced an increase in the number of articles after 1989. The increase in the number of Japan-related articles in this magazine during the period 1996–98 can be attributed to the "Fallows effect," as it appears to coincide with James Fallows' tenure as editor of that magazine. This suggests that the personal interests of a given editor can also have some impact on the volume of coverage.

Reporting on Japan has also dropped in relative terms, especially when compared to the amount of coverage accorded other countries by the *New York Times* (see figure 6-5). While Japan was long a leader in terms of article volume when compared with such countries as China, Mexico, and Canada, especially in the period 1982–95, there has been a precipitous decline in the last five years in the number of articles about Japan in the *New York Times* when compared to these other countries, and a gradual increase in the number of articles about China. Coverage of Mexico, and to a somewhat lesser extent, Canada, remains at about the same level as current Japan coverage. These declines in media, and consequently public and elite interest, have occurred in spite of the fact that Japan is still the number two economy in the world and the United States' second-largest trading partner, and that it maintains a very sizable trade surplus with the United States (see figure 3-1 in chapter 3 by Grimes in this volume).

This brings up another important revelation about newspaper reporting on the relationship during the 1980s. Recent analyses of the determinants of international news flows across a wide range of countries argue that economic factors (especially gross national product (GNP) and trade) are key predictors of the amount of news coverage a country receives, and some have claimed that changes in the global balance of power resulting from the end of the cold war may have even strengthened this tendency.[41] Following these studies, one might expect that American media coverage of Japan, a nation with which it has a substantial trading relationship, would remain high throughout the current period.[42] However, as noted above, American media coverage of Japan has declined even as the trade imbalance has increased. Though many of the news reports of the revisionist period

Figure 6-5. *Coverage of Four Countries by the* New York Times,
1982–2000

Number of articles

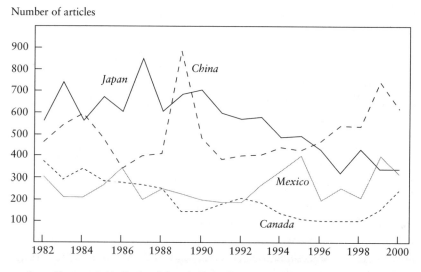

Source: Newspaper Articles Database. Information Access Company, 1982–2000, available from California Digital
Library (www.dbs.cdlib.org/?CSdb=news).

(1982–93) focused on trade, especially the trade deficit and its ostensible
causes, in the last five years (1995–2000) the trade deficit with Japan has
been as high or higher than it was during the peak period of trade friction
(see chapter 3 by Grimes for trends in trade). Yet the American media no
longer seem concerned about this fact. This suggests that the trade deficit
may have been a scapegoat for larger concerns about the state of the American economy overall and its relative strength when compared to that of
Japan, as William Grimes argues in chapter 3 of this volume. As Ronald
Morse, president of the Annapolis International consulting firm once noted,
"As a general rule, American concern with Japan rises and falls with the
fluctuations in U.S. economic prosperity." [43] It would appear that this is also
the case for American media coverage. Once the United States became more
internationally competitive, and a recession ensued in Japan, the American
media moved from "Japan bashing," as critical news reports about Japan
were called, to "Japan passing," as they began paying increasingly more
attention to China (see figure 6-5). This implies, however, that should American fortunes once again take a turn for the worse, the American public,
political elites, and the press may once again turn to that political football
in the relationship—the trade imbalance.

News Gathering Practices and Press-Source Relations

This chapter has outlined the importance of situational changes in the relationship itself and suggested that relative changes in the state of the economies in either or both nations may (in addition to critical events) serve as a key determinant of news flow in the U.S.-Japan relationship. There are, however, other factors that also drive and shape media coverage of the relationship over time—including industry structure and news gathering practices. This chapter now turns to these qualitative factors.

No country has an entirely free and open marketplace for information, of course. Long-term relationships between journalists and official sources are a common feature of reporting in every advanced industrial democracy. So too is a degree of cooperation among journalists themselves (for example, in pool reporting). Sensitive information may become known by an individual journalist or small group of journalists that does not get reported because of concerns about losing a source. In addition journalists may have to negotiate with their sources for the what, when, why, who, and how of a story's dissemination. This is an inevitable part of news reporting, if for no other reason than the fact that official news sources always have access to privileged information that journalists do not. Having said this, however, it is equally important not to underestimate the significance of system differences for the political process and the reporting of that process across otherwise democratic societies such as the United States and Japan. Given space constraints, this chapter will focus primarily on some of the more distinctive Japanese news gathering institutions, as they appear to be outliers when compared to those of many other advanced industrialized democracies.[44]

Differences in U.S. and Japanese Media Environments

Two features of the media environment in Japan are key to understanding its present form: blurred state-society boundaries and a cohesive but insular industry structure. The watchdog and adversarial aspects of the liberal European press that had developed in the nineteenth century served as an early model for the American press. Japanese newspapers were introduced in the mid-nineteenth century to a country with little by way of a civil society and a long history of strict controls on publishing. Meiji-era journalists and leaders were not adversaries, they were both a part of the same elite. Former samurai founded early newspapers, while journalists ran for public office and moved easily into and out of the state bureaucracies. This history shaped early journalists' view of the purpose of the printed press, as they saw themselves as insiders whose ultimate goal it was to push for the modernization of Japan through the enlightenment of the masses.[45]

Even today Japanese journalists differ from their American counterparts in terms of the extent to which they feel that it is important to have an adversarial as opposed to neutral stance in their relationship with key sources.[46] While recent scholarship on the American press acknowledges some of the pernicious effects that excessive reliance on adversarial norms may have on the public and on democracy more generally, rigid adherence to neutrality can also have deleterious results. It may be the case, as can be seen especially in prewar Japan, that in adopting an impartial and nonpartisan position toward political elites, the press becomes a de facto supporter of the state and its policies. This became even more significant, of course, when Japan began its wartime buildup, as the media came to be used as an important part of the state's propaganda machine. After Japan's defeat, its media industry and related media conventions never underwent significant reform at the hands of the Occupation, unlike many other industries that had served the state or worked in close cooperation with it.

The second key feature of the Japanese media environment, a cohesive but insular industry structure, ensures that these close ties to key elites are carefully managed among all major rivals in the industry, and that outsiders (both domestic and foreign) do not gain access. Japanese journalists carry out news gathering as members of exclusive press clubs scattered throughout the country in an estimated 1,000 key government and business organizations. Information flows within the press club system take place not on an ad hoc, case by case, informal or situational basis, but through the formal structures and institutionalized procedures of the news gathering system itself. All insider journalists are provided the same information and make shared agreements about how to report the news. All outside journalists are excluded from this information and left to fend for themselves. To make certain that they preserve this prerogative, the cartel members have worked through their industry association to prevent reform.[47] Although American journalists, particularly those in Washington, are also known to develop close ties with their political sources, in Japan press clubs provide an environment for the institutionalization of such relationships and practices. The structure of Japan's media industry makes it possible to limit those relationships to a small set of media outlets. It is often said that Japanese journalists actually know a good deal more about the details of the political process in Japan than American journalists know about their own system. They do not, however, write about them because they have exchanged access for autonomy.

Press Clubs and Japanese Reporting

For the Japanese journalist, the impact of the press clubs and related news gathering institutions and relations on coverage of bilateral issues is much as it is with respect to local stories—press club members generally have access to information about aspects of the bilateral relationship that they cannot always use. Or, alternatively, they uncritically publish the official line. There is some empirical evidence of the distorting effect the press club system has on Japanese reporting of the U.S.-Japan relationship, especially in terms of two journalistic values—those of objectivity and balance.

How do Japanese news reporting practices influence Japanese reporting of the relationship? To answer this, one turns to a study conducted by the Mansfield Center for Pacific Affairs in 1992 that sought to evaluate and compare U.S. and Japanese newspaper coverage of friction between the two countries in 1989 and 1990.[48] This study, one of the few comparative empirical analyses of news reporting in the United States and Japan, looked at three issues of importance to the relationship—the Structural Impediments Initiative (SII), the FS-X fighter issue, and the purchase of Columbia Pictures and the Rockefeller Center by Japanese investors. American and Japanese reports on each of these issues were evaluated in terms of two traditional journalistic criteria—balance (defined as the degree to which equal representation is given to different parties in a dispute) and objectivity (operationalized as the degree to which the news report avoids either justifying or blaming one side or another in a dispute). The report's conclusion supports the suggestion made here that news gathering practices matter, and more importantly, that Japanese practices may matter more.

The Mansfield study found overall that American coverage of the three issues tended to be more balanced and objective, as well as more detailed and elaborate than Japanese coverage.[49] In terms of balance, the study found that American journalists were far more likely than Japanese journalists to cite sources and to achieve balance by citing arguments from both sides of an issue. In contrast Japanese news reports achieved balance by omitting or ignoring arguments altogether, often merely supplying facts without argument or context. To get a clearer picture of the data on balance, the Mansfield group carried out a second analysis that looked only at those stories which had included some kind of argument. This analysis found that Japanese news stories about the relationship citing substantive arguments were "far more likely to be one-sided than equivalent American reports."[50] They also found that when Japanese news reports cited opinions, they were more often than not those of Japanese government officials and that the facts and opinions they supported were the official Japanese views. Krauss notes that "this characteristic of Japanese newspaper coverage may represent a partial explanation for the apparent confusion and difficulty that many Japanese have in understanding what the United States wants from Japan, or why American pressure is so intense. Not having been exposed to the American perspective, many Japanese may be unable to understand the rationale (right or wrong) behind American demands."[51]

This approach to balance on the part of the Japanese press stems in part from the press club system, which fosters a strong sense of allegiance to sources and a desire to minimize the attention drawn to them. Even when sources are cited, they are rarely cited by name: Japanese journalists usually rely on an elliptical and elaborate code of Japanese that, while understood by elites and other insiders, is not readily intelligible to the general public.[52] The practice of omitting arguments also results from the difficulty club members have in seeking out alternative or opposing views—even official views—while attached to a given club. In Japan journalists are generally assigned to cover a single club and do not have access to other clubs or the official sources covered by them. Moreover, colleagues from the same newspaper who are members in these other clubs are more inclined to feel loyalty to their club than to a journalist from their own newspaper from another club, and less likely to share information that might make a more balanced story possible.

With respect to objectivity in the coverage of bilateral affairs, the Mansfield study found that "Japanese coverage tended to show an allegiance to Japan's position by suggesting that the United States was more to blame for the friction, while American coverage showed no such tendency."[53] In explaining these results, the report once again turns to the critical role of the press clubs, suggesting that although Japanese journalists emphasize factual and noninterpretive stories, they nevertheless are more inclined to derive their stories from official Japanese sources. They conclude that "since Japanese journalists depend more upon officialdom for explanations of what underlies the news than their American counterparts, their interpretation of events inevitably tends to reflect the Japanese government's perspective. It is very likely that this dynamic is reinforced by the general exclusion (only now beginning to end) of foreign journalists from the reporters' clubs."[54]

There is also some evidence suggesting that press club practices affect news coverage even when Japanese journalists are away from the clubs. When Japanese journalists travel abroad, for example with the prime minister or other prominent officials, the tendency is to remain a part of the group of journalists closely tied to the prime minister and his aides, even though these journalists potentially have ready access to the alternative views of American officials.[55] There is also an inclination on the part of Japanese foreign correspondents residing in the United States to continue to practice other aspects of press club reporting while abroad. This is especially the case when it comes to what are known as morning rounds and night attacks (*asagake* and *yomawari*, respectively). While these visits to officials' homes in the early morning and late evening by press club members in Japan ostensibly allow them to gain deep background, many reports on this practice by Japanese as well as Americans have suggested that they are one of the mechanisms by which sources co-opt journalists, instilling a sense of loyalty and allegiance through familiarity. How does the transported Japanese journalist go about his nightly rounds in the United States? According to one former Japanese correspondent, it is not by making rounds to various American officials' homes, but by visiting the homes of Japanese embassy staff or going to the hotels of visiting Japanese officials and dignitaries. In this way, they are able to perpetuate the same kinds of ties developed at home.[56] Still, in spite of the export of such practices, the somewhat limited empirical evidence suggests that Japanese foreign correspondents are less likely to ascribe blame to the United States for some issue when they are based in the U.S. than are press club–based journalists writing from Japan.[57]

Press Clubs and American Reporting

The press clubs and related exclusionary practices not only shape Japanese news reports about the relationship at home and abroad, they also shape foreign news reports about Japan. There are many examples in the postwar period of cases where American and other foreign journalists did not have access to press briefings of important events occurring in Japan, including many happening in the period of heightened American media interest in Japan in the 1980s. Although American press conferences are held by sources, the press clubs control press conferences in Japan. As a result, until quite recently only club members have been allowed to attend them. In one of the most famous cases, when U.S. Ambassador Edwin Reischauer was stabbed in an assassination attempt in 1964, American journalists could not attend the press conference held to discuss the stabbing because they were not members of the metropolitan police press club that was responsible for holding the conference. Similarly, an October 1989 *Newsweek* cover appalled many Japanese by lampooning Japan's "invasion" of Hollywood. The cover contained an illustration of the Columbia Pictures logo dressed in a kimono and the bold headline "Japan Invades Hollywood." (The Japanese language edition of *Newsweek* carried the picture but used the term "advances into" instead of the more offensive "invades"). No foreign journalists were allowed to attend the announcement of Sony's purchase of Columbia, an admittedly sensitive icon of American culture. Foreign reporters covering the Recruit stock-for-favors scandal involving bureaucrats, politicians, and media managers in the late 1980s and the *Aum Shinrikyō* gassing of a Tokyo subway in 1995, likewise did not have access to the press club in the prosecutor's office where daily briefings were given to the Japanese press. Furthermore, although the Imperial Household Agency held daily briefings for the Japanese press on the late emperor Hirohito's illness, in the agency's separate briefings for foreigners it merely released information that was given to Japanese reporters the previous day.[58] Some critics of the foreign press in Japan rightly point out that the general lack of Japanese-language skills among foreign correspondents serves as a major hurdle to their being able to cover Japan accurately. Still, while the lack of local language fluency is a general problem faced by foreign correspondents everywhere, in the case of foreign correspondents residing in Japan, linguistic ignorance is only confounded by the more general lack of ready access to important official sources.

One perverse result of American journalists' exclusion from official Japan is that they have to rely to a very high degree on the uniform reports coming from the mainstream Japanese press that does have access. This practice potentially allows for an extension from the domestic to the international arena of the images and views of Japan and the U.S.-Japan relationship carefully crafted by official Japan. In the early part of the revisionist period, Dutch journalist Karel van Wolferen warned his fellow foreign correspondents in Japan about their overreliance on local reports, admonishing them to take special care not to mistake uniformity for accuracy:

> Our relationship with the Japanese press is extraordinary. It has probably more influence in determining what we write than the local press has on correspondence out of other major capitals. A further insidious aspect of this is that most of us tend to be trustful of this

information because of the uniformity with which it is usually presented. If all the papers come out with the exact same conclusions about a political event and convey the 'voice of the people' in the same key, one is likely to think that they portray more of reality than if some of them said something different. As this applies to most foreigners here, the outside world gets a picture of Japan through a rather uniform filter. Often that picture is very misleading indeed.[59]

As suggested below, however, this mechanism is even more problematic during periods of heightened tension in the relationship such as were experienced during the 1980s or when the press is feeling particularly cynical, especially about its own exclusion.

The exclusion of foreign journalists from the press clubs was perhaps most troublesome in the case of Bloomberg and other financial news services such as Dow Jones and Knight-Ridder. For many years these news services were unable to receive important financial information in a timely manner due to the refusal of Japanese news companies and journalists to allow the American news firms to obtain membership to the Tokyo Stock Exchange press club (the *Kabuto* club) and other relevant press clubs. Economists argue that fair markets depend on the free flow of information, but investors and brokerage houses around the world that were Bloomberg subscribers did not receive a free flow or even distribution of information. In this case Bloomberg's Japanese rival, the *Nihon Keizai Shimbun,* had a significant time advantage in accessing important financial news. Rival foreign companies to *Nihon Keizai Shimbun* were afraid that they might lose subscribers to the Japanese news service. American negotiators even raised the closed nature of the press clubs during the Structural Impediments Initiative talks that took place in 1989–90. Although foreign financial reporters were eventually allowed access to a number of key financial clubs in 1992, this would not have been possible without the concerted effort and occasionally aggressive lobbying on the part of David Butts, the Asian bureau chief of Bloomberg, and the related support from American embassy officials, including the chief of the trade unit of the U.S. embassy's economics section in Tokyo, the U.S. press attaché, and U.S. Ambassador Michael Armacost.

This chapter has suggested that the Japanese press club system affects the quality, quantity, and clarity of news reporting by both Japanese and foreign journalists. In the Japanese case, this influence extends to such journalistic traditions as balance and objectivity, leads to homogeneity in news reporting about the relationship, and results in a tendency to blame the United States when ascribing blame at all. The chapter also finds that press club journalism affects American and other foreign correspondents at two levels. First, the system itself means that foreign journalists do not always have ready access to information about Japan, or are overly dependent on press club-based reports by the mainstream Japanese press, and therefore potentially write fewer, and perhaps more flawed stories. Second, at a more personal level, the feeling of being shut out may also make one more cynical about Japan and the Japanese, resulting in more negative or trivialized stories. As Ivan Hall has argued, "The adamant refusal of reciprocity, flying in the face of burgeoning international interest in Japan and relentless leaps in communications technology, can only lead to an increasingly embittered foreign press corps, whose personal frustrations are bound to affect the tone of their reporting."[60] Similarly, the Mansfield study discussed earlier notes that during a conference held to discuss the study's results, many American journalists "voiced their resentment of a press system which unfairly gave Japanese reporters better access to Japanese officials and other sources than they had."[61] Clearly, exclusion breeds cynicism; whether that cynicism leads to the kind of negative reports common in the 1980s or merely the trivialized accounts of Japan found in the 1990s and today, probably depends on a number of factors, including the state of the relationship itself, as suggested earlier.[62] While neither negativism nor trivialism is productive for the relationship as a whole, neither are the barriers to information that at least partially drive such tendencies.

While foreign correspondents were finally granted access to a larger number of press clubs in 1997, the clubs are still an important factor limiting the flow of information today. Why? To begin, foreign correspondents, as nonregular members of press clubs, are rarely granted access to the institutionalized informal briefings (*kondan*) that occur directly after the extremely formalized and often scripted official press briefings. While these are often ritualized affairs, journalists are less inhibited in asking questions during them than they are during the official press briefings. Not to be confused with the inner circle of elite journalists that an American president or high official might meet with off-the-record as deep background, the Japanese *kondan* are accessible by all regular members of the club, and are part of an attempt to provide a level playing field for cartel members. Though this chapter has focused on the exclusion of foreign journalists from the clubs, an even more problematic omission is the fact that freelance and nonmainstream Japanese journalists still do not have access to them. As

Ivan Hall notes, the Japanese press clubs have a profound impact on the formal structures and working habits of an entire profession, and consequently have a "most baneful impact on the exchange of ideas with other countries."[63]

Bilateral News Flows and Media Impact in the Information Era

So far, this chapter has examined two key factors driving and framing news reporting of the bilateral relationship over time: changes in the balance of (mostly economic) power; and qualitative institutional and structural differences. A third influence on media presentations of the relationship is only beginning to be felt—the rise of new media and information technologies, including computers, cable television, satellite, and most importantly, the Internet. Will these new technologies reshape media coverage of the U.S.-Japan relationship or mass and elite perceptions and knowledge of the relationship in any meaningful way? Equally important, as more actors in the relationship—including citizens, journalists, and political and bureaucratic elites—begin to use these media, what impact will they have on perceptions, opinions, or the knowledge and access imbalances discussed earlier in this chapter? In short, what will be the future impact of the new media on the bilateral relationship and the flow of information between the two countries?

The political potential of the Internet for citizens in both democratic and authoritarian societies is that it makes it possible for them to bypass formal political organizations, the scrutiny of government authorities, and the often predictable fare of the mainstream media, and create an unmediated space within which information and ideas can be debated and exchanged. The Internet is also a useful tool for political elites—including bureaucrats, politicians, and journalists—who can use it to gather and disseminate information about a wide variety of issues. Still, results of early studies into the political implications of the Internet conducted in a variety of countries have produced mixed results. Some, such as Nicholas Negroponte at MIT, have tried to show the ways in which the Internet promotes global democracy and increases political participation.[64] Others, such as Mark Poster, have suggested that the Internet can actually retard citizenship as much as aiding it.[65] Unlike the community gathering places that Habermas has argued helped give rise to civil society and the public sphere in the West, these critics charge that the Internet is a socially isolating technology in its replacement of face-to-face interaction. In addition they argue that as it becomes increasingly commercialized, it will undergo the same kind of centralizing tendencies as the traditional media and that a limited number of large corporations will be allowed to frame political and social agendas on the Internet as they have elsewhere.

While the lively debate about the nature and impact of the Internet on politics and society is expected to continue into the near future, it is nevertheless possible to imagine at least three ways in which the Internet might shape the flow and exchange of information about the U.S.-Japan relationship and the relationship itself. The Internet might be used:

—in the news gathering process by journalists in both countries to supplement or transcend more traditional means of gathering information, including the press clubs discussed earlier;

—by the public and elites as an alternative source of information, thereby influencing not only what people know about the relationship, but how much, an especially critical issue in the American case; and

—by a variety of groups or individuals—especially those currently marginalized by the traditional media, but also government officials, political parties, those in business, and private citizens—in the information dissemination process to shape public opinion and policy debates between the two countries in potentially divergent ways.

Given the relative infancy of this new technology, as well as differences in rates of diffusion and use in the United States and Japan, the estimation of the impact of the Internet on the U.S.-Japan relationship must remain somewhat tentative. Most likely it will be found, as in the case of the traditional media, that the Internet's impact on the bilateral relationship will vary depending on who uses it, how, and for what purposes. The question is not whether the Internet will have an important impact on the bilateral relationship, but how. Three possibilities are considered below:

1. More information overall. The Internet may play an important role in ameliorating the information divide discussed earlier by providing more English-language information about Japan to Americans and more information about the United States to the Japanese. One advantage for Americans is that many Japanese websites, including those of government, media, business, and alternative and grassroots organizations, provide English-language translations and summaries of key topics covered on the sites. This may make it easier for the public, those conveying information to the American public, as

well as policymakers to gain a more nuanced understanding of key issues. It can be expected for this to help reduce misunderstandings and tension, especially at critical junctures in the relationship.

2. More (nonofficial) sources. The development and diffusion of information technology may pluralize communication by creating an increasing number of alternative sources of information on important issues. As more journalists begin to use the Internet in their news gathering, they may become less reliant on the credentialed facts readily provided by official sources on both sides of the Pacific and more willing to incorporate views and sources currently excluded due to time or access constraints. This could potentially result in stories that are more genuinely balanced, and may help to reduce the stereotypes individuals have of certain groups and issues. Additionally, it may be found that the press clubs become less important as sources for bilateral news stories. The Internet has already started to have a visible impact on the way local governments disseminate information in Japan. Some local government officials have begun to place routine announcements on the web where the public can access them almost as quickly as the press club–based mass media. If this practice expands, it can be expected to reduce the information dissemination role of the press clubs and result in a more knowledgeable public.

3. New outlets for grassroots organizations. Grassroots groups in both countries have been using computer-mediated communication (CMC) for a long time to disseminate information about their causes. In the mid-1980s grassroots groups in Japan effectively used international computer networks to influence public opinion to stop the construction of housing for American military personnel in an area near Zushi. In 1995, after several American military soldiers were arrested for raping a young girl in Okinawa, a number of Japanese-language sites were established in order to disseminate information about that issue. Many of them were critical of the American presence and provided English-language summaries of their contents. It is expected that grassroots and other interest groups on both sides of the Pacific will increasingly use the Internet to gather support for and disseminate information about various bilateral and international issues, among them retention of American bases in Okinawa and Japanese fishing of Atlantic bluefin tuna. As various interest groups begin to use the Internet in this way, they should have a visible impact on the relationship as a whole, at times reducing tension and misunderstanding and at times exacerbating already tense circumstances. Additionally this might lead to increased pluralization as it brings a wider range of actors into the political process.

In sum, the Internet offers a number of technological advantages over other types of media that might be useful to all parties in the relationship. It can provide near instantaneous communication, alternative sources of information and an interactive format, as well as search and selection functions, and links to related sites. This ability to provide knowledge on demand will make the Internet an important resource for those interested in the relationship in normal times, and will be critical in times of crisis. At the same time, not only will many users not know how to evaluate the essentially unedited and undigested information they find on the Internet, they will only know about important bilateral issues if they have first learned of them in the traditional print and broadcast media. Thus although it can be expected that journalists, political elites, and the public will make ready use of the Internet in the future, it can also be expected for the Internet to supplement rather than supplant these other media.

Because the traditional media are expected to remain important information sources for the public—especially as the providers of much of the initial information about and interpretation of current issues and events— there is some concern about the current dwindling coverage of the U.S.-Japan relationship by the mainstream and popular American media. Without prior exposure to key bilateral issues and events on television and in the printed press, the public may not be able to benefit fully from the relationship-enhancing potential offered by the Internet. One journalist from the *Washington Post* recently suggested that the Internet potentially could lead to the creation of a two-tiered society for foreign news, by which he means "an ever more knowledgeable elite tapping into a multiplicity of news sources on and off the information highway as distinct from a 'dumbed down' mass of citizens increasingly alienated from once regular links with the outside world provided by newspaper and especially network television news."[66] Ultimately, the Internet's impact on the bilateral relationship may depend in large part on the ability of the traditional media to sustain and foster a public interested in that relationship in the first place.

Summary and Conclusion

This chapter examined the role the media played in the U.S.-Japan relationship over the past half century. The media systems of each country provide the primary filter through which both the public and elites obtain news and information, and are the main vehicle through which most people in each country understand one another. This ability to mediate and construct reality has a considerable impact on how Japanese and Americans view not only the functioning of their own political systems but also how they understand important bilateral and international issues. Indeed, recent research suggests that the media's impact may be greater when it comes to how the public understands foreign affairs than it is with respect to their understanding of domestic issues.[67] A better understanding of the differing ways information is filtered and passed on to the American and Japanese public will result in a reduction in misunderstandings and the mutual mistrust it engenders. It must be recognized that while the media are primarily domestic entities, they have an impact that goes much further than the boundaries of each individual nation.

The media in both countries have operated throughout the postwar period within a number of constraining frameworks: the larger framework of the U.S.-Japan relationship itself, and, perhaps just as important, the framework provided by their own socially and culturally embedded media institutions. While the dynamics of the relationship have shifted over the fifty-plus year period under review here and will continue to shift, each country's media institutions and the basic overall framework largely remains the same. It is likely that even the introduction of the more democratic and two-way information technologies, especially the Internet, will not alter the relationship in any dramatic way, though it may contribute over time to a gradual reduction in the number and types of misunderstandings as more people are able to become better informed about important bilateral and international issues.

Notes

1. *Newsweek*, August 7, 1989.
2. John Dower, *Japan in War and Peace: Selected Essays* (New Press, 1993), p. 329.
3. Ibid.
4. Sidney Verba and others, *Elites and the Idea of Equality: A Comparison of Japan, Sweden, and the United States* (Harvard University Press, 1987).
5. Pippa Norris, *A Virtuous Circle: Political Communications in Postindustrial Societies* (Cambridge University Press, 2000).
6. Robert D. Deutsch and Arthur J. Alexander, "American Images of Japan," *Japan Economic Institute Report*, May 17, 1996.
7. *San Francisco Chronicle* reporter Charles Burress is one of the most vociferous American critics of American media portrayals of Japan.
8. Harold G. Zucker, "The Variable Nature of New Media Influence," *Communication Yearbook 2* (Sage, 1978).
9. Holli A. Semetko, "The Media," in Lawrence LeDuc, Richard G. Niemi, and Pippa Norris, eds., *Comparing Democracies: Elections and Voting in Global Perspective"* (Sage, 1996), pp. 254–79.

10. Dower, *Japan in War and Peace,* p. 319.

11. Pacific Forum CSIS Pacnet No. 35, September 1, 2000. (www.nyu.edu/globalbeat/asia/Pacnet090100.html).

12. The inability to name the Japanese prime minister is perhaps understandable given that Japan has had eleven prime ministers in the last ten years. Noted by Kiyoshi Kawato, professor of economics at Middle Tennessee State University in an online article called "Transformation of the U.S.-Japan Relationship through the Internet" (www.mtsu.edu/~kawahito/ESSAY.html [January 15, 2001]).

13. *Japan Times,* October 7, 1995.

14. "Learning from Each Other: Japan, the United States and the International Knowledge System," International Higher Education, Winter 2000 (www.bc.edu/bc-org/avp/soe/cihe/newsletter.News03/text5.html).

15. Ibid.

16. Stanley Budner, "Communicating across the Pacific: United States and Japanese Newspaper Coverage of Friction between the Two Countries," *Mansfield Center for Pacific Affairs* (Mansfield Center, 1993). See also Ellis S. Krauss, "Media Coverage of U.S.-Japan Relations," in Susan J. Pharr and Ellis S. Krauss, ed., *Media and Politics in Japan* (University of Hawaii Press, 1996).

17. Ibid.

18. Masayuki Tadokoro, "The Media in U.S.-Japan Relations," in Gerald Curtis, ed., *New Perspectives on U.S.-Japan Relations* (Brookings, 2000).

19. K. Ishii, "Is the U.S. Overreported in the Japanese Press?" *Gazette,* vol. 57 (1996), pp. 135–44. See also Stanley Budner and Ellis Krauss, "Bias and Objectivity in Coverage of the U.S.-Japan Relationship," *Asian Survey,* vol. 24, no. 4 (April 1995), p. 355.

20. Tovah LaDier and Isao Kawasaki, "Creating Images: American and Japanese News Coverage of the Other," *Mansfield Center for Pacific Affairs* (Mansfield Center, 1997).

21. Zipangu, *Japan Made in U.S.A* (Zipangu, 1998), p. 78.

22. Ibid.

23. William Watts, "Americans Look at Asia: A Potomac Associates Policy Perspective," *Henry Luce Foundation Project on the Occasion of the 25th Anniversary of the Luce Scholars Program (*October 1999), p. 11.

24. Ibid.

25. Ibid.

26. John Woolley, "Using Media-Based Data in Studies of Politics," *American Journal of Political Science,* vol. 44, no. 1 (January 2000), p. 157. Woolley suggests that there is a potential for bias and error in such data—both media counts and events data. Here the volume counts are used to suggest trends only. Although this chapter largely focused on *New York Times* coverage, it also looked at volume in other (albeit elite) newspapers as well as popular magazines and found largely similar trends.

27. In examining American media volume for the period 1950–2000, the print index for the *New York Times* was hand counted for the period 1950–82, and a computerized index was used for the period thereafter (1983–2000). This analysis was supplemented with a computerized count of the volume of Japan coverage by four U.S. newspapers (*Washington Post, Christian Science Monitor, Los Angeles Times,* and *Wall Street Journal*) and several newsweeklies. Additionally, the number of articles in the *New York Times* on Japan was compared with that on China, Canada, and Mexico for the key period 1982–2000. Finally, to provide a comparative context, the Asahi.com database of newspaper articles published in the *Asahi Shimbun* (sometimes touted as the *New York Times* of Japan) was searched, and similar (though not identical) data on volume on the Japanese side were derived.

The data on media volume were subsequently compared with events data for the same period. A common feature of such data sets is that a single international event (defined as a

158

discrete occurrence with a beginning and an end and an actor and target that has sufficient prominence to stand out from the background of normal developments) is counted only once, irrespective of the number of stories that are written about it. Because the events data are derived from major international wire services, it becomes possible to reduce the potential effects of editorial selection bias or other structural constraints that might potentially distort results obtained from measuring volume alone. For the analysis of events trends, this chapter relied on a study conducted by the now defunct Japan Economic Institute (JEI) that analyzed U.S.-Japan-related events data from two important data sets—the University of Maryland's Global Event-Data System and the somewhat more limited Michigan State University Conflict and Peace Data Bank (COPDAB) database.

28. Bernard C. Cohen, *The Political Process and Foreign Policy: The Making of the Japanese Peace Settlement* (Princeton University Press, 1957), pp. 110–21.

29. Ibid., p. 111.

30. Arthur J. Alexander, "U.S.-Japan Relations since 1948: A Preliminary Analysis of Events Data," *JEI Report*, no. 32 (August 21, 1998), p. 8.

31. Ibid., p. 2.

32. Ibid., p. 5.

33. Andrew Horvat, "Reviewing Revisionism—Judging the Legacy of an Era of U.S.-Japan Acrimony" (www.ajiazaidan.org/english-graphics/3-23/article.html).

34. Ibid. See also Brink Lindsey and Aaron Lukas, "Revisiting the 'Revisionists': The Rise and Fall of the Japanese Economic Model," *Cato Institute Trade Policy Analysis*, no. 3 (July 31, 1998).

35. Ibid.

36. Data are from a search using Japan as the keyword on www.booksinprint.com/bip/Search/history_print.asp. The total for the period from 1981 to 1990 was 1,911 books; the total for the period 1991–2000 was 3,803 books. Admittedly, some of the increase for the latter period is due to the continued publication of books written in the earlier period.

37. Theodore White, "The Danger from Japan," *New York Times Magazine*, July 28, 1985.

38. See, for example, the critical essays on recent *New York Times* coverage of Japan in Zipangu, ed., *Made in Japan* (Zipangu, 1998).

39. Robert Deutch and Arthur J. Alexander, "American Images of Japan," *JEI*, May 17, 1996.

40. Hidehisa Mano, *Tokyo Shimbun*, evening edition January 26, 2001, as cited in e-mail message from the Japan Information Access Project, February 2, 2001.

41. Ibid. See also Pippa Norris, "The Restless Searchlight: Network News Framing of the Post–Cold War World," *Political Communication*, vol. 12 (1995), p. 357–70.

42. See, for example, H. Denis Wu, "Systemic Determinants of International News Coverage: A Comparison of Thirty-Eight Countries," *Journal of Communication* (Spring 2000).

43. Ronald Morse, "The Morse Target: Washington's Movers and Shakers on Japan," Working Paper 2 (Los Angeles: Japan Policy Research Institute, September 1994).

44. See, for example, Pharr and Krauss, *Media and Politics in Japan*; Laurie Freeman, *Closing the Shop: Information Cartels and Japan's Mass Media* (Princeton University Press, 2000); and Ellis Krauss, *Broadcasting Politics in Japan* (Cornell University Press, 2000).

45. James Huffman, "The Meiji Roots and Contemporary Practices of the Japanese Press," *Japan Interpreter*, vol. 11, no. 4 (Spring 1977), p. 460.

46. Budner, "Communicating across the Pacific," p. 25.

47. See Freeman, *"Closing the Shop,"* for details of the press club system.

48. Budner, "Communicating across the Pacific."

49. Ibid., p. 23.

50. Ibid., p. 15.

51. Budner and Krauss, "Bias and Objectivity," p. 355.

52. See Freeman, *Closing the Shop*, for details.

53. Ibid., p. 352.

54. Ibid.

55. Leslie Helm, "All on Board for Miyazawa," *Los Angeles Times*, April 27, 1993.

56. Hiroshi Ando, *Nichibei jōhō masatsu (U.S.-Japan Information Friction)* (Iwanami Shoten, 1991), p. 135.

57. Budner and Krauss, "Bias and Objectivity," p. 352.

58. Richard Read, "In Japan Journalists Act More Like Lapdogs than Watchdogs and Foreign Reporters Get Only Scraps," *Oregonian*, April 12, 1992.

59. *Number One Shimbun*, January 15, 1984.

60. Ivan Hall, *Cartels of the Mind: Japan's Intellectual Closed Shop* (Oxford University Press, 1998), p. 74.

61. Budner, "Communicating across the Pacific," p. 23.

62. See, for example, Zipangu, *Made in Japan*, for a criticism by expatriate Japanese residing in New York of this practice.

63. Ibid.

64. Nicholas Negroponte, *Being Digital* (Hodder & Stoughton, 1995).

65. Mark Poster, "The Net as Public Sphere?" *Wired*, November 1995, pp. 42–43.

66. Claude Moisy, "The Foreign News Flow in the Information Age," Discussion Paper D-23 (Joan Shorenstein Center for Press, Politics, and Public Policy, Harvard University, November 1996), p. 15.

67. Wayne Wanta and Yu-Wei Hu, "The Agenda-Setting Effects of International News Coverage: An Examination of Differing News Frames," *International Journal of Public Opinion Research*, vol. 5, no. 3 (1993), p. 252.

CHAPTER SEVEN

International Organizations

AMY E. SEARIGHT

International organizations (IOs) have played an increasingly important role in shaping relations between the United States and Japan in the postwar period. Their influence has risen dramatically in recent years, resulting in the shift of many issues from the bilateral to the multilateral arena and the prospect that this will enhance overall cooperation between the two countries. IOs have been neglected by many observers of U.S.-Japan relations because their reach extends to many countries simultaneously, and their focus has often fallen on areas outside of the core issues defining the U.S.-Japan relationship. Moreover, for much of the postwar period Japan kept a very low profile in the multilateral discussions within IOs, and the United States frequently resorted to bilateral persuasion and pressure when seeking to influence Japanese behavior.

However, IOs have affected U.S.-Japan relations by empowering Japan in at least three specific ways. First, they fundamentally shaped Japan's rise as a postwar power. The General Agreement on Tariffs and Trade (GATT) and the International Monetary Fund (IMF) laid the foundations for Japan's spectacular economic success, and they shaped Japan's subsequent transformation into a more liberal economy. In addition, the UN framework helped Japanese leaders institutionalize the U.S. security alliance domestically, making it palatable to the Japanese public by embedding it, at least rhetorically, in a UN-centered diplomacy. Second, IOs have served as an outlet for Japan's growing international activism. They have provided opportunities for Japan to translate its rising economic power into political power without alarming its Asian neighbors or disrupting bilateral ties with the United States. As Japan steadily gained economic strength relative to the United States, IOs have helped mediate this power shift by providing compatible and rewarding roles for both powers to play, including a larger degree of shared leadership.[1] Third, Japan has increasingly turned to IOs to bind the United States, in terms of keeping it engaged in multilateral regimes and constraining its unilateral exercise of power. Japan's growing use of these two binding strategies—binding its own emerging power to IOs, and binding the United States to multilateral regimes—has sparked contention in certain areas where American dominance has been challenged, but it has led to even greater areas of coordination and cooperation between the two countries.

International organizations themselves have undergone significant changes in recent decades, growing broader in their scope and authority. These institutional changes, combined with Japan's growing multilateral activism, have shifted many interactions between the United States and Japan from the bilateral to the multilateral arena. However, this shift has been far more pronounced on the economic side than on the security side of the relationship, for two main reasons. First, institutional change in economic IOs, and the trade regime in particular, has been more dramatic and has thus had a larger impact on bilateral relations. Although the United Nations has seen its influence rise in the post–cold war era, it remains peripheral to U.S.-Japan security relations, which are instead defined by the bilateral Security Treaty. Second, Japan has faced quite different trajectories in economic and security IOs. Whereas Japan has risen to become a leading member of GATT, the IMF, and the World Bank, its influence in the United Nations has been limited by its lack of a permanent seat on the Security Council and by domestic constraints that prevent it from actively participating in UN peacekeeping operations.

This chapter begins with a historical overview of the postwar institutions and how they affected Japan and U.S.-Japan relations in the early postwar years. This is followed by a description of three trends in IOs that have been important for redefining U.S.-Japan relations: the institutional development of the organizations themselves, the wavering leadership of the United States, and the growing assertiveness of Japan. These three trends have played out in slightly different ways in trade, finance, and UN security relations, and subsequent sections of this chapter examine the emerging patterns of competition and cooperation in each of these areas. The final section considers these developments in light of international relations theories, and speculates about how IOs will affect U.S.-Japan relations in the future.

In the context of this chapter, IOs are defined as formal international institutions that are set up and run by governments, based on a treaty or explicit agreement, and embodying sets of rules, procedures, and norms that member countries are expected to follow.[2] They also serve as multilateral forums for engaging in discussion and bargaining over issues, and managing conflicts that arise between countries. This chapter focuses on the core organizations that have been involved in managing global economic and security affairs in the postwar era: GATT and its successor organization, the World Trade Organization (WTO); the IMF and World Bank; and the United Nations.

Historical Background

The United States made several institutional choices in the early postwar period that would shape Japan's reintegration into the world system and thereby determine the course of U.S.-Japan relations for years to come. The first was the decision by American policymakers to construct a range of multilateral organizations to regulate interstate relations in trade, finance, and security. At the Bretton Woods conference in 1944, the United States and its allies created the twin pillars of the international financial system: the IMF, which would manage exchange rates and payments imbalances among nations; and the World Bank, which would finance reconstruction and promote investment in developing countries. In trade GATT was established to provide a framework of international trade rules and a negotiating forum for liberalizing trade barriers. In the security domain the United States designed the United Nations as a mechanism for collective security, albeit subject to veto by the five great powers on the Security Council.

Not only did the United States take the lead in designing and building these IOs, but American leadership was critical for their early functioning and maintenance. The United States supported GATT by opening its markets and offering disproportionate tariff cuts in early rounds. In the financial regime it provided the necessary liquidity in the system through the Marshall Plan and other financial outflows, and it allowed other currencies to grow undervalued against the dollar, which hurt its trade competitiveness. Finally, the United States demonstrated its commitment to multilateral peacekeeping in the United Nations in the 1956 Suez crisis, when it worked through the United Nations to organize pressure against its two oldest and closest allies, Britain and France, to withdraw their forces from Egypt and be replaced by multilateral peacekeepers.

American leadership was also crucial for integrating Japan and West Germany into the postwar institutional framework. American policymakers firmly believed that the full participation of Japan and West Germany in the postwar institutions was essential for a stable world order, and they set about convincing their allies to extend institutional membership and other linkages to the former enemy states. The task of reintegration was much easier in the case of West Germany than Japan. Other European countries shared the U.S. belief that the German problem would best be solved by its incorporation into regional institutions, and they acquiesced in U.S. plans for regional organizations (NATO and the European Community (EC)) that would promote new linkages between member states in the region. However, few countries were eager to reestablish trade relations and other ties with Japan, especially since it had already emerged in the prewar period as a formidable trade competitor. This reluctance posed a significant barrier to gaining Japan's admittance to a number of IOs, especially GATT. Although Japan had applied for GATT membership in 1952, many countries continued to resist the idea of including Japan in the liberal trade club, and the United States had to apply strong and insistent diplomatic pressure to gain Japan's admission in 1955.[3] The United States also offered substantial economic incentives to gain Japan's full participation, persuading Canada, Denmark, Finland, Italy, Norway, and Sweden to grant tariff concessions to Japan in exchange for U.S. concessions to them.[4]

With U.S. sponsorship Japan also gained admission to the IMF in 1952, the United Nations in 1956, and the Organization for Economic Cooperation and Development (OECD) in 1964. Japan's entry into these international organizations was a high priority of the Japanese government, and each admission was greeted enthusiastically at home as a symbol of Japan's return to the international community after humiliating military defeat and long occupation. Yet once Japan joined these organizations it remained very passive within them. Japanese leaders felt satisfied with membership status and felt little need to engage in active multilateral diplomacy. Instead Japanese leaders turned inward to focus on economic reconstruction and growth.

A final institutional legacy that would shape the contours of Japan's future international relations came from the U.S. decision to forgo earlier plans for creating a regional security organization in East Asia akin to

NATO. Although American planners in the State Department had initially advocated a Pacific Pact that would provide collective security for the United States, Japan, Canada, Australia, New Zealand, and the Philippines, it abandoned the idea in the face of opposition from its potential allies, including Japan.[5] Instead, the United States forged separate bilateral alliances, creating a hub-and-spoke system with the United States at the center and several countries in the region serving as spokes, including Japan, South Korea, the Philippines, and Australia and New Zealand. For economic relations, the United States relied on global economic organizations to link Japan and other countries in the region to the rest of the world. The United States provided additional bilateral economic help by opening its markets to Japanese goods. This reliance on a bilateral security framework and global economic multilateralism left Japan rather isolated diplomatically from its Asian neighbors. It also left Japan heavily dependent on the United States for its security and economic needs. Unlike Germany, which could forge closer ties to its neighbors and expand its international role through regional institutions, Japan would have to rely on global IOs if it were to seek a more active and independent voice in world affairs.

Japan thrived in this institutional framework. With GATT and the IMF serving to open markets abroad and stabilize exchange rates, Japan could focus its efforts on export-led economic growth, which it did with spectacular success. Although many countries had taken advantage of an exception in GATT (Article 35) that allowed them to continue discriminating against Japanese goods, this treatment became difficult to sustain under pressure by the United States and other GATT members that had opened their markets to Japanese imports. By the mid-1960s most countries had relinquished their restrictions and granted Japan full GATT treatment. The Bretton Woods exchange rate regime was especially beneficial to Japan in the first twenty-five years. The fixed rate of exchange between the yen and the dollar meant that as the dollar grew more inflated over time the yen was increasingly undervalued, and this helped Japanese goods penetrate foreign markets. Japan began to mount massive current account surpluses that destabilized the Bretton Woods system and contributed to its demise, yet it faced no obligations under IMF rules to bear the burden of adjustment.

In security affairs, Japan's bilateral security relationship with the United States meant that it could focus its energies on economic reconstruction rather than rearmament. A multilateral security arrangement like the Pacific Pact would have been far more costly and domestically divisive, since it would have required a larger defense contribution from Japan and would have posed a higher likelihood that Japan would be drawn into regional military conflicts. At the same time, the United Nations served a useful function in domestic politics, as Japanese leaders skillfully deflected criticism of Japan's overwhelming security dependence on the United States by invoking UN Centrism (*kokuren chūshinshugi*) as a core principle of foreign diplomacy.[6] The concept was never clearly defined and had little substantive import, but it resonated with the deep strain of idealism and support for the United Nations in Japanese public opinion.[7]

Japan thus benefited enormously from participating in these IOs, perhaps more than any other country in the early postwar period. Yet Japan assumed a very low profile within them. Japan showed virtually no interest in shaping the policy agenda of IOs or actively engaging in their management. And, just as the presence of Japan did little to shape IOs, the institutional rules or norms of IOs had little direct impact on Japan in the early postwar period. Japan's compliance with the rules and norms of GATT and the IMF was slow and uneven, and further Japan often found ways to comply with the rules yet avoid the anticipated consequences of trade or financial liberalization. The United States found that it could achieve better results in opening up Japan through bilateral pressure. Japan's passivity in multilateral affairs, and U.S. reliance on bilateralism in dealing with Japan, meant that IOs were not all that relevant in defining the U.S.-Japan relationship. Although IOs were vitally important to Japan's economic success and its diplomatic standing in these early years, it would take several decades before they would become a central feature in U.S.-Japan relations.

Trends over the Postwar Period

The impact of IOs on postwar U.S.-Japan relations has been shaped by three interrelated trends: the decline and subsequent strengthening of IOs, the wavering of American leadership, and the transformation of Japan's multilateral behavior.

International Organizations

The first trend is the institutional development of IOs over time, and in particular the strengthening of major IOs in recent decades. International organizations have grown in size and number, and many have become more legalistic and binding. As a result a growing proportion of international interactions take place within the institutional framework of IOs, including interactions between the United States and Japan.

The trend toward more expansive and more powerful IOs has not been a uniform, steady process. Institutionalization and legalization has waxed and waned over the postwar period, and has developed differentially across regimes. The core postwar IOs were originally designed with greater powers of legal authority than they would actually exercise; in the trade regime, the highly legalized International Trade Organization never materialized, and was replaced by the much more slender institutional framework of GATT. All of the major postwar IOs declined in effectiveness and relevance in the 1970s before rebounding in various ways a decade or so later. The collapse of the Bretton Woods fixed exchange rate regime in the early 1970s removed many of the legalized obligations that members used to face in monetary policies. Dispute settlement procedures in GATT fell into almost complete disuse from the mid-1960s until the early 1970s,[8] and the widespread use of gray area and nontariff measures further diminished the relevance of GATT in the 1970s. In the United Nations, peacekeeping operations stalled in the face of cold war rivalry and the rise of nonaligned states, resulting in its growing irrelevance to conflict management in the 1970s–80s.[9]

However, in recent decades these IOs have reemerged as central arenas of international management, and many areas have undergone significant institutional change. Separate international developments have driven change in economic and security regimes. The advance of economic integration gave rise to new incentives for institutionalized cooperation in trade and finance. As economies become more intertwined, the advantages of coordinating national policies to facilitate further economic transactions increase. Moreover the costs of a state violating prior agreements rise as trade and investment grows. Consequently, governments are more willing to strengthen existing institutions and to build new ones to facilitate policy coordination and harmonization and to make agreements more binding.[10] The second major international change was the end of the cold war, which has profoundly affected security relations and the role of the United Nations. The collapse of the Soviet bloc gave rise to a host of local conflicts between and within newly emerging states, and Western intervention in these conflicts could no longer be justified with reference to the communist threat. The UN Security Council thus assumed a central role in dealing with these conflicts since it could organize and legitimate multinational peacekeeping efforts.[11]

However, institutional development has varied substantially across different regimes. The most dramatic changes have occurred in trade IOs, with the growing legalization of the GATT regime coinciding with the dramatic growth of regional trade IOs. Change has also been significant in the IMF and World Bank, although the expansion of legal obligations and international oversight has affected developing countries far more than the lending countries. In other areas, notably security affairs, institutional development has been much more slow and uneven. The major trends are reviewed below.

PROLIFERATION AND EXPANSION. IOs have spread their coverage in several ways: they have grown more universalistic in membership, broader in scope, and they have proliferated in number. First, the membership in the core postwar institutions has grown considerably in size and diversity. Change has been especially dramatic in the economic IOs, with a growing number of developing countries joining and assuming more obligations of membership in the 1960s through 1980s. GATT, for example, began with twenty-three original signatories in 1947, and almost tripled in size by the end of the Kennedy Round two decades later. Today, GATT's successor organization, the WTO, has 140 members representing over 90 percent of world trade. Developing countries joined in large numbers in the 1960s and 1970s, and today 80 percent of all WTO members are developing countries or former socialist economies.[12] East Asian countries were slow to join GATT. By 1970 only Japan, Indonesia, Malaysia, and South Korea were members. Singapore and the Philippines followed later in the decade, and Thailand and Hong Kong joined in the 1980s. The Bretton Woods organizations likewise saw membership rise and become more diverse in the 1960s. The IMF began with twenty-nine governments signing the 1945 Articles of Agreement; by 1980 it had 138 members, and today it has 182.[13] Even the United Nations saw membership rise dramatically in the first twenty years, more than doubling from fifty-one members in 1945 to 118 in 1965. Today membership stands at 189 countries.[14]

International organizations have also proliferated in number, creating a much denser institutional landscape in world politics. They increased in number from about 100 in 1945 to over 600 by 1980.[15] New areas of international concern such as environmental protection and human rights have given rise to a range of new organizations, many of them embedded in the UN institutional framework.[16] However, much of the institutional growth has occurred at the regional level. These include a host of regional trade agreements such as the EC and European Union (EU), North American

Free Trade Agreement (NAFTA), Southern Cone Common Market (Mercosur), and Asia-Pacific Economic Cooperation (APEC), as well as other forms of economic cooperation like OPEC, the European Monetary Union (EMU), and regional development banks. They also include a number of regional security organizations that have arisen over time, like the Association of Southeast Asian Nations (ASEAN), the Organization for Security and Cooperation in Europe (OSCE), and the ASEAN Regional Forum (ARF). Regional organizations are often designed to mesh with the rules and norms of overarching global IOs, producing a complex yet complementary layering of different levels of institutionalization in many areas. However, institutional growth has been highly uneven across regions. Whereas western Europe has become densely institutionalized, and governments in North America and Latin America have created a range of economic, human rights, and security institutions, East Asian regional organizations remain sparse, informal, and comparatively weak. For Japan, this means that the major global IOs in economics and security remain the most useful institutional arenas for pursuing a more activist multilateral diplomacy, even in the service of regionally based interests.

The scope of many IOs has also broadened considerably. Rules have expanded to cover a wider range of issues and have reached deeper into policy areas once thought to be exclusively domestic domains of governance. The trade regime provides the most striking example of this trend. Whereas the original GATT rules and early trade negotiations dealt with border measures like tariffs and quotas, subsequent rulemaking in the Tokyo and Uruguay Rounds moved behind the border to address such issues as technical regulations and health standards, government procurement practices, domestic enforcement of intellectual property rights, and domestic regulatory regimes in telecommunications and other service sectors. The Bretton Woods financial organizations expanded their regulatory scope in the developing world as they shifted their focus from postwar reconstruction and exchange rate management to providing development assistance that was increasingly linked to international oversight of domestic policies. In the United Nations as well, the norm of sovereignty has eroded as human rights issues have been elevated in importance and have been used as legal justification for intervening in a range of international conflicts.

LEGALIZATION OF INTERNATIONAL ORGANIZATIONS. In many areas, the rules and norms of international organizations have been increasingly formalized into legalistic obligations. Rules have grown more precise and binding, and greater authority has been delegated to third parties to enforce and elaborate these rules.[17] These changes, where they have occurred, have moved IOs closer to something akin to domestic legal systems and away from their previous modus operandi as informal clubs in which powerful actors devise ad hoc solutions to problems that arise between them. The legalization of international rules in the trade regime exemplifies this trend. GATT had grown more legalized in the Tokyo Round, as rules specified more precise obligations in a range of areas. However, the legal reforms undertaken in the Uruguay Round substantially increased the judicialization of the regime. Under GATT, a country that felt another member had violated the rules could file a complaint, and if the matter could not be settled through bilateral consultations, the dispute would be adjudicated by a panel made up of third-party representatives. However, any country, including the loser of the panel process, could block the adoption of an adverse panel report. Countries could also delay the process in various ways. Under the new system, the adoption of a negative ruling no longer requires the agreement of the losing country, although countries have recourse to a review by an appellate body. After that, however, panel recommendations become binding, and countries are obligated to take any required remedial actions within a specified time frame.

Legalization has occurred in many other areas of international relations, notably the judicialization of the human rights regimes through the creation of regional human rights courts, the UN International Crimes Tribunals, and efforts to establish an International Criminal Court. Although the IMF and World Bank lack judicial forums, they have nevertheless become more legalized over time. Conditionality agreements have become more precise and binding. Other aspects of project lending in the World Bank, such as environmental impact assessment and treatment of indigenous peoples, have been written into legal obligations attached to loans and become subject to international oversight by the World Bank Inspection Panel.[18] Still, these changes affect recipient countries rather than major shareholders. As will be seen, the primary significance of the legalization trend for U.S.-Japan relations is that it increases the binding power of IOs, and GATT-WTO in particular, which has proved valuable to both countries but especially to Japan.

Wavering U.S. Commitment to Multilateralism

Despite its early leadership and support of IOs, the United States' commitment to multilateral cooperation began to waver over time, declining significantly in the 1970s and 1980s before rebounding somewhat in recent years. The story is familiar. The postwar economic resurgence of Europe and Japan led to a decline in the relative position of the United States and thereby weakened the American commitment to bearing the costs of sustaining the effective functioning of IOs. The earliest and most dramatic demonstration of declining U.S. leadership came in 1971, when President Nixon unilaterally suspended U.S. commitments under Bretton Woods to redeem gold for dollars and imposed a 10 percent tariff surcharge on imports that would remain in place until other countries agreed to revalue their currencies against the dollar. Both actions were explicit violations of the international monetary rules agreed to in the Bretton Woods charter, and signaled that the United States was unwilling to shoulder the burden of adjustment of the monetary system, which would have required reining in its budget deficits. This led to a complete collapse of the fixed exchange rate system in early 1973. However, the United States continued to support the Bretton Woods institutions, as they redefined their missions to focus on structural adjustment lending to developing countries. In particular, U.S. leadership ensured that the IMF retained a central role in managing financial crises that threatened the global economy.[19]

In trade the executive branch remained committed to negotiating further tariff liberalization and supporting GATT, but Congress increasingly insisted that actions be taken to counteract what were perceived as unfair trading practices of Japan and other states. This led to growing unevenness in U.S. trade policy and its commitment to its obligations under GATT. On the one hand, the United States continued to take the lead in pushing for further trade liberalization, launching the Tokyo Round (1973–79) and the Uruguay Round (1986–94) of multilateral negotiations. However, the United States was far less generous than it had been in earlier GATT rounds. American negotiators were much more concerned about securing equivalent concessions from major trade partners and expanding GATT coverage to agriculture and other areas of U.S. export interest.[20] Moreover, as the United States trade position deteriorated in many sectors, it showed increasing willingness to violate GATT rules and norms by resorting to voluntary export restraints and other measures designed to protect the domestic market. Further, Congress instituted new mechanisms under Section 301 of the 1974 Trade Act, and the more aggressive provision of Super 301 in 1988, that signaled to other countries that the United States would not rely on GATT legal mechanisms to pursue its trade complaints. Yet in the Uruguay Round, the United States agreed to legal rules that bind it to multilateral dispute resolution, thereby making unilateral retaliation under Section 301 an explicit violation of the rules.

The United States further revealed its ambivalence about the GATT system by pursuing regional strategies of trade liberalization. Discouraged by the slow pace of multilateral negotiations on issues of deeper integration in the Uruguay Round, the United States turned to its neighbors to negotiate the comprehensive NAFTA in 1992. The United States also took a much greater interest in APEC, elevating the annual meeting to an executive-level summit in November 1993, and pushing the following year for a more formal and binding set of trade commitments.[21] By pursuing a two-track policy, simultaneously building up regional institutions while working toward strengthening and expanding the GATT system, the United States was signaling Japan and other countries that its commitment to GATT was not absolute.

U.S. leadership also declined considerably in the United Nations as the Reagan administration and subsequent congressional leaders lost faith in the management and collective decisionmaking of the institution. The growing membership of developing countries and nonaligned states in the United Nations in the 1960s and 1970s resulted in a sharp rise in anti-American rhetoric and voting behavior. The United Nations had become a "dangerous place," in the famous words of former UN ambassador Daniel Patrick Moynihan. President Ronald Reagan responded by appointing Jeane Kirkpatrick as his first UN Ambassador (1981–85), who adopted an openly confrontational diplomatic style and aggressively promoted narrowly defined U.S. interests. U.S.-Japan relations in the United Nations also hit a low point; according to Robert Immerman, "Kirkpatrick never saw fit to visit Japan for UN-related talks during her four-year tenure."[22] Dissatisfaction with the United Nations was also brewing in Congress, culminating with the passage of the Kassebaum amendment that mandated that the United States withhold UN funds unless a weighted voting system was adopted on budgetary matters, or U.S. dues were limited to 20 percent of total contributions. Reagan withheld U.S. dues in 1986, and in the mid-1990s Congress again refused to pay the full amount of UN dues, demanding further bureaucratic changes and a reduction of the U.S. contribution.[23] However, after the cold war had ended the United States helped revitalize the United Nations by again turning to the UN Security Council for legitimation and collective management of a range of conflicts and humanitarian interventions, in places like the Persian Gulf, Somalia, Haiti, and Bosnia. Its failure to secure a UN mandate for NATO actions in Kosovo was an important departure from this trend, and caused an unusual degree of strain with Japan in their otherwise cooperative UN relations.

In sum, U.S. multilateral leadership dropped precipitously in the 1970s–80s, but it has since reemerged, albeit in a somewhat different form. Whereas previously the United States was generous in its willingness to shoulder the costly burdens of leadership, today it strives to maximize its gains while minimizing its contributions. Other countries, notably Japan, have picked up the slack. Given the institutional architecture devised by early postwar American planners, with the strongly embedded norms of multilateralism and collective management, this inevitably leads to demands by the new contributors for a larger voice in decisionmaking and greater credit for their support.

Japan's New Assertiveness

In contrast to the United States, Japan has been slowly but steadily increasing its support and leadership of IOs in the latter half of the postwar period. In the 1980s the two countries became mirror images of each other, with the United States seeking to decrease its financial burdens and Japan seeking to raise its contributions.

Throughout the 1950s–70s, Japan was remarkably passive in multilateral affairs. In most areas, Japan remained deferential to the United States rather than seeking an independent voice. Although Japan began to assume more obligations of membership in the 1970s and 1980s, such as improving its rule compliance in GATT and IMF and contributing more financial support to various international organizations, it remained relatively quiet about the policy direction and the management of these IOs. Beginning in the 1980s, however, Japan's passivity began to dissolve as it embraced a much more assertive set of multilateral policies. In GATT Japan became newly aggressive in its bargaining tactics in the Uruguay Round and in its behavior in multilateral dispute resolution. Japan played the leading role in establishing APEC as a supplementary framework to promote trade and other economic cooperation in the region. In the IMF and World Bank, Japan first raised its financial status, climbing to the rank of second-largest contributor in both institutions, and subsequently began to raise its voice in substantive debates over lending policies and institutional reforms. In the United Nations, Japan began actively lobbying for a permanent seat on the Security Council, and it backed this campaign with growing financial support to the United Nations and by undertaking a larger role in peacekeeping operations.

Japan's emerging activism has been driven by two primary sets of concerns. The first was a desire to increase its international status and influence. Japanese political elites wanted symbolic recognition of Japan's new status as an economic superpower, and they sought political status to match Japan's rising economic might. Japan turned to IOs as convenient, effective outlets for exerting more influence. Other options were limited: Japan is still constrained, at least domestically, from using military force to exercise its power and enhance its prestige and influence. Moreover, a multilateral strategy allows Japan to raise its profile and assert its priorities without alarming its Asian neighbors, which remain wary of the independent expression of Japanese power. Germany dealt with the problem of postwar reconciliation with its neighbors by binding itself to regional economic and security institutions—the EC and NATO—through which repeated interactions gave rise to growing trust between former enemies. Lacking a similar regional institutional framework, Japan has had to rely on the larger IOs as well as bilateral initiatives to overcome historic mistrust and antagonism. Recently, it has engaged in efforts to build regional organizations to facilitate cooperation in economic and security affairs, but it has been limited to leading from behind and to building loose organizational forums rather than binding institutions so as not to arouse the suspicions of other Asian countries about its motives. By binding its power to multilateral IOs, Japan hopes to assume a more prominent yet nonthreatening role in world affairs.

At the same time Japan has sought to bind the United States to IOs, in two ways—through engagement and entrapment. First, in the face of the wavering commitment of the United States to global multilateralism, Japan has sought to keep the United States actively engaged in IOs in order to sustain multilateral cooperation. Much of Japan's new multilateral activism in the late 1980s and 1990s, and its continued willingness to defer to the United States in core areas of leadership, have been motivated by a desire to reinvigorate or sustain American interest in investing in IOs. Second, Japan has sought to bind the United States to multilateral rules that would constrain the unilateral exercise of its power. This strategy has been especially important in trade relations, but Japan has also sought to curb U.S. dominance in international development and financial affairs by raising its voice in the World Bank and IMF.

These goals have played out somewhat differently in shaping Japan's behavior toward trade, finance, and security international organizations, as discussed in the next section. However in each case, they have led to a remarkable transformation in Japan's multilateral diplomacy, as Japan shed its passive and reactive approach and began using its economic clout and a more independent voice to redefine its role in IOs.

Emerging Cooperation and Conflict in Economic and Security IOs

The interplay of the three trends described above—the institutional strengthening of global IOs, the wavering and recent resurgence of U.S. multilateral leadership, and Japan's growing activism and assertiveness in multilateral affairs—have redefined bilateral and multilateral relations between the United States and Japan in a number of significant ways. However, changes in economic relations have been much more significant than change on the security side of the relationship, with trade and finance IOs playing an increasingly central role in managing issues between the two countries while the United Nations remains peripheral to U.S.-Japan interactions in security affairs. Japan's strategies to raise its profile in economic IOs have been more successful than its efforts to gain influence in the United Nations, and this has meant that economic relations have been more deeply affected by IOs than the security relationship. This section explores the emerging patterns of cooperation and competition across different regimes, paying particular attention to the ways in which Japan has sought to redefine relations with the United States through institutional strategies of multilateral engagement.

Trade

The growing impact of IOs on U.S.-Japan relations has been most pronounced in the GATT-WTO trade regime. Whereas the United States used to rely almost exclusively on bilateral pressure to open up Japan's markets and ease competitive export pressures, and Japan remained largely passive in multilateral negotiations and dispute resolution, both countries now turn with growing frequency to the multilateral forum provided by GATT-WTO, and to a lesser extent APEC, to influence each other's trade behavior. The shift from bilateral to multilateral engagement in trade issues has produced important changes in trade relations between the two countries, in part due to the centrality of trade in the U.S.-Japan relationship. The level of intergovernment interaction over trade issues has always been high, so any shift in the modus operandi of these interactions is likely to produce a noticeable impact on relations. Second, the GATT-WTO regime has undergone the most significant institutional change in the latter half of the postwar period, with the widening of its scope and the legalization of its rules described above. Third, and most importantly, this is the area in which Japan's multilateral behavior has changed most dramatically, which in turn has influenced the institutional development of the trade regime itself and has transformed its interactions with the United States over trade issues. The sources and consequences of Japan's behavioral shift in the trade regime are thus central to understanding emerging patterns of conflict and cooperation in trade.

Japan shifted to a more assertive multilateral diplomacy in all of the major IOs, but its behavior changed earliest and most dramatically in GATT. Throughout the Kennedy and Tokyo Rounds of tariff negotiations, Japan had remained very passive in multilateral bargaining, taking few actions to shape the talks or push them toward a successful conclusion.[24] Japan assumed a low, defensive posture, seeking to minimize concessions it would have to give away rather than trying to maximize concessions received or exert its influence in the process of rulemaking. However, in the Uruguay Round (1986–93) the Japanese government, under the leadership of the Ministry of International Trade and Industry (MITI), began to assume a far more assertive and cooperative negotiating posture. Japan led the effort to reform the rules on antidumping to make them less trade-restrictive. Japan also joined the EU in pressuring the United States to accept constraints on the use of unilateral actions in trade disputes. Japan was a strong early supporter of U.S. efforts to expand the bargaining agenda to include services, intellectual property, and investment, and it took an active role in the early negotiations in these areas. Japan offered a very liberal proposal early in the round to eliminate all tariffs on industrial goods, and it made timely and generous offers on industrial tariffs and services throughout the negotiations. The one area where Japan remained defensive was in the agricultural negotiations, because the liberalization of rice represented a sensitive political problem for the government. Japan dealt with this problem by sitting on the sidelines while the United States and EU engaged in battle and forged a compromise, and then Japan negotiated its own compromise agreement that provided limited market opening in rice.

Another significant change was Japan's embrace of multilateral legal procedures to resolve disputes in GATT and the WTO.[25] In its first three decades of GATT membership Japan had maintained an extremely low profile in GATT dispute settlement. When targeted by a complaint, Japan preferred to settle cases early in the legal process, before a panel was established or a decision was reached. Prior to 1986, Japan had brought only two

Table 7-1. *Multilateral Dispute Resolution before and after the* World
Trade Organization (1995)

	Complaints brought by Japan		Complaints brought against Japan	
Period	Against the United States	Against others	By the United States	By others
1955–79	1	0	2	2
1980–86	0	1	6	3
1987–94	1	2	1	3
1995–2000	5	3	5	7

complaints to the GATT. One was an exceptional case in which the United States had invited Japan to file a complaint against it as a way to pressure internal government agencies,[26] and the other case involved French restrictions on Japanese VCRs, which Japan chose to settle by offering a voluntary export restraint. In the mid-1980s Japan, however, began turning to the GATT legal process with greater frequency and resolve. Japan litigated two cases against the EC involving antidumping complaints, winning a partial victory in one and a full legal victory in the other. These set the stage for Japan's greater legal activism in the years following the Uruguay Round. Japan filed seven complaints against other countries, four against the United States, and it requested a panel in all but one case (table 7-1).

Japan also began insisting on multilateral dispute resolution when it was on the receiving end of complaints. Thus when the United States complained about the trading practices of Fuji Film, Japan refused to even discuss the matter outside of consultations held at the WTO. Japan's success in the film case further emboldened it to insist on multilateral rather than bilateral dispute resolution in subsequent trade conflicts with the United States. Furthermore, Japan's willingness to settle disputes prior to a panel ruling drastically declined. Before 1994, seven out of the nine cases brought by the United States against Japan were settled prior to a legal ruling. After 1995, only one out of four cases was settled (a fifth case is still pending).[27]

Japan's new assertiveness in GATT-WTO arose from several sources. First, changes in Japan's economy and trade policy, many of which were brought about by GATT itself, produced a new commitment to upholding and expanding international trade rules. Participation in GATT and other economic IOs had transformed Japan into a much more liberal economy. Tariffs and other trade barriers had been negotiated down over successive rounds of multilateral bargaining. Even more importantly, the extensive framework of administrative controls over the economy, which ironically had been bolstered by U.S. Occupation policies,[28] had been gradually dismantled by the government to bring Japan in compliance with GATT and other IO rules. Japan's early compliance with multilateral rules had been slow and uneven, and often required the additional leverage of bilateral U.S. pressure. Nevertheless, by the 1980s Japan had emerged as one of the most compliant members of GATT, and this gave Japan new confidence and clout to bargain aggressively and use multilateral dispute settlement. Whereas in earlier rounds Japan had assumed a low posture and bargained defensively to minimize losses, in the Uruguay Round it could concentrate on an offense-centered strategy.

A second impetus was the changing behavior of the United States. The sharp turn toward more aggressive unilateralism in U.S. trade policy in the 1980s exposed the weaknesses of Japan's traditional reliance on a bilateral approach to dealing with trade conflicts. Japan had long sought to manage trade disputes with the United States by doling out piecemeal concessions and agreeing to trade restraints. However the growing list of trade demands on the U.S. side, and the tougher threats of sanctions that accompanied them, convinced Japanese trade officials that a new strategy was needed. A turning point in their thinking came with U.S. retaliation under the Semiconductor Trade Agreement that had been negotiated in 1986. Japan had signed a secret side letter to the agreement that included a market share goal of 20 percent for foreign semiconductors, and when Japan failed to meet that goal the following year the Reagan administration imposed $300 million in punitive tariffs on Japan. Trade officials were deeply angered that the market share goal, which they had understood to be voluntary, was used as the basis for heavy-handed retaliation.[29] Japan's response to this growing U.S. unilateralism was to shift to a strategy of aggressive multilateralism. Japan brought the semiconductor case to GATT, although it withdrew its complaint after the United States partially removed the tariff sanctions. However, in the Uruguay Round negotiations it joined forces with the EU to insist on new legal rules that require countries to use multilateral legal procedures to resolve disputes covered by WTO rules, rather than resorting to unilateral measures. These rules were aimed directly at the United States and its use of Super 301. Japan also sought, with limited success, to strengthen restrictions on the use of antidumping protection as a way to limit the expansive use of antidumping protection by both the United States and the EU.

A third factor that spurred Japan's multilateral activism was the legalization of the trade regime in the new WTO. The stronger legal remedies instituted in the WTO, in particular the binding force of its rulings and the stricter timetables under which it operates, have made this venue more attractive to Japanese trade officials seeking to pursue Japan's trade interests. Japan has used these procedures to litigate disputes involving automobiles against Indonesia, Brazil, and Canada in the WTO. However, half of all complaints lodged by Japan in the WTO have been against the United States. Its biggest victory came with the 1995 automobile dispute, when Japan took advantage of the new legal constraints to charge the United States with the illegal use of unilateral import surcharges on automobiles and auto parts. [30] Japan's win was not a legal victory, since the case was settled bilaterally before a panel was established, but it represented a significant political victory. The EU and Australia sided with Japan in the complaint, adding multilateral weight against the use of unilateral measures by the United States.[31] And the legal leverage provided by the WTO suit appeared to be effective in convincing the United States to back down from most of its demands in the bilateral negotiations, and Japan hoped that it would serve as a deterrent to future recourse to unilateral actions in bilateral disputes.

In sum, Japan has showed a new willingness to use GATT-WTO rule-making and rule enforcement to directly confront and challenge the United States. However, it has done so very much within the normative institutional framework of the regime. GATT and other international organizations have fundamentally shaped Japan's integration into the postwar world economy, and its gradual transformation has deepened its commitment to the liberal norms of GATT. Japan's adherence to the liberal norms of GATT-WTO has also shaped its stance toward the formation of new regional economic institutions. Japan played the leading role, albeit a behind-the-scenes one, in the formation of the Asia-Pacific Economic Cooperation forum in the late 1980s. Although Australia, Japan's partner in launching the venture, resisted early American involvement in the trade group, Japan insisted on U.S. inclusion and repeatedly reassured Washington that it had no intention of creating an Asian-only trade group.[32] Indeed, Japan's central motivation in building APEC was to keep the United States committed to liberal multilateral trade in the region, at a time when the United States was pursuing narrower regional initiatives in negotiating NAFTA. Further, Japanese trade officials hoped that the regional multilateral organization would provide a viable framework for transitioning from "development through U.S. dependency" to "development through role sharing cooperation in the region."[33] In other words, Japan was not seeking to displace U.S. leadership in the region; rather it sought joint leadership, and it viewed strengthening of liberal multilateralism in GATT-WTO and APEC as the best way to achieve this. Japan has remained committed to the "open regionalism" of APEC and has resisted calls from Malaysia for a more regionally exclusive bloc. However, the United States is not the only partner that Japan must engage in the region. China has been seeking a larger role in regional trade affairs, and recently proposed a Free Trade Area (FTA) between China and ASEAN. Japan responded with its own proposal for an FTA with ASEAN, and suggested a web of FTA including South Korea that would encompass the whole region. Negotiating these FTAs would not be easy, since many of these countries are natural trade competitors and most have domestically sensitive sectors that would strongly resist liberalization.[34] Nevertheless, the emerging discussions over regional FTAs may signal a new trend in Japan's regional trade strategy, as it shifts from engaging the United States multilaterally in the region to focusing on containing the economic and political influence of China.

Finance

New patterns of U.S.-Japan interaction have also emerged in the IOs governing financial relations and multilateral development assistance. Change has been less dramatic in multilateral finance than in trade, in part because financial IOs have been less central to U.S.-Japan relations. The most important monetary issues between the two countries, such as managing exchange rates and other areas of macroeconomic policy coordination, remain outside the institutional scope of the IMF and World Bank (see chapter 3 by Grimes and chapter 8 by Posen in this volume). Nevertheless, both countries have important stakes in how the major financial IOs manage developmental assistance and international financial crises, and these stakes have grown as the IOs have come to play a larger role in managing these issues. Their ability to influence multilateral policies in these areas not only enhances their international prestige but also shapes their relations with developing countries on the receiving end of multilateral assistance. Japan has responded to the growing centrality of IOs, and its rise in financial power, by seeking a larger role in jointly managing multilateral financial policies. U.S.-Japan interactions in the IMF and World Bank have thus grown more important and more complex, as each country seeks to advance its agenda without disrupting the overall cooperative framework that has long characterized multilateral financial relations between the two countries.

Japanese officials initially focused on enhancing Japan's prestige by raising its financial status in the World Bank and IMF, and gave little thought to how any newly acquired leverage would be used. In the early 1980s Japan climbed from the rank of fifth-largest shareholder in the World Bank to become the second largest in 1984, and it reached number two status in the IMF in 1990.[35] Japan's new financial clout in these agencies coincided with the broadening scope of their lending policies, with both agencies adopting more stringent and intrusive conditionality requirements. These policy shifts were driven by American officials and economists in the World Bank and IMF, who reflected the emerging "Washington consensus" that trade and financial liberalization were essential ingredients of effective development policies.[36] However, Japanese officials grew increasingly uncomfortable with the neoliberal emphasis of multilateral lending policies. They wanted more credit for Japan's economic model, and for its financial support of the IOs. Japan thus began mounting cautious challenges to both the normative underpinnings and the institutional structure of the financial international organizations.

Japan's first target was the World Bank.[37] In the early 1990s Japan began questioning the neoliberal economic model that shaped the bank's lending policies, arguing that its own development experience had relied on state guidance of market forces rather than the free-market orthodoxy underlying World Bank policy prescriptions and conditionality requirements. At Japan's insistence and funding, the World Bank undertook a major study of the economic miracles of East Asia. Although the Japanese model of directed credit and industrial policy received minimal credit for the regional economic success in the final report, it nevertheless signaled Japan's willingness to engage in substantive debate over multilateral development policies.

The 1997 Asian currency crisis spurred a bolder effort by Japan to reform the IMF. Not only did Japan openly criticize the one-size-fits-all approach of the IMF in its rescue packages, but it proposed the creation of a separate institution, an Asian Monetary Fund, that would supplement the IMF and provide more regionally based leadership in the event of a financial or currency crisis. Japan quickly dropped the idea when it came under strong criticism by the United States and the IMF, both of which argued that a separate fund would compete with IMF lending and thus weaken the IMF's leverage in demanding economic reforms in Asia in exchange for loans. However, Japan did not entirely abandon its attempt at regional monetary cooperation. First, Japan created the Miyazawa fund in 1998, which provided $30 billion in emergency lending to regional economies. Then, it reformulated and scaled down its earlier proposal of a regional lending facility, and the plan reemerged at a meeting of regional financial leaders in Chiang Mai in May 2000.[38] The so-called Chiang Mai initiative is an agreement among the ASEAN+3 countries (ASEAN plus Japan, China, and South Korea) to establish a network of bilateral swap agreements between central banks that could be used to fend off speculative attacks on their currencies. This time Japan managed to gain tacit approval for the plan from the United States and the IMF as well as China. Greater emphasis has been placed on complementarity and direct policy linkages with the IMF, as well as mutual surveillance of regional economies. Japanese officials hope that this will be a first step toward the creation of a regional facility that would act as lender-of-last resort in a financial crisis. However, the credit lines established under the plan will amount to only $2.5 billion, a tiny fraction of the $100 billion envisioned in the Asian Monetary Fund (AMF) proposal (based on Japan's expected contribution alone).[39] In short, although Japan seems determined to proceed toward building regional mechanisms to promote greater monetary stability, it is clearly taking pains not to alienate the United States and IMF in the process.

Japan has also articulated a more independent voice in multilateral discussions over reforming the IMF in the wake of the Asian crisis. It has consistently emphasized the need for greater surveillance and less stringent conditionality in IMF policies, and has supported the use of capital controls by countries seeking to insulate themselves from destabilizing financial flows.[40] Although Japan articulated its views on these issues in G-7 meetings and other forums, in the end it deferred to U.S. leadership and signed on to a G-7 proposal of IMF reform that closely follows the U.S. blueprint and does little to address the issues raised by Japan. Still, Japan has undertaken two other initiatives that have increased its visibility and leadership in the IMF. First, it put forth the name of a former Finance Ministry official, Eisuke Sakakibara, as a candidate for managing director of the IMF, a position that has traditionally been awarded to a European national.[41] Japan secured nominal support from ASEAN countries for Sakakibara's candidacy, although the position went instead to the German official Horst Koehler. Second, Japan has championed the cause of East Asian countries seeking stronger representation in the IMF through a revision of the quota system. These actions suggest that Japan is increasingly comfortable articulating its interests and seeking more responsibility and credit sharing for international financial management, especially in Asia. Despite this growing activism, however, Japan remains reluctant to directly challenge U.S. leadership in multilateral financial affairs.

United Nations

The United Nations has been less important in defining U.S.-Japan relations than IOs in trade and finance, and there are few signs that this will change in the near future. In contrast to the major economic IOs, the United Nations remains an arena in which the United States and Japan are mutually supportive and generally noncompetitive. Japan has developed a more independent voice within the organization and has sought to raise its profile and influence, but it has not been able to break through to the status of the major powers on the Security Council. Japan thus remains a relatively minor player in UN deliberations, and has little leverage over the United States in multilateral decisions involving UN security issues. The limitations on Japan's influence in the United Nations, combined with the centrality of the U.S.-Japan security treaty in defining bilateral and regional security ties, means that the United Nations remains peripheral to U.S.-Japan security relations despite its growing role in managing post–cold war security affairs.

Japan has tried in various ways to raise its status in the United Nations, with limited success. As it had in the IMF and World Bank, Japan began by raising its financial contributions in the 1980s. In 1973 Japan's contribution had risen to account for over 7 percent of the UN budget, which was the third-largest contribution behind the United States and Soviet Union. By 1986 Japan had surpassed the Soviet Union to become the second-largest contributor.[42] In the late 1990s Japan's financial contribution had risen to over 16 percent of the UN regular budget, which was larger than the combined contribution of the four permanent Security Council members other than the United States.[43]

Japan also began taking initiatives designed to strengthen the effectiveness of the institution and thereby sustain multilateral commitment to its activities. Its most significant effort was made in response to the threat of disengagement by the United States. When the Reagan administration withdrew the U.S. contribution to the United Nations in the mid-1980s, Japan proposed a "wiseman's group" to study organizational reform and find ways to improve its administrative design and budgetary procedures. The adoption of the group's recommendations by the General Assembly, which included a 15 percent personnel cut and a consensus rule in budgetmaking, paved the way for the Reagan administration to gradually resume U.S. payments to the United Nations.[44] A second set of initiatives taken by Japan throughout the 1980s aimed at strengthening the role of the Secretary General in resolving disputes and preventing conflicts from emerging. Its proposals centered on expanding the authority of the Secretary General to send fact-finding and other missions in troubled areas, and limiting the prerogatives of the Security Council to veto such moves.[45]

Japan also began to develop a more independent voice in its voting behavior in the UN General Assembly. In earlier decades, Japan had voted with the United States as much as 80 percent of the time. However, by the mid-1980s the rate had fallen to 37 percent.[46] The outbreak of the oil crisis in the 1970s had led Japan to distance itself from the United States and its allies and take positions that were friendly to Arab nations and hostile to Israel.[47] Japan began to drift away from U.S. voting in other areas as well, including issues relating to human rights and disarmament of weapons of mass destruction.[48] However, in the UN Security Council Japan's voting behavior has been much closer to the United States.[49] Japan, with the strong support of the United States, has repeatedly been elected to the Security Council as a nonpermanent member, and in this position it has consistently voted in support of U.S. positions.[50]

In the 1990s Japan made the attainment of a permanent seat on an expanded Security Council the centerpiece of its UN diplomacy. The United States supported its bid for a permanent seat, in large part because it could rely on Japanese support on major issues raised in the Council. However, U.S. vocal support, while consistent, has not been backed by serious tactical effort or political muscle. Reforming the Security Council raises a host of problems, the most troublesome of which has been the intense wrangling among regional powers vying for any additional seats, and the resistance of middle powers that do not want to be overlooked in decisionmaking. In particular the United States is concerned that extending veto power to many more players will lead to paralysis and hence undermine the effectiveness of the Security Council.[51] Thus while the United States supports the addition of Japan and Germany to the permanent membership of the council, its support has been tempered by the difficulty of achieving a workable solution.

Japan's strategy in pursuing a seat has not been able to overcome these obstacles. Moreover, Japan's domestic constraints on expanding its UN peacekeeping role continue to pose a serious barrier to its political aspirations. Japan's initial strategy in the 1980s was to expand its financial contributions and also begin contributing to peacekeeping operations by sending civilian observers to Afghanistan, the Iran-Iraq conflict, and

Namibia. The Ministry of Foreign Affairs (MOFA) hoped that this gradual expansion of support would eventually translate into broad acceptance by other UN members that Japan deserved a seat on the council. The eruption the Persian Gulf crisis in 1990 exposed the flaw in this strategy. Japanese leaders were paralyzed by the crisis. Domestic legal constraints posed by the peace constitution prevented Japan from contributing military personnel to the conflict, but the government was also slow to offer financial support for the multilateral operation. Japan came under strong international criticism as a result, and the question of Japan's ability to engage fully in UN operations emerged as a serious barrier to Japan's diplomatic ambitions in the organization.

The Japanese government tried to address this problem by amending its domestic laws to enable its participation in multilateral military action. Its first legislative attempt failed, when a UN Peace Cooperation Bill submitted to the Diet in October 1990 was withdrawn a month later. The bill, which would have authorized Self-Defense Force (SDF) participation in multilateral enforcement as well as peacekeeping operations, suffered from a lack of support among the public and even within the ruling Liberal Democratic Party (LDP). The government tried again the following year, this time making deployment conditional on a cease-fire agreement and restricting participation to activities completely separated from combat operations. The government finally secured legislative approval in spring 1992.

The new Peacekeeping Operations (PKO) bill enabled Japan to expand its peacekeeping role but did not solve the basic problem of Japan's limited participation, since Japanese personnel are kept well out of harm's way. Meanwhile, the United Nations expanded its peacekeeping operations to conflicts in which cease-fire agreements have not been reached in places like Somalia and Bosnia, resulting in a continuing gap between UN peacekeeping demands and Japan's contributions.[52]

Japan thus faces a dilemma. Expanding its peacekeeping role remains politically difficult to achieve at home, and further raises concerns among key Asian countries like China and South Korea, whose diplomatic support would be essential for obtaining a Security Council seat. At the same time, the limited nature of Japan's current contributions has diminished support among key potential allies such as France, which maintains that Japan's assumption of permanent member status would require full participation in peacekeeping operations.[53] This has also led to some opposition to Japan's bid in the U.S. Congress, although the State Department remains strongly supportive of a Security Council seat for Japan and has not pressed Japan to expand its military role in peacekeeping.[54] Given these difficulties Japan is unlikely to attain a permanent seat and thereby increase its diplomatic leverage in the foreseeable future, and U.S.-Japan relations in the United Nations will probably remain mutually supportive on most issues but of limited significance for either country.

Furthermore, the reemergence of the United Nations as a meaningful site for multilateral security decisionmaking has created new problems that have made it more difficult for the Japanese government to maintain domestic support for its increasingly activist role in the organization. First, the wave of international criticism directed at Japan in the Persian Gulf crisis, despite its $13 billion contribution to the multilateral operation, led many Japanese to question the value of its UN checkbook diplomacy without generating much support for greater participation in UN peace-keeping, since the operation in the Gulf was viewed as primarily an American initiative designed to serve the strategic interests of the United States and a few of its allies in the Gulf. Most Japanese believed that Iraq's invasion of Kuwait had minimal relevance for Japan, and would have preferred that the United Nations pursue a diplomatic rather than military solution. Second, Japan's economic stagnation throughout the 1990s has led to growing pressure from within the ruling LDP to reduce Japan's financial contributions to the United Nations. Finally, NATO's actions in Kosovo, and its decision to circumvent the Security Council, further undermined Japanese confidence in the effectiveness and legitimacy of the United Nations in managing multilateral security affairs. Like the Gulf war, the Kosovo crisis served to highlight the inadequacy of the United Nations in reining in the unilateralist tendencies of the United States. Although the United States chose to act in concert with a few allies in these crises, it was not willing to bind itself to multilateral mechanisms, such as joint command structures or Security Council deliberations, if it was not completely confident that it could control or dominate the outcomes. The structural power of the United States in multilateral security affairs and the weakness of Japan's position leaves Japan with few options to change this situation. As a result, Japan faces growing internal pressure to reduce its UN commitments, rather than seeking to softly challenge U.S. leadership and constrain U.S. unilateralism as it has done in the economic IOs.

Future of U.S.-Japan Relations in a More Multilateral Context

How have these trends affected U.S.-Japan relations? What do they mean for the future of the relationship? On the whole, the picture that emerges from this analysis is an optimistic one. The declining relevance of economic bilateralism has its down side, namely that short-term, ad hoc solutions to nagging problems become somewhat more difficult to devise. However the growing role played by IOs in structuring not only U.S.-Japan relations, but an ever-growing web of international interactions, creates incentives for the United States and Japan to work together in pursuit of common goals in a multilateral context.

Shift from Bilateralism to Multilateralism

The most visible impact of the changing role played by IOs has been the declining relevance of bilateral frameworks for managing issues and coordinating policies, at least in the economic sphere. This shift has been especially striking in trade relations. The expanding agenda of GATT-WTO has opened up new areas for multilateral negotiation and litigation, including financial services, government procurement, and intellectual property rights. More importantly, the transformation of GATT into the broader and more legalized WTO has weakened bilateral options on both sides for managing trade conflict. More rules mean less room for negotiated, ad hoc solutions to trade problems. The new rules prohibit the use of voluntary measures like export restraints and import expansion agreements to settle disputes over market access, and they also limit the ability of the United States to threaten unilateral sanctions to resolve disputes. For Japan this has made multilateral dispute settlement preferable to one-on-one negotiations in a growing number of cases. For the United States as well, the more expedited and binding legal process in the WTO provides greater leverage in many disputes, since legal victories now include a specified timetable under which the losing country must implement remedial actions, and failure to do so can lead to multilateral authorization of retaliatory measures. The United States, after all, had been the leading advocate of tougher legal remedies for multilateral dispute resolution, and in dealing with Japan it was increasingly frustrated with finding ways to ensure meaningful compliance with negotiated agreements. As a result, both sides have turned to multilateral dispute procedures with growing frequency. Whereas Japan used the WTO process to its advantage in the 1995 auto dispute and the 1996

Fuji Film case, the United States achieved legal success in disputes over alcoholic beverages and apples, and it has threatened WTO legal action to gain leverage in negotiations over telecommunications and government procurement.[55] Meanwhile, bilateral trade disputes handled outside the WTO have virtually evaporated. Future trade relations will be defined almost entirely by the multilateral rules and procedures of the WTO.

Multilateralism is also a growing feature of the U.S.-Japan relationship in international finance. Here, however, the major change has been the rise of new areas of policy coordination and rivalry in multilateral management, rather than a shift of existing issues from bilateral to multilateral venues. Prior to the 1980s, Japan simply followed the U.S. lead in the IMF and World Bank, but its shift to a more independent and assertive role in these IOs means that multilateral policies have emerged as a new site of conflict and cooperation. Acting through a single set of international organizations has meant that each cannot impose their own unilateral preferences on development policies and financial crisis management, but rather they must reach some agreement over policies and institutional structure. Growing financial integration in the world economy, and new regulatory challenges posed by recent banking crises and the campaign launched against international terrorism, will further deepen the linkages between the two governments on international financial issues and pave the way for even greater coordination and cooperation in multilateral venues in the future.

U.S.-Japan security relations have been less affected by these trends, although recent developments may signal that important changes are ahead. The United Nations has expanded its role in peacekeeping and peace enforcement operations in the post–cold war period, but Japan's limited participation in these ventures has prevented it from attaining the degree of influence that it enjoys in economic IOs. Thus on multilateral security issues the United States focuses its attention on more activist countries, and in particular the other veto-wielding members of the Security Council, knowing it can generally count on Japan's political and financial support. The bilateral U.S.-Japan security treaty remains the primary institutional framework for defining the major interests and obligations of each country in matters related to Japan's defense and vital interests in the region.

Japan's initial response to the September 11 attacks on the World Trade Center and Pentagon bears this out. Eager to avoid a repeat of the diplomatic isolation it faced in the Gulf war, Japan quickly responded with new legislation that would allow its Self-Defense Forces to take part in rearguard action to support U.S. forces in retaliatory military action in the Middle East.[56] The government chose to amend the 1999 guidelines on Japan-U.S. defense cooperation by extending the geographical scope of military emergencies in which Japan can aid U.S. forces, rather than expanding the PKO law to allow Japan's defense forces to participate in collective security actions. This avoided the need for a UN resolution authorizing military action before Japan could take part, and framed Japan's participation in terms of its bilateral security cooperation with the United States rather than UN-based collective self-defense.

However, a shift toward greater multilateralism in U.S.-Japan security relations could come from several possible developments. If Japan were to succeed in its quest for a permanent seat on the Security Council, or if it would expand its military role in UN peacekeeping operations, Japan would suddenly become much more relevant to multilateral security issues. As in financial relations, this would lead to an expansion of U.S.-Japan interactions on multilateral issues, rather than a displacement of bilateral cooperation with multilateral ventures. Either of these developments would increase Japan's independence and influence while simultaneously strengthening U.S.-Japan security cooperation. The steps taken by Japan in the wake of the September 11 attacks have already made Japan a more valuable ally in multinational security cooperation. Moreover, they opened the door to further revision of the PKO law to enable Japan to engage in a broader range of activities, including the use of weapons for self-defense and the protection of civilians, in UN-sponsored collective security operations. This could significantly boost Japan's relevance in multilateral peacekeeping activities, and should also strengthen its case for a permanent seat on the UN Security Council. Alternatively, the creation of multilateral security mechanisms in Asia could subsume areas of the bilateral treaty. To date the ASEAN Regional Forum (ARF) is the only region-wide security institution, and it remains an informal "talking shop" rather than a mechanism for defining security commitments. There is growing consideration of creating other regional security forums, but a serious substitute to the U.S.-Japan alliance does not appear likely to emerge anytime soon.

Impact on Cooperation

The growing multilateral dimension of U.S.-Japan relations raises another set of questions, namely, how does this affect the substance and strength of the U.S.-Japan relationship? Does a shift to multilateralism in the economic realm lead to more cooperation or conflict? Does a change in venue make a difference in shaping interests and adjusting actions? Competing perspectives in international relations theory offer opposing views on these questions. Whereas realists view IOs as sites of conflict rather than cooperation, liberal institutionalists contend that international institutions serve to mitigate conflict and promote cooperation, and their strengthening is thus likely to broaden and deepen cooperative ties.

Realists' pessimism about cooperation derives from their view of the international system as inherently competitive and dangerous, and their deep skepticism about the impact of international institutions to change these dynamics. As stated recently by Kenneth Waltz, "Realists believe that international institutions are shaped and limited by the states that found and sustain them and have little independent effect."[57] In this view, the United States created postwar institutions in trade, finance, and security when it was at the height of its power, and it designed and managed them to privilege its own interests. As underlying power relations shift over time, realists expect that rising powers like Japan will challenge these American-made institutional frameworks and seek changes to suit their own interests. The end of the cold war should further unravel cooperation, since it eliminates the strategic incentives for countries within the Western alliance to pursue joint gains vis-à-vis the rival Soviet bloc.[58] From a realist perspective, therefore, Japan's growing activism in IOs is a natural outgrowth of its rising power and desire for prestige and influence, and Japan should be expected to instigate greater challenges in multilateral affairs in the future.[59]

Liberal institutionalists are far more optimistic about the emergence and persistence of cooperation, even between major powers like the United States and Japan. Unlike realists, who see competition as endemic to world politics and thus view most interactions as zero-sum games, liberals see a wider harmony of interests among states and believe IOs play an important facilitating role for states pursuing mutual gains. IOs are the products of cooperative bargains, and also serve as venues through which further bargains can be made and sustained. Liberal theory offers two different mechanisms through which a virtuous circle of sustained and growing cooperation may arise. The first is based on a functionalist logic that emphasizes the role played by international organizations in reducing transaction costs and providing information, enabling member states to conclude and enforce mutually beneficial agreements. Once established, IOs create momentum for further cooperative bargains by providing the institutional machinery and cross-issue linkages that can facilitate further dealmaking.

A second set of arguments drawn from sociological variants of liberal institutionalism point to ideational changes that can occur through a country's participation in an international regime. The normative underpinnings of IOs may come to shape actors' conceptions of the most appropriate and effective policies, and thereby transform their interests and their preferred policy strategies. For example, exposure to liberal trade norms in the GATT regime may over time shape the preferences of national trade officials for free trade policies. Ongoing participation in IOs and the regimes in which they are embedded may also shape broad conceptions of state identity and its appropriate role in world politics. Leaders may come to view their state as a member of an international community in which it has reciprocal obligations with other members. This kind of socialization is not automatic, and Japan's participation in various regimes provides both positive and negative examples of normative change. On the one hand, Japanese trade officials involved in GATT affairs have grown increasingly committed to its underlying liberal trade and legalistic norms, and now regularly refer to the WTO as the "constitution of world trade."[60] And many commentators have noted the powerful normative impact that UN declarations and conventions have had on the Japanese government and public, such as way the UN International Women's Year (1975) galvanized domestic support for legislation to end gender discrimination. On the other hand, Japan's involvement in the World Bank and IMF led to normative conflict rather than convergence in development philosophies, and Japan's long-standing participation in the International Whaling Commission has not changed its ideas or interests regarding the harvesting of whales.

Both realist and liberal institutionalist arguments find some support in the developments described in this chapter, but overall the picture that emerges justifies the optimism of liberal institutionalists in the constructive role played by IOs in adjusting mutual expectations and promoting harmonious international relations. Although particular instances of U.S.-Japan conflict have been on the rise within IOs, their institutional strengthening has helped contain and resolve those disagreements while embedding them in a broader framework of institutionalized cooperation. In trade, for example, the United States and Japan bring more complaints to GATT-WTO, but a broader view reveals that the overall level of conflict is constant or falling. First, as argued above, much of the new conflict simply represents a change in venue, as disputes that would previously have been taken up in bilateral negotiations are now brought to GATT-WTO instead. Second, taking disputes up in the WTO is likely to lessen trade tensions in the targeted area in the long run.

Bilateral negotiations often produce repeated iterations of particular disputes as one side seeks to extend prior agreements or revive unresolved complaints. Thus negotiations over things like apples, automobiles, and semiconductors can drag on for years and years. New WTO rules are likely to settle these issues with a higher degree of finality, and will generate multilateral pressure against the loser to end the conflict.

Third, the rise in legal complaints is probably small in proportion to the growing volume of transactions covered by an expanding set of GATT-WTO rules. Deeper cooperation is likely to be followed by more visible conflict, but the broader picture should not be lost. This point can be expanded to include Japan's emerging activism in agenda formation and rulemaking. In the Uruguay Round and recent talks in Seattle, Japan has challenged U.S. priorities and interests in several areas, most notably its advocacy of antidumping reform. At the same time, however, Japan actively supports U.S. initiatives in many areas, most recently in rules governing e-commerce. Although disagreements between the United States and Japan over international trade rules are likely to continue, they are also likely to find expanding areas of common interest, especially on issues involving access into developing country markets. China's accession into the WTO is likely to boost U.S.-Japan cooperation in these endeavors.

In the financial IOs, Japan's growing willingness to challenge the United States over multilateral policies and management provides some support for realist predictions that rising powers will challenge hegemonic control of international regimes. Japan has clearly been driven by a desire for more prestige and influence in international financial affairs, and it has begun flexing its muscles and articulating a more independence voice. Japan's actions have also made explicit its intention to use financial IOs to enhance its leadership in East Asia. Nevertheless, disagreements that have arisen between the two countries have been easily contained. Japan accepted the compromise position put forth by the World Bank in its report on development policies in East Asia, despite its emphasis on market-friendly policies. Japan quickly withdrew its AMF proposal after it drew fire from the United States and the IMF, and reworked it into a much less ambitious version that was acceptable to the United States. Japan ultimately followed the U.S. blueprint for reforming the IMF without demanding that its own reform priorities be met. In short Japan remains surprisingly cooperative, despite real differences in development ideology and regional economic and political interests.

In fact much of Japan's growing activism has been directed toward keeping the United States actively engaged in multilateral affairs. With its enormous economic, political, and military weight, the United States remains essential to the effective functioning of global IOs, and maintaining a high level of American involvement and commitment thus remains a priority for Japan. Examples of this engagement strategy abound. Japan stepped up its financial support of international organizations when the United States demanded greater burden sharing from other countries. Japan initiated institutional reform at the United Nations when American dissatisfaction with the organization led it to the brink of financial and political disengagement. In GATT-WTO, Japan provided strong, early support for U.S. efforts to launch the Uruguay Round and formulate an expansive agenda for the negotiations. Although Japan also challenged the United States by bringing antidumping reforms to the table, in the end it backed down from its most significant demands in order to reach a conclusion of the round. Moreover, Japan's efforts to build a nonexclusive trade grouping in APEC were designed to keep the United States engaged in liberal trade with East Asia, and this also explains Japan's resistance to Malaysia's proposal of an exclusive East Asian trade bloc.

At the same time Japan seeks to bind the United States through IOs in another way—to constrain U.S. behavior through the application of multilateral rules, and the insistence on multilateral norms of collective management. This strategy of entrapment has been most effectively used in GATT-WTO, since the new rules prohibit the unilateral exercise of economic force in most trade disputes, and thus can be used to trap the United States into multilateral legal procedures, where its political and economic leverage is severely limited. However, Japan's subtle but growing insistence that the United States curb the unilateral imposition of its own ideas and priorities on the World Bank and IMF and abide by a more collective management style in these IOs is another example of this strategy.

In order to achieve this double bind of both engagement and entrapment, Japan performs a careful balancing act. While it uses the leverage of IOs to press the United States into forgoing the unilateral exercise of its power and ceding some joint management to Japan, it cannot push too hard or it risks provoking U.S. defection, and thus institutional collapse. Japan's challenges are thus tempered by the larger gains that come with the cooperation anchored by IOs. These gains have risen with the inclusion or deepening participation of East Asian countries, especially China. Although liberal institutionalists have argued that increasing numbers in IOs can make decisionmaking difficult and thereby reduce cooperation, membership expansion also increases the magnitude of joint gains from cooperation, and thereby makes it more valuable.

By binding the powerful to cooperative outcomes, economic IOs have provided a valuable mechanism to promote cooperation between the United States and Japan, against a backdrop of broader cooperation among many. Although realists are correct to point to Japan's rising power as an important determinant of its behavior, they cannot explain the persistence and strengthening of IOs, or the continued willingness of Japan to defer to the United States in many areas. Liberal institutionalists account for these changes by demonstrating their value in producing joint gains. At this point in time, liberal theories appear to capture more accurately the dynamics of multilateral behavior and institutional change that are redefining the economic side of the U.S.-Japan relationship. Much hinges, however, on how Japan chooses to pursue its binding strategies in the future.

Notes

1. The classic statement on the dangers of power transition is made by A. F. K. Organski and Jacek Kugler, *The War Ledger* (University of Chicago Press, 1980). Organski and Kugler argue that rising powers destabilize the international system and lead to the outbreak of war.

2. IOs represent one end of a spectrum of international institutions, which range from informal conventions and decentralized regimes, to specific contracts and international treaties, to the formal organizations considered here.

3. As a compromise, Japan was granted provisional GATT membership in 1953, which did not obligate members to extend GATT treatment to Japan in its trade relations. For U.S. efforts to gain Japan's admission to GATT, see Tatsuo Akaneya, *Nihon no Gatto Kanyū Mondai (The Problem of Japanese Accession to the GATT)* (Daigaku Shuppankai, 1992), pp. 83–117.

4. According to F. V. Meyer, "The U.S. was willing to give twice as much by way of scheduled concessions as she received, just as she had done to secure the general agreement in the first place in 1947." F. V. Meyer, *International Trade Policy* (St. Martin's Press, 1978), pp. 141–42.

5. Masaru Kohno, "Limits of Neoliberal Institutionalism: Learning from the Failure of Multilateral Institutions in East Asian Security."

6. Shortly after Japan joined the United Nations, Foreign Minister Nobusuke Kishi pronounced a UN-centered diplomacy as one of the three basic principles of Japan's foreign policy; the other two were cooperation with other democracies, and maintaining Japan's position as an Asian country. Sadako Ogata, "The United Nations and Japanese Diplomacy," *Japan Review of International Affairs* (Fall/Winter 1990), p. 143; Yasuhiro Ueki, "Japan's UN Diplomacy: Sources of Passivism and Activism," in Gerald L. Curtis, ed., *Japan's Foreign Policy after the Cold War: Coping with Change* (M. E. Sharp Inc., 1993), p. 348.

7. Ueki, "Japan's UN Diplomacy," pp. 348–50.

8. For a description of the rise of antilegalism in GATT in the 1960s, see Robert E. Hudec, *The GATT Legal System and World Trade Diplomacy* (Salem, N.H.: Butterworth Legal Publishers, 1990), pp. 235–50. Hudec reports that between 1959 and 1970, only ten legal complaints were filed, compared to forty complaints filed in the previous seven years.

9. This has been observed by John Gerard Ruggie, among others; see John Gerard Ruggie, *Winning the Peace: America and World Order in the New Era* (Columbia University Press, 1996), p. 70.

10. Miles Kahler, *International Institutions and the Political Economy of Integration* (Brookings, 1995); Robert O. Keohane, "Multilateralism: An Agenda for Research," *International Journal* 45 (Fall 1990), pp. 731–64.

11. In the twelve years between 1988 and 2000, forty new peacekeeping operations were launched, compared to only thirteen peacekeeping missions launched in the previous twenty-five years from 1945 to 1980. See www.un.org/depts/dpko/view.htm.

12. Renato Ruggiero, "Whither the Trade System Next?" in Jagdish Bhagwati and Mathia Hirsch, eds., *The Uruguay Round and Beyond* (University of Michigan Press, 1998), p. 137.

13. Beth A. Simmons, "The Legalization of International Monetary Affairs," *International Organization*, vol. 54, no. 3 (Summer 2000), pp. 573–602.

14. See www.mofa.go.jp/policy/un/pamph2000/reform.html.

15. Robert O. Keohane, "Institutional Theory and the Realist Challenge after the Cold War," in David A. Baldwin, ed., *Neorealism and Neoliberalism* (Columbia University Press, 1993), p. 285.

16. On the growth of environmental IOs, see John W. Meyer and others, "The Structuring of a World Environmental Regime, 1870–1990," *International Organization*, vol. 51, no. 4 (Autumn 1997), pp. 637–38.

17. These characteristics—obligation (or legal boundedness), precision, and delegation—are the dimensions of international legalization used in the definition of Abbott and others, "The Concept of Legalization," *International Organization*, vol. 54, no. 3 (Summer 2000), pp. 401–20.

18. Judith Goldstein and others, "Introduction: Legalization and World Politics," *International Organization*, vol. 54, no. 3 (Summer 2000), p. 390.

19. The United States also relied on the IMF and World Bank to finance and manage the economic transformation of eastern Europe and the former Soviet Union in the early 1990s.

20. Another shift in U.S. negotiating strategy was the willingness to move away from the principle of nondiscrimination by negotiating separate codes regulating nontariff measures that would apply only to signatories. A number of these plurilateral agreements were negotiated in the Tokyo and Uruguay Rounds.

21. An ambitious agenda of trade and investment liberalization, and a multispeed timetable for implementing commitments, appeared to be confirmed at the Bogor Summit in 1994. However, subsequent implementation of the Bogor commitments has been disappointing.

22. Robert M. Immerman, "Japan in the United Nations," in Craig C. Garby and Mary Brown Bullock, eds., *Japan: A New Kind of Superpower?* (Washington: Woodrow Wilson Center Press, 1994), p. 187.

23. Congress demanded that the U.S. contribution be reduced from 25 to 22 percent of the administrative budget, and reduced from 30.4 to 25 percent of the peacekeeping budget. A compromise agreement was reached in December 2000 that meets U.S. demands on its contributions to the general budget, and reduces U.S. peacekeeping dues to 26 percent.

24. The following description of Japan's behavior in successive rounds of multilateral trade negotiations in GATT is drawn from Amy Searight, *MITI and Multilateralism: The Evolution of Japan's Trade Policy in the GATT Regime* (Stanford University, 1999).

25. On Japan's behavior in the GATT-WTO dispute resolution, see Searight, *MITI and Multilateralism*; and Saadia M. Pekkanen, "International Law, the WTO, and the Japanese State: Assessment and Implications of the New Legalized Trade Politics," *Journal of Japanese Studies* 27 (Winter 2001), p. 41.

26. The case involved Zenith color television sets. The United States encouraged Japan to lodge a GATT complaint against a U.S. court decision that held Japanese tax subsidies to be

grounds for countervailing duties. The U.S. government was upset with the court ruling and it cooperated with all GATT members in issuing a ruling within a few days.

27. Taking complaints against Japan brought by other countries as well as the United States, Japan settled twelve out of seventeen cases prior to a panel ruling between 1955 and 1994; after 1995, Japan settled only three out of ten, with two cases still pending.

28. For a recent analysis of the economic legacy of postwar Occupation policies, see John W. Dower, *Embracing Defeat* (W.W. Norton, 1999), pp. 525–46. For an insider's account of Occupation policies, see Leon Hollerman, "International Economic Controls in Occupied Japan," *Journal of Asian Studies* 38 (August 1979), pp. 707–19.

29. MITI trade officials repeatedly stressed this point in interviews.

30. The Clinton administration had demanded that Japan further open its automobile and auto parts sectors. In May 1995 the United States threatened to impose 100 percent punitive tariffs on Japanese luxury automobiles, and Japan immediately responded by filing a complaint in the WTO (WT/DS6/1, United States—Imposition of Import Duties on Automobiles from Japan under Sections 301 and 304 of the Trade Act of 1974).

31. The EU and Australia requested to join in the consultations under Article 22 of GATT due to their concern over U.S. unilateral measures in the dispute. See WT/DS6/2, United States—Imposition of Import Duties on Automobiles from Japan under Sections 301 and 304 of the Trade Act of 1974—Request to Join Consultations under Article 4.11 of the DSU.

32. Yoichi Funabashi, *Asia Pacific Fusion* (Institute for International Economics, 1995), pp. 61–64.

33. Report issued by the Study Group for Asia Pacific Trade Development (the so-called Sakamoto Report), cited in Funabashi, *Asia Pacific Fusion*, p.59.

34. Both China and Japan have proposed that their FTAs with ASEAN be completed within a decade, so even if the economic and political problems can be solved they will not emerge in the near future. Anthony Rowley, "ASEAN, Japan Already in Talks for an FTA," *Business Times Singapore*, December 10, 2001, p. 2.

35. Dennis Yasutomo, *The New Multilateralism in Japan's Foreign Policy* (St. Martin's Press, 1995), p. 66. Japan's current IMF quota represents 6.32 percent of total shares, second to the U.S. quota of 17.63 percent. Voting rights are closely correlated with quotas (6.2 percent for Japan; 17.20 percent for the United States). See (www.imf.org/external/np/sec/memdir/members.htm).

36. Robert Wade, "Japan, the World Bank, and the Art of Paradigm Maintenance: The 'East Asian Miracle' in Political Perspective," *New Left Review* (May-June 1996), p. 5; Dennis Yasutomo, *Japan and the Asian Development Bank* (Praeger Publishers, 1983) pp. 162–64.

37. Wade, "Japan, the World Bank," provides an excellent account of this challenge. See also Yasutomo, *The New Multilateralism*, pp. 74–81.

38. The meeting was an annual meeting of the Asian Development Bank.

39. Japan already had bilateral swap agreements with South Korea ($5 billion) and Malaysia ($2.5 billion); under the Chiang Mai initiative it has negotiated agreements with Thailand ($3 billion), the Philippines ($3 billion), and expanded its swap arrangements with South Korea (with an additional $2.5 billion) and Malaysia (an additional $1 billion). Red Woods, "Currency Swaps—Toward Asian Integration?" *United Press International*, May 17, 2001.

40. For further discussion of disagreements over IMF reform, see Marc Castellano, "Tokyo, Washington Clash over Reshaping IMF's Role," *JEI Report*, January 7, 2000, p. 10–11.

41. By long-standing tradition, the role of leader at the IMF is filled by a European national, and the top job at the World Bank goes to an American.

42. Ogata, "The United Nations and Japanese Diplomacy," p. 145.

43. Masayuki Tadokoro, "A Japanese View on Restructuring the Security Council," in Bruce Russett, ed., *The Once and Future Security Council* (St. Martin's Press, 1997), p. 129.

By 2000 Japan's contribution was over 20 percent. Nobumichi Izumi, "UN Security Council Needs Japan's Voice," *Nikkei Weekly*, October 2000.

44. Immerman, "Japan in the United Nations," pp. 187–88; Ogata, "The United Nations and Japanese Diplomacy," p. 148; Ueki, "Japan's UN Diplomacy," p. 353.

45. Ogata, "The United Nations and Japanese Diplomacy," pp. 149–50.

46. Tetsuo Urano, *Kokusai Shakai no Hen'yō to Kokuren Tohyo Kodo 1946–85 (Changing International Society and UN Voting Behavior)* (Kokusai Chiiki Shiryo Senta, 1989). Cited in Ogata, "The United Nations and Japanese Diplomacy," p.156.

47. This included abstaining from the infamous resolution equating Zionism with racism.

48. Soo Yeon Kim and Bruce Russett, "The New Politics of Voting Alignments in the General Assembly," in Bruce Russett, ed., *The Once and Future Security Council* (St. Martin's Press, 1997), p. 47. In Kim and Russett's quantitative analysis of UN voting behavior in the mid-1980s and early 1990s, Japan's voting pattern puts it in a voting cluster that includes many of the more independent or neutral Western countries in Scandinavia, South Europe, and Australia and New Zealand. The U.S. cluster includes the United Kingdom, France, and Germany, as well as Israel and Canada. See Kim and Russett, pp. 41–48. According to Ueki, "On disarmament issues, Japan tends to vote affirmative at the United Nations when the United States votes affirmative; it tends to abstain when the United States votes negative." Ueki, "Japan's UN Diplomacy," p.352. Kim and Russett make a stronger claim that Japan has distanced itself from both the United States and the former Soviet Union on disarmament issues; see Kim and Russett, p. 47.

49. Kim and Russett, "The New Politics," p. 53; Barry O'Neill, "Power and Satisfaction in the Security Council," in Bruce Russett, ed., *The Once and Future Security Council* (St. Martin's Press, 1997), pp. 70–76.

50. Japan has been elected to serve eight two-year terms on the UN Security Council in 1958, 1966, 1971, 1975, 1981, 1987, 1993, and 1997.

51. Japan has proposed expanding council members from fifteen to twenty-four, but the United States had long insisted that twenty-one members is an absolute upper limit for the council to continue functioning effectively. Last year, however, Ambassador Richard Holbrooke announced that the United States would consider greater enlargement of the council; see Barbara Crosette, "U.S. Ready for Much Larger Security Council," *New York Times*, April 4, 2000, p. A-4.

52. Peter J. Katzenstein and Nobuo Okawara, "Japanese Security Issues," in Craig C. Garby and Mary Brown Bullock, eds., *Japan: A New Kind of Superpower?* (Washington: Woodrow Wilson Center Press, 1994), p. 62.

53. Aurelia George, "International Peacekeeping and Japan's Role: Catalyst or Cautionary Tale?" *Asian Survey*, vol. 35, no.12 (December 1995), pp. 1102–118.

54. In 1994 the U.S. Senate passed two resolutions stating that the United States government should not support Japan's bid for a permanent seat. The second one passed unanimously, and called on Japan to "fully engage in any form of peacekeeping or peacemaking operation." See "Ministry Official Discounts Senate Resolution," *Daily Yomiuri*, July 19, 1994, p.1.

55. Personal communication, Director of Office of Japan, U.S. Commerce Department, January 2001. An agreement on telecommunications was reached in July 2000; government procurement talks are ongoing. See also Richard Lawrence, "It's Japan Trade Policy Time Again," *Journal of Commerce Online*, July 27, 2000.

56. The government passed two laws in the wake of the September 11 terrorist attacks. The first authorizes the government to dispatch Self-Defense Forces to noncombat areas to provide rearguard logistical support to U.S. and other forces, such as intelligence gathering and transport of fuel, food, and medical supplies, as well as humanitarian aid to refugees. Moreover, SDF forces will be permitted to carry and discharge weapons in self-defense during these activ-

ities. The second law enables the SDF to guard U.S. bases and government facilities in Japan, activities that are currently restricted to domestic police forces.

57. Kennth N. Waltz, "Structural Realism after the Cold War," *International Security,* vol. 25, no. 1 (Summer 2000), p. 18.

58. For realist arguments that emphasize strategic incentives for institutionalized cooperation in the face of a common enemy, see, for example, Joanne Gowa, "Rational Hegemons, Excludable Goods, and Small Groups: An Epitaph for Hegemonic Stability Theory?" *World Politics*, vol. 41, no. 3. (April 1989), pp. 307–24.

59. Kenneth N. Waltz, "The Emerging Structure of International Politics," *International Security* (Fall 1993), pp. 44–79.

60. Interviews, various MITI officials, conducted July–September 1995, August 1998.

CHAPTER EIGHT

Finance

ADAM S. POSEN

Economic relations between the United States and Japan have been characterized by substantial tensions in the postwar era, yet this has not damaged the underlying security relationship or critically harmed the multilateral economic framework. In fact these two economies have become more integrated over time even as these tensions played out. These tensions, however, have required an enormous expenditure of political capital and officials' time on both sides of the Pacific and have led to forgone opportunities for institution building and policy coordination.[1] They have deepened since Japan caught up with the United States around 1980, and Japanese and U.S. firms began increasingly to compete for profits and market share in the same sectors. Moreover, as both the U.S. and Japanese economies continue to mature—both in terms of the age of their populations and their industrial mix—they will likely face even greater tensions between them over allocating the management and costs of industrial adjustment.

Financial liberalization and integration could change all this. At present, U.S. and Japanese corporate governance and investment behavior appear to be converging toward the arm's-length, market-based, U.S. approach to financial markets. If this trend continues, it will not only reduce tensions in the near term by facilitating the resolution of specific disputes, but it could also forge common interests between domestic interest groups across the

Pacific while giving those groups more power relative to their respective governments. Over the longer term, convergence would also produce common U.S. and Japanese policy goals in relation to international capital flows and investment. Finally, for a transitional period, convergence should simultaneously increase U.S. influence and improve Japanese economic performance, a combination that has been difficult to attain since the first oil shock.

Convergence between the U.S. and Japanese financial systems, however, is not a foregone conclusion. The general question of whether the decline of national models is inevitable remains open[2]—and the specific outcome of the interaction between Japanese political economy (arguably the most distinctive among industrial democracies) and financial liberalization (arguably the most transformative aspect of globalization) already is unfolding as a critical case study.[3] Even if most would agree that some form of liberalization has taken place in Japanese as well as American financial markets, scholars disagree over whether the Japanese form of liberalization is distinct from the American, whether this liberalization is likely to be the victim of political backlash (in either country), or whether financial sector change is likely to transform the rest of Japan's economy.

This chapter is focused on a related but more policy-oriented question: If it is assumed that the current trends toward liberalization in and convergence between the U.S. and Japanese financial systems persist, how will this affect U.S.-Japan relations? This chapter presents evidence of convergence toward the increasingly deregulated U.S. system over the past fifteen years, and argues that this trend is likely to persist and probably accelerate. The chapter assumes as well that the case need not be made here on the pure economics of why the more liberal model is likely to confer efficiency gains (at least in the short run). It is not presumed that the ongoing academic discussion of globalization and its effects has been settled. For purposes of policymaking, however, if this convergence assumption proves incorrect in the coming years, it almost certainly would mean that financial issues would be only a very minor factor in U.S.-Japan relations (as it was until recently), or simply one of many sectoral disputes with dynamics with which scholars are familiar, having no special implications. Several hundred billion dollars have already been bet by Japanese and American investors on the belief that financial liberalization and convergence will occur, so it seems worth exploring the implications of this likely possibility.

The impact of financial convergence on U.S.-Japan relations has been limited to date. Despite the breathless rhetoric about globalization, the concern with which some observers viewed the growth in Japanese holdings of U.S. government debt, and the incidence of severe banking system problems in both countries, neither government has been able to extract much in the way of leverage over the other from financial sector developments. This may not come as a surprise to most observers, but it is worth documenting. This chapter argues, however, that many of the key deregulatory measures have only taken effect in Japan since the response to the 1997–98 recession, and that those, combined with the looming financial crisis awaiting Japan's undercapitalized banking system, will change matters.[4]

Specifically, American foreign direct investment (FDI) into and influence on the Japanese financial sector is likely to mount in the coming years and will reinforce American soft power over the ideas driving international financial arrangements. This combination of financial flows and ideational factors has already radically shifted the setting of the U.S.-Japan trade agenda and the willingness of both governments to engage in exchange rate intervention. The underlying forces of liberalization will be reinforced by a shift in capital flows—both short term out of Japan when a financial crisis hits, and longer term from the United States into Japan when American financial firms take a role in recapitalizing and rebuilding the Japanese financial system. While a nationalist political backlash against FDI into Japan may raise tensions temporarily, the underlying economic forces will ultimately drive the United States and Japan into closer cooperation in terms of results on financial issues.[5]

These financial developments are unlikely to have much direct impact on U.S.-Japan security relations, but they are likely to exemplify and feed many of the themes about the broader relationship identified in this project. The themes include: economic issues growing less contentious between the two countries; military power becoming less important as a factor in determining bargaining power between the United States and Japan; and nongovernmental actors and international organizations continuing to increase their role in the relationship at the expense of the two states.[6] The recent announcements by the Japanese government of unprecedented support for the United States on the national security side of the relationship in the aftermath of the September 11 attacks do nothing to significantly alter these trends. In the end the low returns on Japan's vast pool of capital are unsustainable, especially if some major Japanese banks feed Japanese savers' fears by going bankrupt despite the government's attempts to coddle them along. A lessening of pressure from the United States on Japan for bank reform in response to coalition politics will only postpone the day of reckoning a few months—

and may add to the likelihood of crisis preceding policy rather than vice versa.

Financial Liberalization in the United States and Japan

For this chapter, the independent variable influencing the U.S.-Japan relationship is finance, both the state of financial capabilities within the two countries as well as financial flows between them. The source of variation is the long, slow process of deregulation, first in the United States, second, and even more slowly, in Japan. Until 1980 there was little change of import on this front in either country. The size and turnover of international capital flows only significantly expanded beyond that necessary for trade in the mid-1980s.

Accordingly, this section gives a brief history of domestic financial deregulation and response in the United States and in Japan, followed by an overview of the development of trans-Pacific capital flows, emphasizing the last fifteen to twenty years. Underlying developments in both countries are four facts. Both systems

—started out with strict regulations separating banking and securities activities;

—started out with the vast majority of domestic savings in bank accounts and limits on the returns that could be paid depositors;

—faced fundamentally unprofitable banking systems once these barriers began to erode;

—suffered through banking crises caused by financial firms' reaction to partial deregulation and lax supervision.

Speaking of convergence, thereby acknowledging a gap between national forms of both corporate finance and savings behavior and regulatory practices, does not rule out basic similarities between systems. It is these similarities, arising out of the economic logic of what financial systems can and cannot do that gives rise to the convergence.

United States

The U.S. financial system was characterized by decentralization of both financial institutions and regulators, with additional divisions between types of financial firms and between states' rules.[7] The response to the 1929 stock market crash and the Great Depression had led to the creation of many legal barriers between firms, most notably the Glass-Steagall Act of 1933, preventing both interstate banking and the conduct of investment and commercial banking under one roof. Additionally, the Bank Holding Company Act of 1956 plugged any holes in Glass-Steagall's rules, preventing commercial banks from holding stock in nonfinancial firms. Interest rates paid on individuals' deposit accounts were limited by Regulation Q. Savings and loan institutions (S&Ls) were required to invest only in long-term housing loans, and therefore were limited in their risk taking and profitmaking, but received the right to offer a little more to their depositors in recompense. The Securities and Exchange Commission was one of several regulators of financial markets, including state-level regulators who controlled both the life and casualty insurance industries (and still do).

Deregulation began in earnest with the Garn-St. Germain Depository Institutions Act, effective September 1983. This act legalized interest-paying deposit accounts and money market funds (MMFs), products already well under way as the inflation of the 1970s had made Regulation Q interest rate limits untenable. The use of certificates of deposit (CDs) had been deregulated by 1973. Garn-St. Germain also removed all statutory limits on real estate lending, opening up the S&Ls' mortgage market to competition but in return allowing the S&Ls to engage in commercial and consumer lending. Unfortunately, this regulatory pandering—giving each piece of the banking sector something, rather than encouraging exit of some banks—sowed the seeds of what became the S&L crisis. Losing their traditional high-margin business, and presented with the opportunities to make loans in areas where they were unprepared to evaluate credit risks, the S&Ls ramped up real estate lending as part of an early 1980s boom. Commercial banks also shifted into lending to small and medium enterprises collateralized by land as they lost their best clients to the rise of commercial paper (CP) as a low-cost, short-term financing option. Meanwhile, more depositors switched their assets into money market funds, CDs, and mutual funds, all of which made banks and S&Ls compete harder for loanable funds.

The collapse of the market for real estate in the mid-1980s cut directly into the capital of most S&Ls and many banks. As a measure of the change in real estate prices, Friedman notes that the vacancy rate for commercial offices was 4 percent at the height of a recession in 1980, but 18 percent despite a recovery by 1986.[8] The affected banks and S&Ls behaved just as economic theory would predict. Until supervisors enforced matters, the banks and S&Ls invested in higher risk, high return projects in hopes of restoring their capital, they rolled over outstanding bad loans to avoid writing them down, and they stopped lending to high quality borrowers with safe low returns. These financial firms also rapidly escalated deposit interest rates, figuring that any losses would be covered by deposit insurance.

U.S. supervisors unfortunately did some gambling on resurrection of their own, waiting to shut down banks and S&Ls with insufficient capital in hopes that better economic times would allow them to recoup their losses. This only allowed the problem to grow until it was necessary for large-scale government action to consolidate, recapitalize, and close failed institutions, and to begin selling off foreclosed real estate assets.[9] In August 1987 the Competitive Equality Banking Act put $11 billion into recapitalizing the Federal Savings and Loan Insurance Corporation, but this ended up being just the start of what became an estimated $159 billion hit (about 3 percent of a year's U.S. gross domestic product (GDP)) to taxpayers for cleaning up the mess, with final legislation coming only in 1993.

One positive outcome of this sequence was an increase in the sophistication of U.S. savers, including a rising awareness that the limits per account on deposit insurance really would be upheld, and might come into play, as well as a greater appreciation for risk and for self-allocation of funds. As can be seen in figure 8-1, the allocation of U.S. household wealth has shifted significantly over this period. The share of transaction accounts and other once standard bank accounts has steadily declined. CDs are held by half as many savers as at the height of their popularity. Retirement accounts, mutual funds, and individual equity ownership have risen to compensate, as life insurance's share in savings has remained stable. The rise in share of the equity portion appears to be less than one-for-one, with the runup in the U.S. equity market of 1994–2000 again indicating a healthy sense of discounting by American savers.

A similar process was under way on the corporate finance side. After commercial paper became standard for the largest American corporations, displacing short-term bank loans, the high-yield (junk) bond market grew to provide securitized financing for riskier businesses. The minimum size for American companies to go directly to the markets for financing, either to issue a bond or to go public with an equity issue, declined throughout the period. This gave rise to the growth in the volume of NASDAQ and to lower demand for long-term bank lending. To manage their risks, as well as to offer differentiated products, American financial firms including banks began to create derivative securities and to securitize an increasing share of loans. Investors and borrowers could go directly to financial markets for lower costs of intermediation, or even without intermediation, to an unprecedented degree.

Figure 8-1. *Allocation of U.S. Household Wealth, 1989–98*

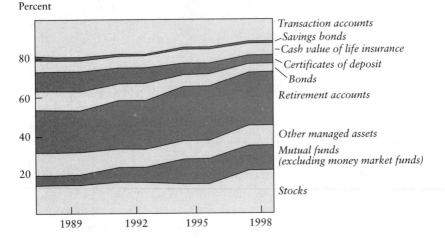

Percent

Source: "Recent Changes in U.S. Family Finances: Results from the 1998 Survey of Consumer Finances," *Federal Reserve Bulletin*, January 2000.

The United States' reactive approach to financial deregulation extended beyond the response to the S&L crises. The largest commercial banks slowly took on more capabilities by sending petitions to the Federal Reserve, as, in an early example, Bankers' Trust did by engaging in some investment banking activities. Bank holding companies were allowed to merge across state lines or acquire out of state banks, as recognized in the Riegle-Neal Interstate Banking and Branching Efficiency Act of September 1995 (taking effect in June 1997). In November 1999, after two decades of lobbying, Congress passed the Graham-Leach-Billey Act, effectively repealing Glass-Steagall and the 1956 Bank Holding Company Act. The expected effect is the emergence of a number of financial supermarkets, like Travelers-Citibank-Salomon Smith Barney, offering a complete range of services. Some critics remain concerned that the risks to financial stability that Glass-Steagall was meant to prevent will reappear. The Federal Reserve has announced that it has moved to the use of bank-reported Value-At-Risk (VAR) models to assess the soundness of banks' portfolios, instead of examining the portfolios themselves, in what it deems a necessary response to the complexity of banks' diversification and securitization. The question is open whether such self-regulation will be effective. U.S. banks are still prohibited from having shares in nonfinancial companies directly on their balance sheets, though they now may be held by other parts of their holding companies.

Japan

The Japanese financial system traditionally featured indirect financing of industry, with a concentrated banking sector and underdeveloped capital markets.[10] As in the United States, there was compartmentalization between securities and banking activities, because the postwar occupying authorities imposed a law modeled on Glass-Steagall.[11] The banks had competition for depositors from the Postal Savings System, which doubled in size over the last fifty years, and now takes in two-thirds as many deposits as the entire private banking sector. Since Postal Savings funds were made available to the government for use in the Fiscal Investment and Loan Program, and since the Postal Savings system was regulated by the Ministry of Posts and Telecommunications in *de jure* cooperation (*de facto* competition) with the Ministry of Finance (MOF), it offered a slightly higher rate of interest as well as an implicitly superior government guarantee. Also, like the United States, all interest rates on deposits were regulated, but they were capped at much lower levels relative to lending rates and to returns on capital, as a conscious effort to subsidize investment.

There were strong limits on corporate finance in return for the lower cost of funds. Much of capital was administratively allocated by the MOF, the Ministry of International Trade and Industry (MITI), and other agencies through the banks because demand exceeded supply.[12] Only NTT, the telephone monopoly, Japanese National Railways (government owned), and electric utilities were encouraged to issue corporate bonds. All other private firms had to put up private collateral with a trust bank and then pay a securities firm for the privilege of selling a bond. The long-term credit banks provided most of the long-term lending for industry. Unlike in the United States, where the separation between banking and securities businesses arguably was a spur to financial innovation, in Japan financial innovation was limited by the MOF.

The MOF's idea of financial stability meant controlling exit as well as entry to the financial market, and in so doing the regulators took a limited view of disclosure in their perceived interest(s) of stability.[13] Steil and Vogel paint very similar views of MOF regulators as proud of their power and prestige, protective of the firms under their supervision, even more protective of their administrative discretion, and clearly associating market competition with unnecessary risk.[14] As one example of this view, deposit insurance was kept informal, without any specified limits, because the real objective was to never have any banks fail, so no deterrent effect on savers was desired.

Yet the same economic forces working on U.S. banks and securities houses were also increasing competitive pressures on the Japanese financial system. As Ogata notes, since the mid-1960s there were growing private capital markets worldwide, growing Japanese government bond markets, diversification of the savings instruments available to savers, gradual erosion of compartmentalization, and then phased deregulation of interest rates paid depositors starting in 1985.[15] Japan's persistent balance of payments surplus made capital controls less relevant, forcing banks to make their own decisions on credit allocation. By the mid-1980s the same process that had hit the American S&Ls and small banks had begun in Japan. Japan's small banks were at least as ill prepared to adapt their credit assessment as their U.S. counterparts, and they had even fewer options for shrinking or changing their business lines.

The best Japanese nonfinancial firms were going directly to capital markets, whether at home or abroad, and were driving down margins on banks' lending and demanding cheaper capital. The commercial paper market, for example, was created in 1988 when 2.2 trillion yen were issued in the first year, before going on to average around 9 trillion yen a year in the 1990s.[16] In 1989 and 1990 literally no domestic yen bonds were issued by any firms other than NTT or electric utilities, because all corporate borrowers had gone to the euroyen markets. Banks were also getting squeezed on the deposit side, at least in terms of interest rates. In 1985–86, 150 trillion yen went into high-yielding ten-year time deposit accounts at Postal Savings (instead of banks).

As their American counterparts did, Japanese banks ramped up lending to small and medium enterprises (SMEs) on the basis of real estate collateral, feeding into a property boom. As Shimizu carefully documents, up until 1983 total lending to all SMEs in Japan was about equivalent to the total lending to large firms.[17] SME lending then began to rise for the remainder of the decade, reaching a level three times that of lending to larger firms by 1990. With the MOF committed to there being no exit from the financial markets and banks still holding a large amount of (decreasing margin) loanable funds, banks had to chase new areas for lending. The three long-term credit banks made the biggest shift in lending toward SMEs and real estate since they had the sharpest fall-off in loan demand.

The collapse of the Japanese stock market in 1990 and again in 1992, followed by steady declines in land prices, triggered the financial crisis with which Japan is still coping today. Underlying, however, was the inherent problem of partially deregulating financial markets, neither allowing banks to change their business lines nor to close, while their old margins and old methods of credit evaluation eroded. MOF bank supervisors waited to close banks in hopes that an upturn in the economy would bail them out. Japanese bank regulators still believed that stability was defined as no failures. Meanwhile, in response to the moral hazard of having too little capital and too much deposit insurance, Japanese banks rolled over outstanding bad loans rather than writing them off and continued to lend on real estate well into the 1990s.

The *jūsen*, the real estate lending companies owned by consortia of banks to handle small scale mortgages, were the first to visibly collapse under the cycle of bad loans, depreciating collateral values, and credit contraction, feeding further local SME business collapses and bad loans. MOF inspectors admitted in 1991 that 40 percent of their outstanding loans were nonperforming, but gave the *jūsen* a ten-year regulatory window to deal with the problem. Four years later in 1995, the share of nonperforming loans on the *jūsen*'s only slightly smaller balance sheets had risen to 75 percent. Cargill, Hutchison, and Itō put it very well:

> The resolution of the *jūsen* industry [in 1995] was fundamentally flawed and illustrated to the market the [Japanese] government's unwillingness to objectively assess and manage the financial crisis. It illustrated that the convoy system was still operational by imposing the greater part of the resolution burden on the banking system. The intense public negative reaction to the small amount of taxpayer funding included in the plan gave the regulatory authorities the rationale to continue a policy of forgiveness and forbearance. As a result, the government became very reluctant to propose the use of public funds to resolve the financial distress. This reluctance to use public funds further delayed resolution of the nonperforming loan problem and thereby substantially increased the ultimate resolution costs.[18]

The difference between the American and Japanese regulators' initial response was only in degree, not in kind,[19] but the difference in degree was enormous. American regulators, with prompting from legislators, tackled their S&L problem within five years from when it started and at a cost of 3 percent of GDP, and the problem was limited to some regions and types of banks. Japan, by contrast, is now into its eleventh year of systemwide financial fragility, and the expected cost to the taxpayer is on the order of 100 trillion yen, or 20 percent of a year's GDP. Between the surprise failures in fall 1997 of Yamaichi Securities (the number four Japanese securities firm) and Hokkaido Takushoku Bank (a major regional bank on the north island), and the passage of a package of bank reform legislation a year later, Japan teetered on the edge of outright financial crisis.[20]

With the arrival of Prime Minister Keizō Obuchi's government in July 1998 following an LDP election setback in an upper house election, some real financial reforms were put in place. In a bill passed in October 1998, the government began to address recapitalization of the Japanese banking system with public funds. In addition to a new commitment to stricter supervision (see below), the government arranged for all but one of the largest banks, and most of the second-tier banks, to take strictly conditional capital injections by April 1, 1999, based on new balance sheet inspections. The Japanese government received in return preferred shares that would allow the regulators to take over the bank or vote out management if the mandated capital adequacy ratio was not met. The trend of financial disintermediation in Japan was stopped and partially reversed as a result.

The MOF, now very much discredited with the electorate, was held accountable for mismanagement as a bank supervisor. In June 1998 the ministry was reorganized, and the Financial Supervision Agency (FSA) was spun off with responsibility for the banking system. Within the MOF, the banking and securities bureaus were combined into a "Financial Planning Bureau."[21] Combined with the granting of independence from the MOF to the Bank of Japan, effective February 1998, the MOF became a shadow of its former self. Nevertheless, the Japanese tendency toward centralized regulation remained, and the FSA became the Financial Services Agency in 2000, with the addition of the securities industry to its portfolio and the movement of the Financial Planning Bureau to it from the MOF. The nationalizations of the bankrupt Long-Term Credit Bank and Nippon Credit Bank in fall 1998 demonstrated the new FSA's resolve.

As in the United States, much of the Japanese securities deregulation proceeded down an independent track, neither impeded nor hurried by the country's banking crisis. Steil offers ample evidence that through 1995, Japanese securities markets had offered only the "illusion of liberalization."[22] In November 1996 then Prime Minister Ryūtarō Hashimoto announced his plan for "big bang" deregulation of financial markets. This plan promised a series of deregulatory initiatives through 2001. These included allowing price competition on brokerage commissions and other financial fees, removal of limits on individuals holding bank accounts abroad or trading foreign currencies, removal of restrictions on the trading

Figure 8-2. *Allocation of Personal Savings in Japan, 1985–98*

Percent

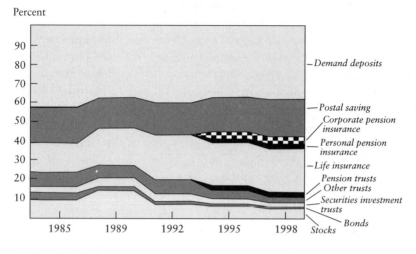

Source: Bank of Japan.

of derivatives, and allowing cross-sectoral competition between banks, securities houses, and insurance companies. Given the implementation lags for any deregulation initiative, it is difficult to say as yet what the ultimate state of the Japanese financial system will be once the banking crisis is resolved.

Japanese savers have suffered some hard lessons in recent years, and perhaps as a result their savings behavior has if anything grown more conservative (see figure 8-2). Demand deposits at banks and in Postal Savings have continued to account for around 55 percent of Japanese household savings throughout the 1980s and 1990s. Holdings of equities and bonds, which did rise in the 1980s with the asset price boom, have been halved since then. In fact, security and investment trusts have not been growing, despite some deregulation measures meant to encourage their growth. As discussed below, it is the Japanese savers' unwillingness to move their money to seek out higher returns that allows Japan to withstand its financial problems, explains the lack of political demand for resolution, and is the major drag on the forces for convergence.

Financial Flows between the United States and Japan

It is often observed that capital flows between nations and the desire to control or maximize inflows is a major concern of economic policy today. The U.S.-Japan relationship putatively is affected by the huge flows between the two countries. Yet trans-Pacific financial flows have developed fitfully against this backdrop of slow deregulation and temporary crisis in the U.S. financial system, and slower deregulation and ongoing fragility in the Japanese financial system. Tokyo is one of the world's major financial centers, and financial firms there allocate vast quantities of savings, but it remains relatively underdeveloped versus London and New York. In both the United States and Japan, the banks and firms who hold savers' money are actually engaged in vast international transactions—securitized mortgages in the United States, for example, are resold worldwide, commercial paper and interbank markets run twenty-four hours globally to maintain liquidity for the largest corporate players—but domestic savers still invest domestically.

So the capital flows between the world's first- and second-largest economies, between the world's biggest net debtor and biggest net creditor, have not shown the same growth as global finance overall. Direct banking flows would be expected to decline in relative importance as better corporate borrowers seek out disintermediated finance via securities.[23] It is clear that U.S. bank claims on (loans to) Japan have been steadily declining since the height of the bubble, from $1.7 trillion outstanding to $220 billion, one-eighth of where it started. As a percent of total U.S. banks' claims on foreigners, the decline over the period is from 24 percent to 3.5 percent, or to one-seventh of the initial share. This lack of direct exposure may explain the relative lack of concern in some American quarters about Japanese financial problems. U.S. banks' liabilities to Japan show a more mixed picture since 1988—the amount outstanding has fluctuated between $1.05 trillion and $1.9 trillion, first declining from 1988 to 1991, then rising again from 1994 to 1998. This would seem to reflect changing borrowing costs, where of late the carry trade of borrowing from Japanese banks charging near zero nominal interest rates and reinvesting elsewhere is profitable. Even as the level of borrowing rose to surpass old highs, however, the share of Japanese lending in U.S. bank liabilities abroad remained largely steady in the 11 to 13 percent range.

Moving to the holdings of equities, a different pattern emerges. The total sales and total purchases of U.S. corporate stocks by Japanese investors have both been growing strongly since mid-1995. Both spent the 1990–95 period fluctuating between $10 billion and $25 billion per month.[24] Since then equity flows have grown steadily to a little more than $100 billion per month in purchases by Japanese, a little less than $100 billion in sales. The net purchases (or sales) have been largely undisturbed by this five- or six-fold increase in capital flow, remaining at essentially zero, though varying month-to-month from positive to negative. Even ten years of monthly flows

Figure 8-3. *U.S. and Japanese Foreign Direct Investment, 1989–99*

Billions of yen

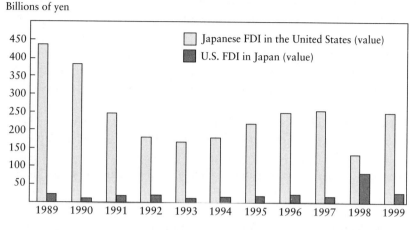

Source: *Balance of Payments Monthly*, Bank of Japan.

in the billions do not add up to large quantities of American equities in Japanese portfolios if the net each month is plus or minus $5 billion or less.

Conversely, foreign direct investment is a form of capital flow with implications beyond those suggested by its small volume. It is a flow that tends to be lasting, it often involves corporate control and transfers of technology and management techniques, and it has a visible political symbolism that many more liquid financial flows lack. Countries often have mixed feelings about foreign direct investment. If inflows come, the country can fear being taken over; if inflows do not come, the country can ask itself what makes it unattractive. Similarly, if FDI flows out, the country can worry about exporting jobs, but if no FDI goes out, it can worry about missing out on opportunities left to others. As discussed below, the United States and Japan have experienced all of these concerns.

Figure 8-3 gives the picture of annual flows of FDI to the United States from Japan, and vice versa. FDI from Japan to the United States was very high in the late 1980s, as the yen was strong and Japanese assets were very expensive relative to American ones. Despite the apparent attractiveness of the U.S. economy in the 1990s to foreign investors, the relative expensiveness of American companies and the relative lack of investment funds in Japan due to the recession there kept FDI below $2.5 billion a year. Meanwhile, American FDI into Japan remained a trickle throughout this period, though 1998 and 2000 were record years for the inflow. To put the numbers in perspective, Japanese FDI outflow to the

United States in 2000 was five times the U.S. FDI inflow to Japan in the record year.[25] If there is an asymmetry in U.S.-Japan financial flows that might be exploited or politically sensitive, this would be the one, especially since it is so persistent.

Another financial flow that is much remarked on for its asymmetry is the vast Japanese holdings of American treasury bonds. Even as Japanese issuance of government debt grew enormously over the 1990s, less than 6 percent of Japanese government bonds (JGBs) were held outside of Japan.[26] Meanwhile, Japanese holdings of American treasury bills and notes during America's runup of debt in the late 1980s reached over 40 percent of the total. Several people on the U.S. side worried about American dependence upon Japanese capital, while some Japanese officials and politicians made vague threats at times of dumping T-bills in retaliation for American actions.[27] Yet, net monthly sales of U.S. Treasuries by Japanese investors rarely exceeded $50 billion, and only once exceeded $100 billion, since January 1988. This is hardly a prepossessing number for a national debt numbered in the trillions and, until recently, issuing billions of dollars of new treasuries every month. The only large net sales sustained for more than a month were in late 1995 and in 1997–98, which again makes sense as times of acute financial distress lead investors to meet cash calls by selling their most liquid assets. The economic fundamentals rather than any political agenda seem to be the main driver of Japanese net sales of U.S. Treasuries, and they remain low versus the stock outstanding.

Effect of Financial Developments on U.S.-Japan Relations

The American and Japanese financial systems have been going through much the same process of liberalization, but with the United States starting earlier and moving faster.[28] As outlined in the previous section, this process has included for both economies a banking crisis and an abrupt rise in inward FDI from the other country (with the U.S. experiencing them first) and Japan still in the throes of both transitions as of summer 2001. The Japanese Big Bang financial deregulation initiatives, if carried through, would tear down the walls separating investment from commercial banking, and smaller investors from the markets, much as the long succession of legislation coming through the U.S. Congress in the 1980s and 1990s eventually repealed Glass-Steagall. Cross-border equity flows, FDI, and sales of U.S. Treasuries all grew over the 1990s, without clear secular trends, consistent with integrating financial markets.

Despite this tendency toward convergence, or at least staggered movements down the same path, there were two important divergences. First, Japanese savers' behavior changed less in line with financial deregulation than American savers' behavior, and actually became more risk averse over the 1990s. Second, and perhaps not unrelated, the American process of liberalization was accompanied by increasing confidence in the U.S. financial model and its benefits as the process went on, while in Japan the opposite reaction was felt. Undoubtedly, these contrasting confidence effects were largely the result of the diverging growth and unemployment performance of the two economies over the period.[29] Nevertheless, the divergence in confidence also reflected the different starting points of the two financial systems, with the American adjustment to liberalization more one of degree, while the Japanese adjustment was definitely one of kind.

These similarities and differences made themselves felt in U.S.-Japan economic relations over the last twenty years, but primarily within their own realm. That is, there were examples of conflict and cooperation over: the pace of deregulation in Japan in relation to U.S. exports and direct investment; the response to overt Japanese financial fragility in 1997–98; and how changes in the market influenced the financial regulations and model that the two countries could advocate in Asian emerging markets. There was, however, little evidence of either financial flows (from Japan to the United States, in the form of Treasuries purchases) or financial confidence (waxing in the United States, waning in Japan) granting leverage by one country over the other in broader economic discussions, let alone in matters of national security. In general even in the decade since the end of the cold war, security aspects of U.S.-Japan relations have run on a separate track.[30] The declining importance of G-7 summits and of macroeconomic policy coordination is evident throughout the 1980s and 1990s as well, but appears to be driven by the rise of markets and the decline of interventionist ideology across all the industrialized economies.[31]

Relations over Financial Regulations and Financial Services Trade

In theory banking regulators should form a relatively close fraternity, if not an epistemic community across national borders. They share a similarity of goals and pressures, a common sensibility, and often direct experience working together through numerous international forums, postings in each others' countries, and training efforts through the Bank for International Settlements and the International Monetary Fund.[32] In today's integrated financial markets, they have little choice but to exchange information—not only are subsidiaries of Japanese financial firms active in U.S. markets (and to a lesser degree, vice versa), but loans between Japanese and American banks, and movements in asset prices in each country, tie financial stability within one country to the other. This is a classic example of interdependence, where openness and integration increases both capabilities and vulnerabilities. Since the creation of the Basle Capital Adequacy Standard for Banks in 1996, commercial banks active in international markets have been subjected to a clear common standard of evaluation for the asset side of their portfolios. This standard was created with the participation and assent of both American and (grudgingly) Japanese regulators.

However, when push came to shove in U.S. and Japanese financial markets in the 1980s and 1990s, relations between regulators were not entirely smooth. As described in Steil, Japanese financial regulators made entry extremely difficult for American financial firms through use of discretionary power and their relationships with domestic incumbents.[33] During the late 1980s, the major Japanese banks became the world's largest due to their enormous deposit bases, but they also had some of the lowest returns on assets.[34] Japanese regulators refused to listen to warnings that consolidation was coming, however, being able to point to the simultaneous American difficulties during the S&L crisis. In a particularly notable example of lack of coordination in day-to-day supervision, the MOF learned in August 1995 that one employee had caused huge losses (and hidden the evidence thereof) in Daiwa Bank's New York operations. Neither Daiwa's U.S. operating officers nor the MOF regulators informed the Federal Reserve until six more weeks had passed, during which time Daiwa's counterpart banks were at risk. In the first half of 1998, when fragility in the Japanese banking system peaked, American regulators ring-fenced most Japanese banks in the New York markets, excluded them from the Fed's discount window, and asked them to have on-hand cash sufficient to cover their overnight balances.[35] While this was in no sense intended as a political or threatening act, it clearly conveyed the message that American bank regulators had a far different and more pessimistic view of Japan's banks than did their own regulators.

Particularly striking is that Japanese regulators evidently did not learn from the policy mistakes of the American S&L crisis. Posen characterizes both the Japanese and American financial crises as following a similar dynamic, right down to the regulators' slow response:

[T]he grounds for crisis are laid with protection of the banking system from competition (for example, Japan's convoy regulations), followed by partial gradual deregulation. Turning to policy response, banking supervisors allow a credit boom for lower-quality borrowers to occur in hopes of restoring bank profitability when the large, good borrowers go directly to capital markets. Of course, this just adds to the potential trouble on bank balance sheets when things go south. Regulators observe the bad loans, but keep quiet due to the banks' implicit or explicit offers of direct benefits and future employment, as well as bureaucratic disincentives to delivering bad news, and simple lack of experience with accurately evaluating risky loan portfolios. When the bust comes, supervisors engage in forbearance, meaning that they allow banks time to carry nonperforming loans rather than demanding write-downs. The interaction of moral hazard on the part of the banks and regulatory forbearance on the part of supervisors is what causes the spiraling accumulation of bad loans. This was the story in the United States in the 1980s. And despite this cautionary example, this was also the story in Japan in the 1990s.[36]

Given that U.S. regulators already had been taken to task for the S&L crisis in a litany of congressional hearings, central bank sponsored conferences, and published policy analyses by 1992, it is impossible to claim that Japanese regulators and politicians were not warned against repeating American mistakes.[37] The warnings became only more public and specific as the 1990s progressed, and the size of the Japanese bad loan problem swelled.[38] Cynical observers will not be surprised, because there is no room in this standard financial crisis story for learning; rather the incentives to inaction are universal given the situation. Yet the inability of this knowledge to transfer successfully between regulatory peers is an important cautionary note about the limits of coordination and expertise as influences on policy.

The great size of the Japanese banking problem, taken against the background of Japan's economic stagnation in the 1990s and the Asian financial crisis of 1997–98, made it an issue of enormous salience in U.S.-Japan macroeconomic policy discussions. In fact there was little dispute on either side of the Pacific that both Japan's stagnation and Asia's crisis were in some part caused by the banking problem. Sakakibara recalls that in the summer of 1998, "Washington demanded clear plans to dispose of banks' bad loans and additional stimulus measures. However, Tokyo could not immediately present practical measures in line with the request."[39] The Diet session had closed, and an upper house election was due in July. The yen was in sharp decline against the dollar in this atmosphere, and on June 17, the United States and Japan intervened jointly to support the yen at 137.60 per dollar. "As suspected by Rubin and others, the effects of joint [exchange rate] intervention did not last long. In August, the yen started to weaken again toward the high [dollar value] of 140 yen per dollar."[40] As noted in the previous section, partial bank reform and recapitalization had to wait until October 1998 to be passed by the new Japanese Diet.[41] The financial fragility in Japan had drawn in the U.S. Treasury, normally removed from banking issues, and the MOF's International Finance Division, also normally separated from such concerns. The situation had also provoked the one major concerted foreign exchange intervention of Robert Rubin's tenure as treasury secretary contrary to his declared skepticism for such measures and his strong dollar policy. This added to the sense that U.S. foreign exchange intervention was a favor to elicit the October 1998 legislation.

The escalation of Japan's domestic financial problem into a matter for the highest levels of economic diplomacy was preceded and accompanied by a sharp decline in the civility—public and private—of U.S.-Japan economic relations between 1996 and 1999. Japanese officials publicly complained of being lectured to by domineering and insensitive U.S. officials. American officials felt frustrated by Japanese government intransigence against using what appeared to be obvious remedies to a situation of even more obvious crisis.[42] Vice Minister of Finance Eisuke Sakakibara and Deputy Treasury Secretary Lawrence Summers became poster children in their opposite countries for the degree of tension. Notably, all of this escalating conflict occurred despite the relative lack of trade disputes at the time even with a widening bilateral U.S. trade deficit, and therefore the absence from the discussion of the normally more conflictive U.S. Trade Representative, Department of Commerce, and Congress.

Even more importantly, neither the public conflict nor the concerted intervention nor the common knowledge and transnational forums available to economic policymakers produced much in the way of policy change in Japan. While the American demands or suggestions did give the Obuchi government some of its agenda for fall 1998, as well as add to its sense of urgency, what is striking is how partial and slow the response still was to the international attention paid to a domestic Japanese economic problem.[43] This slowness persists despite the combination of resolution being in Japan's overall economic self-interest, having significant international spillovers on the United States and Japan's Asian neighbors, and (along with economic stimulus in Japan) being one of the foremost goals of over-all U.S. international economic policy.

Trade in financial services in recent years has emerged as an area of growing, though still limited, importance in bilateral U.S.-Japan and in multilateral trade negotiations. This is in part because the United States recognizes this as a sector where it has a clear competitive advantage.[44] Another factor is the pure motivation to improve Japan's economy because much of its weakness and differences with the United States stem from the low returns to capital and the limited power of shareholders in the Japanese economy.[45] These discussions have not really differed much from other trade negotiations, and in fact the deals in this sector have attracted less attention than such matters as steel, auto parts, and plate glass did in the United States.

The most significant negotiation to date was over access of American insurers to the Japanese market. Japanese insurance had long been cartelized, with three sectors, traditional life, traditional nonlife, and a third sector for smaller or more innovative products.[46] In July 1993 insurance was named as a priority sector under the U.S.-Japan Framework Talks. In October 1994 an agreement known as the Framework Agreement on Insurance Sector Measures was reached. There were clear differences between the MOF's implementation of the agreement and what American negotiators believed they had signed, so negotiations resumed in 1995. In April 1996 a new insurance business law was passed in Japan, along with a number of supplementary measures, and then additional deregulation and access was granted as part of the WTO Financial Services Agreement of December 1997. The main result has been to get American firms access to the Japanese auto insurance market, along with the right to differentiate policy rates on the basis of age, and to have the policies sold independently rated for soundness. American firms also gained control of most of the third sector, where new products are offered. Still, as of fiscal year 1998 foreign insurers held only 4.6 percent of the total market versus a usual foreign firm market share of 10 to 33 percent in the rest of the G-7.[47]

Relations over Capital Flows

The largest swing in capital flowing between the United States and Japan in the last twenty years has involved U.S. Treasuries and Japanese government bonds. During the 1980s the U.S. government accumulated an unprecedented amount of public debt in peacetime as a result of the Reagan fiscal policies, while the Japanese government slowly but steadily paid off the expanded public debt it issued in 1975 after the first oil shock. The picture reversed completely in the 1990s, with the U.S. federal government steadily reducing its deficits and then its stock of outstanding debt through annual surpluses. The Japanese government ran up an even larger debt-to-GDP ratio over the course of the 1990s, though more through tax revenue shortfalls than through intentional deficit spending to counter the recession. These vast movements in the stocks of government debt available to the market, however, conceal a major asymmetry in the flow of capital between the two countries.

Put simply, Japanese and other foreign investors purchase a great deal of U.S. Treasury bills and notes, while U.S. and other foreign investors purchase only a small fraction (currently, about 8 percent) of Japanese Government Bonds (JGBs) issued. Interestingly, Japanese shares and purchases seem to move in tandem, which is consistent with the view of small net sales of Treasuries by Japanese investors without multimonth trends. Nevertheless, when the U.S. public debt was at its height in 1988–90, Japanese purchasers made up 50 percent of total foreign buyers, and they already held upward of 40 percent of the outstanding debt. In 1990-92 Japanese investors hit hard by the bubble's burst no longer had spare cash to put into Treasuries, and dropped out of the market. Since 1992, as cash continued to be tight, strong availability has led to JGBs replacing Treasuries as the main inflow into Japanese investors' portfolios.

As previously noted, the perception that Japanese holdings of U.S. public debt gave Japanese officials a means of threatening U.S. policymakers—that Japan could dump Treasuries, and thereby roil U.S. markets and drive up U.S. interest rates—was widely held in both Japan and the United States, though more so in the former. The facts are undeniable that the U.S. economy was importing a great deal of capital annually, that this capital inflow allowed U.S. investment and consumption to exceed domestic production and savings, and that Japanese savers hold a lot of the assets that were sold to gain the capital. The interpretation that links these as something controllable by conscious policy, however, is flawed analytically and unsupported by the historical record. The basic problem is that capital flows are the result of thousands of decentralized individual decisions to buy and sell, and those decisions are largely driven by economic fundamentals. At the margin that moves markets, and beyond, they are not up to the discretion of policymakers on either side of the Pacific.

Japanese savers hold their assets overwhelmingly in low-risk, low-return demand deposits and life insurance, with a large portion of those assets automatically invested in JGBs. Japanese banks and other financial firms on their own accounts are the major owners of U.S. Treasuries in Japan. In their portfolios, these highly liquid bonds play a key role in the settlement of payments, as well as being a store of value. While it is true that a depreciation of the dollar would lead to capital losses on Treasuries holdings in yen terms, a rise in interest rates on JGBs would have similar effects, so there is no truly risk-free asset available to these firms, and it therefore pays to diversify. To claim that these investment decisions would be subject to government direction is mistaken, even in Japan. Were the Treasuries to be somehow dumped in large measure at once by Japanese banks, they would have to replace the safe assets in their capital with something of equivalent security. Japanese regulators would also have to somehow come up with a justification for telling financial firms to shed the world's most liquid security, one without credit risk.

Of course, the U.S. government could do something to cause rational individual investors to sell off Treasuries. It is perfectly sensible that the policies of a debt-issuing government could have a direct effect on the perceptions of investors, and that the perceptual shift would be widely shared. It is this threat of losing the faith of international capital markets that disciplines the monetary and fiscal policies of many emerging markets.

Yet there are two related reasons why this theoretical possibility is unlikely to be a factor in U.S.-Japan relations today and in the future. First, there is nothing distinctive about the Treasuries owned by Japanese as opposed to other foreign, or for that matter American, investors. A policy that is likely to bring about sales of U.S. debt is going to be perceived at first approximation similarly by all holders of that debt. European or even American capital can leave the United States just as easily as Japanese capital can, so the issue becomes one of the general economic effects of a policy shift, not one of bilateral foreign relations. Second, the fact that a large amount of Japanese savings are invested in U.S. Treasuries does not mean that the United States is in any sense dependent upon Japan to fund its debt. Just as the sustainability of the U.S. current account deficit depends upon its overall level and not any particular bilateral trade balance, the inflation and currency risks of Treasuries determine their demand, and the particular composition of who holds them is largely irrelevant. Were Japanese savings for foreign policy reasons to go en masse into another safe asset to substitute for U.S. Treasuries, such as JGBs or German *Bunds*, this would drive down the returns on that substitute asset for those already holding it, and would induce those people to increase their holdings of U.S. Treasuries.

This lack of leverage from capital flows in and out of the U.S. Treasuries market can be seen in the historical record. The Japanese share of Treasuries purchases has been steadily declining, with a sharp fall in 1990–92, and large net sales in 1996–98. There is no evidence of the United States being more accommodative of Japanese demands on policy as a result during those periods. There is also no sign of any particular Japanese policy decisions being the source of the sales, while the economic events in Japan raising investors' need for cash explains these movements easily. Meanwhile, total American public debt has been declining markedly over the second half of the 1990s, and there is no evidence of a secular decline in Japanese influence over U.S. economic policy. The same logic held in the opposite direction when the U.S. public debt rose over the 1980s. The Plaza Accord of 1985 and the Louvre Accord of 1987, and the macroeconomic coordination associated with them, would seem to indicate that mounting U.S. debt did not bolster Japanese resistance to American economic demands, let alone increase the ability to force changes in U.S. policy.[48]

Foreign direct investment is the other main type of capital flow to merit discussion as a potential influence on U.S.-Japan relations. As discussed earlier, cross-border portfolio equity flows remain small between the United States and Japan and movements in trans-Pacific bank loans seem to be driven by medium-term economic factors. In 1986–91 the declining dollar and the rise in Japanese asset values led to the first large inflow of Japanese investment into the United States.[49] Coming at a time of unemployment, historically large trade deficits, and perceived lack of competitiveness, there were numerous episodes of popular backlash against foreign takeovers. Despite various debates in Congress, however, no legislation was passed to counter the inward investment, and no efforts were exerted in bilateral U.S.-Japan talks to curtail the flow.

It is incredible to think of the transformation in attitudes. Ten years later, there is hardly a stir when recent FDI flows into the United States have dwarfed the previous record annual inflows of 1989–90.[50] When Senator Ernest Hollings tried in the summer of 2000 to make the takeover of Voicestream by Deutsche Telekom a national security issue, he lost a Senate vote 99-1. Honda had an advertising campaign in the late 1990s showing a red, white, and blue Civic automobile, declaring how much of the car was made in U.S. plants that Honda owned.

In Japan significant FDI inflows began only in 1998, and public attention was drawn to such notable acquisitions as Renault taking over Nissan, and Ripplewood Holdings purchasing the nationalized Long-Term Credit Bank

(LTCB) (later Shinsei Bank). There was some publicly vocalized discontent, especially when both firms quickly and visibly engaged in non-Japanese corporate behaviors, such as laying off workers (Renault) and refusing to roll over Sogo department store's loans (Ripplewood). There has also been some greater resistance from parts of the Japanese government than seen in their U.S. counterparts, but the Ministry of Economy, Trade, and Industry (METI) is on record wanting to encourage more inward FDI.[51] Whether this resistance to FDI will be transitional on the part of Japanese citizens and officials (as it was in the United States), or whether the opening for inward FDI is a temporary one created by the weakness and insecurity of the current Japanese economic situation, remains to be seen. As is argued in this chapter's conclusion, that sort of weakness is likely to increase in Japan in the near future, particularly in the financial sector, which will probably increase the acceptance and inflow of FDI.

Relations over the Financial Model for Emulation

U.S.-Japan relations take place at a number of levels. In economic matters the ideational issue of who has the better model has at times played a critical role. There is the matter of relative self-confidence in bilateral relations on the part of the policymakers in light of their nation's economic performance, and therefore their support or perceived competence at home.[52] While important, this factor alone is too narrow a consideration of the economic model debate's impact. Such assessments encompass a richer range of ideas than just pointing to the most recent national growth and trade statistics, and influence a broader range of specific issues besides general bargaining confidence or popular tensions. The relative merits of financial systems, with the arm's-length, market-based, securitized model on the U.S. (or U.K.) side versus relationship-based, mixed claims, bank dominant model on the Japanese (or German) side, have been heatedly discussed by academics, businesspeople, policymakers, and pundits over the entire period this chapter analyzes. As will be described, the running state of this debate has directly influenced such aspects of U.S.-Japan relations as the frequency of coordinated exchange rate intervention, the composition of capital flows between the U.S. and Japan, and the bilateral economic agenda in terms of respective national wish lists.[53] Examination reveals that the underlying economic and political factors driving convergence have led to lasting effects of the American dominance in these financial ideas in recent years, whereas the earlier ascendance of the Japanese financial model in the discussion had negligible long-term impact.[54]

Exchange rate levels and volatility have been a major source of frustration for governments since the end of Bretton Woods—rarely is an economy's exchange rate at the desired level, and it never stays put if it gets there. For government officials accustomed to allocating credit and controlling domestic interest rates, like those of the MOF, intervention to stabilize exchange rates is consistent with a general distrust of markets and a belief that they can be controlled. For government officials who have experience with the financial markets and are more accustomed to rules-based rather than results-oriented government action, like those of the U.S. Treasury, intervention to stabilize exchange rates is deemed likely to be ineffectual or counterproductive.[55] Ideology appears to matter more than trade exposure in determining this outlook, as the United States some time ago became a more open (as measured by [imports+exports]/GDP) economy than Japan, and some U.S. export industries have to compete as much or more on price than some high-value-added Japanese manufactures.

The liberalization of international financial markets, starting with the lifting of capital controls in the United States in 1980 and running through deregulation of individuals' foreign exchange holdings in Japan in 1998, has prompted an explosion in the volume of daily foreign exchange transactions. The objective question of whether, under what conditions, sterilized foreign exchange rate intervention will be effective, given the size of the market, is still under debate, though most contemporary macroeconomists are skeptical.[56] For the U.S.-Japan relationship, however, the emerging American view that intervention is unlikely to produce desirable results clearly has not only limited the frequency of concerted intervention in the 1990s, it has eroded some support for exchange rate targeting in Japan.

Sakakibara describes wistfully how a series of concerted and then unilateral exchange rate interventions to weaken the yen against the dollar in 1995 and 1996 failed to have noticeable effects, and how the U.S. Treasury was reluctant to intervene even once to slow the yen's fall in June 1998.[57] *Keidanren*, the Japanese association of large businesses, has dedicated a diminishing amount of space and effort to the exchange rate issue in recent statements about desired policy. This decreasing emphasis occurred even against a backdrop of the Japanese and American governments (but not the Bank of Japan [BOJ]) seeming to agree that a weaker yen would be desirable, if linked to bank reforms. On April 5, 2001, Haruhiko Kuroda, Japan's vice minister of international finance, wrote an article that appeared in the *Asian Wall Street Journal* tying the yen's decline that month to fundamentals, and indicating that intervention would not be forthcoming.

Though political pressures from Asian neighbors opposed to yen weakness made him back off that position the next day, it was a leading indicator that the incoming Koizumi government would not be making currency moves a major part of its economic agenda.

Beliefs about financial systems also influenced the form of capital flows between the two countries over the last two decades, but asymmetrically. The core issue was over corporate governance. Japan's main bank system was one of mixed claims by stakeholders over corporate enterprises—lenders sat on corporate boards, held stock in the firm, intermediated relationships with other companies, and stepped in to change strategy or management during times of corporate distress.[58] In contrast U.S. corporate governance by outsiders had many divisions between investors and management, an absence of cross-shareholdings, an emphasis on shareholder rights and dividends to the exclusion of other stakeholders, and a combination of bankruptcy and hostile takeovers to deal with corporate distress. Amidst concerns for American competitiveness, the well-known business strategist Michael Porter, writing in the *Harvard Business Review* in 1992, was one of many to decry the "short-termism" of American management due to the emphasis on financial markets and share prices in decisionmaking. As late as 1995, Fukao could write:

> As Japanese manufacturers began to show their strength in international markets, potential problems in the governance of U.S. corporations were brought to light [for example, executive compensation, lack of monitoring]. In addition, the short time horizons of U.S. managers, the possible deleterious effects of mergers and acquisitions on the long-term viability of U.S. companies, and the massive layoffs of white-collar workers in the recession of 1991–92 all draw public attention to problems in U.S. corporate governance.[59]

One practical upshot of this state of the debate in the late 1980s and early 1990s was a generally held belief that there was little point in U.S. foreign direct investment into Japan as there was almost no possibility of American firms or partial owners successfully integrating into the web of relationships that made the Japanese economy go.

In hindsight it appears obvious that the disadvantages of American short-termism were at a minimum exaggerated, as were the advantages of Japanese relationship financing. W. Carl Kester was ahead of the curve among academic contributors to the debate (albeit now unintentionally sounding ironic), writing in 1996 that "over-investment in declining core industries, excess manpower, excess product differentiation, and speculative uses of excess cash, among other problems, appear to be at least as problematic in Japan as in the United States."[60] Today, after more than a decade of Japanese bad loans, low returns on capital, and collapsing asset values, Kester's view is commonplace.[61] Yet this view should not be dismissed as merely a matter of jumping on the bandwagon of good American economic performance relative to Japan.

The assessment of the relative advantages of various financial systems was always ultimately an empirical question, and one regarding specific predictions about the behavior of banks, securities, and nonfinancial firms— not just aggregate economic performance. The weight of analysis in recent years has been to argue that the Japanese financial system never quite performed the way it was supposed to do in theory, while American finance did function pretty much as expected once deregulation began.[62] The exodus of Japan's best businesses from bank relationships to direct financing on capital markets, and the sudden entry of questionable Japanese SMEs into ample access to loans, described in the last section of this chapter, should not have taken place if the Japanese financial system did offer in practice the benefits it was supposed to in theory.

The comparison with what occurred in the economic models debate on the side of manufacturing, as opposed to financial systems, is enlightening. At the time that U.S. businesspeople and policymakers were suffering from concerns about international competitiveness in the second half of the 1980s and the first half of the 1990s, American management practices, particularly in manufacturing, came under at least as much scrutiny as financial practices.[63] Such ideas from Japan and continental Europe as just-in-time inventory, quality circles, and team and lean production techniques, were widely adopted in American companies. Japanese home country plants as well as factories under Japanese ownership or management in the United States were visited and studied in detail as models. While widespread calls for change in American financial practices were in the end largely ignored in terms of American policy or business decisions, at least as difficult and costly changes were made adopting foreign high-performance work organizations. Also unlike on the financial side, these changes in American manufacturing and work organization have persisted and spread in the last decade, even as overall U.S. economic performance began to exceed that of Japan.[64] It would be too much of a Whig interpretation of history to suggest that the more economically sensible idea always eventually wins in the market of decisionmaking. Nevertheless, this comparative spread of the

Japanese manufacturing model and the American financial model, affected but not determined by relative macroeconomic performance in the two countries, does give credence to the presumption that learning does take place among both business practitioners and economic researchers.

The real world upshot for U.S.-Japan relations of this intellectual victory by the end of the 1990s for arm's-length, market-based finance has been profound, and is still gaining momentum. One aspect has been the growth in recent years of FDI into Japan, even as the overall world market has been betting on American domestic production and investing accordingly. This has been matched by policies proposed by the Japanese Ministry of Economy, Trade, and Industry, and calls from domestic interest groups in Japan, to make further changes in corporate governance to encourage and accommodate inward investment, including mergers and acquisitions. In the early 1990s Japanese multinationals set up foreign subsidiaries to deal with matching U.S. accounting rules and insider trading constraints, until Japanese regulations on consolidated accounting caught up with U.S. practice in 1998. Cross-shareholdings have begun to be unwound, following a METI-sponsored law in 1999 to make it easier for both banks and non-banks to sell off reciprocal equity without running into prohibitive capital gains. American investors have come to believe that they can in some instances discern the value and connections of Japanese businesses and acquire effective control, and venture funds in Japan have grown as a result.[65]

This increased flow in FDI and convergence in approaches to corporate governance has two related effects. First, it has created new domestic private sector lobbies in each country, as well as splits within the Japanese and U.S. governments, that can form transnational alliances for particular policies.[66] So on the Japanese side, the leadership of Sony Corporation has publicly pushed for the addition of outside directors to Japanese corporate boards and the pursuit of shareholder value. Also, Keidanren has called repeatedly for changes in the 100-year-old commercial code to allow share repurchases by companies, which would also increase the friendliness of Japanese financial markets to American merger and acquisition activity. These efforts have been backed by METI, while the MOF has been silent or opposed. On the American side, there has begun to be a meaningful version of the China lobby on Japanese trade issues; that is, American firms with enough investment over the wall in Japan to have an interest in directly opposing protectionist tendencies in Congress or the U.S. administration. For example, American insurance companies have taken a significant share of the Japanese auto insurance market, and American auto firms have extensive stakes in Japanese producers, and these new interests have changed the tone and terms of the current auto parts negotiations.[67]

The second impact has been on the bilateral trade agenda between the United States and Japan, particularly in terms of American agenda setting. With the rising credibility of inward FDI as a factor, the American priorities have shifted since the mid-1990s in terms of types of goals and sectors pursued, to holding negotiations on sectors such as finance and telecommunications that will leverage structural change in Japan. This is to be distinguished from sectors for negotiation being chosen because of either their perceived strategic significance to the American economy[68] or because of their politically charged visibility as constituting a sizable share of the bilateral trade imbalance.[69] The ultimate goal of the policy is to increase sustainable Japanese growth for the sake of international financial stability and broad foreign policy goals from the U.S.-Japan alliance, not to reduce the bilateral trade deficit per se.

This recent policy shift reflects a fundamental change in ideational and interest group factors likely to last, driven by financial factors, and so far seeming to transcend parties.[70] Current Bush administration U.S. Trade Representative Robert Zoellick has pointed to the negotiations conducted over NTT access charges by former Clinton administration Deputy U.S. Trade Representative Richard Fisher in late 2000 as an example of what should be done in the future. This was clearly an instance where the change bargained for was likely to help Japan grow, help Japanese businesses become more competitive, and not going to cause an immediate large-scale boost in Japanese imports of American goods. Keidanren and METI both publicly supported reductions in access charges as the negotiations went on, despite the Japanese Ministry of Posts and Telecommunications' strong opposition. The Laura Tyson–chaired Council on Foreign Relations Task Force on U.S.-Japan Economic Relations, which, though bipartisan, was popularly seen as a blueprint for Japan policy if there would have been a Gore administration, conveyed much the same message:

> Two broad areas of reform should be a major focus of economic dialogue between the American and Japanese governments during the next several years—reforms that improve the [Japanese] climate for direct investment and financial market reforms affecting how capital is raised and allocated [by Japanese businesses]. [71]

The Institute for National Strategic Studies Special Report of October 2000, known as the Armitage-Nye Report, also bipartisan but popularly seen as a blueprint for Japan policy in the Bush administration, shared the fundamental message that what was good for Japanese economic growth would be in American national interests, without the trade balance being a major factor to take into account.[72] Bush administration Treasury Secretary Paul O'Neill picked up on the progrowth rhetoric for Japan in his first months in office, and emphasized cross-national outreach to private-sector leaders in Japanese business as another source for convergence. Going forward, this finance and FDI driven agenda is one with a more clearly win-win economic attitude, with much less likelihood for trade tension between the United States and Japan, with a much larger role hoped for from nonstate actors, and with much different priorities for what changes in Japanese economic structure would be considered desirable by the United States.

Impact on U.S.-Japan Relations

Since financial deregulation began in the United States, the effect of financial liberalization and convergence in the United States and Japan on the two countries' relationship has been mixed. In the last twenty years, there has been extensive financial deregulation in both countries, enormous growth of international capital markets, and of overall financial flows between the United States and Japan. As well there has been an increase in investors and corporations on both sides of the Pacific taking advantage of market liberalization. Yet there were many areas where financial change had little impact. Instances of Japan or the United States exerting direct leverage on the basis of financial advantage upon the other on overall economic policy, let alone on broader security issues, are unavailable. The much watched sizable Japanese holdings of U.S. Treasury bills and notes proved to have little influence on U.S. behavior, or even on U.S.-Japan tensions, as they waxed and waned. Considering the more cooperative aspects of the relationship, banking and other financial regulators failed to learn from each other's mistakes, and often failed to communicate with each other, despite the existence of an international framework for so doing. Exchange rate management became far less frequent and concerted since the late 1980s, even as the volatility of the yen-dollar exchange rate increased (though the causality may have run from the latter to the former).

Still, the increasing intellectual consensus that convergence on the U.S. financial system does reflect beneficial (if disruptive) economic forces has caused a marked shift in the agenda for U.S.-Japan economic relations more narrowly defined. This shift can be dated from when Japan's banking system breakdown became publicly apparent, in the *jūsen* mini-crisis of 1995 through the present day. Underlying this intellectual flow has been a significant increase in the willingness of both countries' multinational corporations and banks, as well as of American (if not Japanese) savers, to bear market risks for the sake of large efficiency gains. A key marker of this development has been the expansion of American FDI into Japan, particularly in the financial sector, after decades of Japan taking in little or no FDI, and the MOF precluding any entry, domestic or foreign, into the Japanese financial system. Japan's inability to resolve its financial difficulties—such that they visibly exceeded the cost and duration of the 1980s U.S. S&L collapse, and that they were allowed to persist during and impede resolution of the Asian financial crisis—underscored the partial nature of its financial liberalization and the cost to Japanese national interests of leaving matters unfinished.

This dating of a surge in the importance and acceptance of financial convergence is essentially coincident with the emergence of the American New Economy of the late 1990s, and the paying down of the United States public debt. One could claim that the shift in behavior toward inward FDI by Japanese companies, or in agenda from trade opening to growth and financial stability among American officials, really is just another reflection of changing relative growth perceptions overall. Yet as discussed earlier, the persistence in the United States of Japanese models for manufacturing long after the relative decline in Japanese growth, indicates that the specific case for financial convergence rather than some general American triumphalism is at work here, as does the apparent irrelevance of Japanese Treasuries holdings.

The intellectual battle is likely to be as settled as such battles ever are over the course of the next year or two. As can be seen in figure 8-4, which plots the Nikkei and Dow Jones stock averages, it can be argued that the United States ran up as much of a bubble in stock prices in the late 1990s as Japan did in the late 1980s. It has been a repeated question from Japanese press and politicians—what will happen to the U.S. economy when their bubble bursts? It is already being seen that a securitized, less-bank-dependent, more liquid, and risk-taking financial system does not transmit financial shocks with the same persistence to the real economy that a less diversified, collateral-based, less liquid system does. Instead of feedback from asset prices on

Figure 8-4. *Performance of Dow Jones and Nikkei Stock Indexes, 1980–2000*

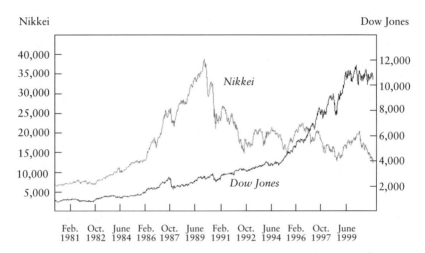

Source: For Dow Jones (http://finance.yahoo.com/m1?u); for Nikkei (http://finance.yahoo.com/m2?u).

lending and credit in a never-ending cycle as Japan has experienced, the United States is having rapid sell-offs and reallocation of capital.

The substantive impact on the U.S.-Japan relationship to date of this recent acceleration of financial convergence is clear. On the Japanese side:

—support for financial convergence grew;

—private-sector lobbying for changes in the laws affecting corporate governance increased;

—receptivity to American FDI expanded;

—nongovernmental allies for American advocates of financial change gained strength.

On the American side this convergence encouraged:

—a new prioritization of economic policies toward Japan;

—bilateral negotiations for trade and regulatory liberalization focused on areas relevant to Japan's investment climate instead of those traditionally seen as more linked to the bilateral trade deficit;

—the U.S. Treasury's increased willingness to put on pressure and, if necessary, accept higher tensions for restoring financial stability in Japan, even as trade disputes receded;

—American financial firms' sudden lobbying on U.S.-Japan issues, largely in favor of reducing tensions where possible.

In general, for both countries traditional trade disputes receded in importance even as the bilateral trade deficit expanded, and on the financial side efforts moved toward setting rules of the game for domestic actors rather than negotiating numerical outcomes.[73]

Is this change likely to persist, or will some form of political backlash turn it around despite the intellectual momentum behind the trend?[74] There certainly is resistance in some powerful parts of Japan to further financial liberalization, especially as it would compel closures of some politically connected businesses and rising unemployment transitionally. At the time this chapter was written, the Japanese Financial Services Agency was escalating a dispute with the American-owned and managed Shinsei Bank. The Japanese regulator wanted the American bank to support failed borrowers, which by the bank's criterion should be cut off. [75] Off the record, some Japanese officials and business representatives have responded to calls for increased U.S. FDI in the banking sector as part of a conspiracy to buy Japanese assets at fire-sale prices.[76]

The pace of implementing agreed upon liberalization is also up for grabs, and the reluctance to decisively deal with the current banking crisis is widespread, even among advocates of banking reform. With regard to the U.S. and IMF response to the Asian financial crisis of 1997–98, Japan and many of its neighbors feel abused or ignored by American policymakers and by financial markets. To the extent that advocacy of financial liberalization is seen as American triumphalism, disregarding the earlier success stories of Asian growth, and is conflated with acknowledged IMF mistakes in the handling of specific structural adjustment programs or in sequencing capital account liberalization, there is the potential for intellectual counterarguments. In the United States there are critics as well. Some public interest nongovernmental organizations (NGOs) are committed to opposing globalization, for ideological or cynical reasons. Japan bashers are alive and well in the Congress, very concerned about the bilateral trade deficit, U.S. market access in specific industries, and the protection of constituent businesses and workers. Between these two is the potential for an alliance against exporting the American financial model and American FDI to Japan.

Though they may make for a prolonged and volatile transition, these forces for backlash are unlikely to win out over the basic economic factors at work. The Japanese government faces an imminent choice between managing a controlled implosion of its financial system or outright financial crisis.[77] A controlled implosion would entail announcing and enforcing a write-off of the 20-plus percent of GDP in bad loans currently held by the Japanese banking system; recognizing that numerous bankruptcies of SMEs will result; shutting down or consolidating undercapitalized banks; recapitalizing those that remain; and selling off the accumulated collateral (mostly real estate) from defaulted borrowers—in short a radical shrinking of the Japanese banking system with convergence on the U.S. model.[78] As described above, the primary problem with Japanese banking has been the inability to force banks to exit as most good borrowers and some savers have left the system. Until exit is forced, the bad loans problem and the low returns to capital throughout the Japanese economy, as well as the drag on consumption from uncertainties about asset prices and job security, will persist.[79] Alternatively, an outright financial crisis in Japan would mean noticeable capital flight, a sharp decline in the value of the yen and of Japanese financial assets, the removal of savings and capital from the Japanese banking system, and a difficult to arrest spiral downward in Japanese investment and growth.[80]

The alternative of muddling through is no longer available to the Japanese government precisely because of the partial financial deregulation and international capital market integration they have already undertaken. There simply is too much American and liquid Japanese capital ready to leave Japan quickly should returns collapse or financial transparency be reversed. In fact the Japanese government has set up its own deadline by its commitment to enforcing mark-to-market accounting on the banks for the fiscal year ending March 31, 2002. This will conclusively reveal the extent of the banks' capital losses and weak loan portfolios. Of course, the regulators could renege on this commitment, but such a renege would be so obvious and clearly motivated by fear that it might prompt the very crisis they are trying to avoid.

It is evident that the events of September 11, 2001, have postponed this day of reckoning both by making some Japanese investors less willing to hold dollars and by giving Japanese officials an excuse on which to blame the current low ebb of the Japanese stock market. Still, these delays will only open up further the gap between returns accruing to Japanese savers and the higher returns with lower risks in the United States and elsewhere. Somehow this would be arbitraged, unless the Japanese government further ramps up its public debt to make up the difference, but that too would eventually provoke a financial crisis through a fiscal channel. Meanwhile, more months with bad loans accumulating and Japanese asset prices falling make it likely that a major bank or two will fail despite the government's best efforts, and visibly add to the government's bill—if, as has historically been the case, the dollar returns to strength once military action proves successful (and as of year-end 2001, the yen was declining against the dollar), this will remove the other brake on the process of forced liberalization through crisis.

No matter how and when exactly such a financial crisis hits Japan in the next couple years, it will force the inward FDI, if not the outright leveraged buyout, of the Japanese financial sector by American capital and financial management. There will be no one else with the money, the skills, or the appetite for risk to salvage the system—and the assets of Japan will be available in a fire sale. So either by choice, or by crisis, Japan will complete its financial convergence upon the U.S. model, with all the long-term effects to ease tensions and decentralize foreign policy decisions in the U.S.-Japan economic arena discussed here. Unfortunately, if the transition to that situation of congruence is made through a Japanese financial crisis, the intervening spillovers on the security relationship from U.S.-Japan financial convergence as well as on the world economy will likely be quite large. Both the Japanese and U.S. governments may come to regret their mutual decision in September 2001 to put Japanese national security cooperation ahead of financial convergence (and therefore reform pressure on Japan)—what seems like a close alliance today may just demonstrate that it is a false priority to make Japan's primary contribution to the U.S.-Japan relationship come on the security rather than the economic front.

Notes

1. In the language of the introduction to this volume, the general picture is one of tension (instead of harmony), but more cooperation than conflict in terms of results, although there were mutual gains missed.

2. Suzanne Berger, "Introduction," in Suzanne Berger and Ronald Dore, eds., *National Diversity and Global Capitalism* (Cornell University Press, 1996). This piece notes (skeptically) that convergence might occur because of economic opportunism and competitive deregulation, open borders and markets, belief in liberal ideas, or direct international pressures on countries and domestic demands. For a different set of arguments why national models will fail to converge overall, see also Adam S. Posen, *Restoring Japan's Economic Growth* (Institute for International Economics, 1998), chap. 6.

3. See Frances McCall Rosenbluth, *Financial Politics in Contemporary Japan* (Cornell University Press, 1989), and Steven K. Vogel, *Freer Markets, More Rules: Regulatory Reforms in Advanced Industrial Countries* (Cornell University Press, 1996), for two somewhat opposing interpretations that agree this is a test case for globalization and for its effect on domestic political economy.

4. Adam S. Posen, "Japan 2001—Decisive Action or Financial Panic," *IIE Policy Brief 01-4* (Institute for International Economics, 2001), explains why the banking system is likely to have an overt crisis in Japan, though partial policy responses in the past have averted or delayed such an outcome.

5. Chapter 5 by Schoppa in this volume illustrates how greater tensions in domestic politics over the Japanese or American government's stance on a given issue can still lead to increased cooperation as a result.

6. Though, in this issue area, financial developments still leave the United States relatively advantaged versus Japan.

7. Benjamin Friedman, "Japan Now and the United States Then: Lessons from the Parallels," in Ryōichi Mikitani and Adam S. Posen, eds., *Japan's Financial Crisis and Its Parallels to U.S. Experience* (Institute for International Economics, 2000).

8. Friedman, "Japan Now and the United States Then."

9. Robert Glauber and Anil Kashyap, "Discussions of the Financial Crisis," in Ryōichi Mikitani and Adam S. Posen, eds., *Japan's Financial Crisis and Its Parallels to the U.S. Experience* (Institute for International Economics, 2000).

10. See Shijurō Ogata, "Financial Markets in Japan," in Suzanne Berger and Ronald Dore, eds., *National Diversity and Global Capitalism* (Cornell University Press, 1996). Takeo Hoshi and Anil Kashyap, *Corporate Financing and Governance in Japan: The Road to the Future* (Massachusetts Institute of Technology Press, 2001), give a provocative historical argument that many of these attributes, and the whole *keiretsu*-Main Bank system in Japan, was a recent, partly American creation.

11. Benn Steil, *Illusions of Liberalization: Securities Regulation in Japan and the EC* (London: Royal Institute of International Affairs, 1995).

12. Vogel, *Freer Markets, More Rules.*

13. Friedman, "Japan Now and the United States Then," p. 41, notes that until 1995 on the official records no Japanese bank had an operating loss, a patently unbelievable situation.

14. Steil, *Illusions of Liberalization,* and Vogel, *Freer Markets, More Rules.*

15. Ogata, "Financial Markets in Japan."

16. Steil, *Illusions of Liberalization.*

17. Yoshinori Shimizu, "Convoy Regulation, Bank Management, and the Financial Crisis in Japan," in Ryōichi Mikitani and Adam S. Posen, eds., *Japan's Financial Crisis and Its Parallels to U.S. Experience* (Institute for International Economics, 2000).

18. Thomas Cargill, Michael Hutchison, and Takatoshi Itō, *Financial Policy and Central Banking in Japan* (Massachusetts Institute of Technology Press, 2000), p. 53.

19. What is interesting and frustrating, naturally, is that Japanese regulators appeared to learn nothing from the mistakes made in the United States, despite explicit attempts to communicate those. This point is revisited later in this chapter.

20. Posen, *Restoring Japan's Economic Growth,* chap. 4, describes the situation and its dynamics at the time.

21. Jennifer Holt Dwyer, "U.S.-Japan Financial Market Relations in an Era of Global Finance," in Gerald Curtis, ed., *New Perspectives on U.S.-Japan Relations* (Japan Center for International Exchange, 2000).

22. Steil, *Illusions of Liberalization.*

23. Borrowers that are not as good are unlikely to have access to international capital markets, and likely to be dependent upon loans from their local bank.

24. This appears to be a tiny fraction of the outstanding bank liabilities, but the equity number is a monthly flow whereas the bank liabilities are an outstanding stock.

25. American Chamber of Commerce in Japan (ACCJ), *U.S.-Japan Business White Paper 2001* (Tokyo, 2001). Among the G-7, the next highest ratio of FDI outflow-to-inflow is 2.8 for Germany, while all the rest of the G-7 members are below 1.5.

26. No figures are available on how many of these are held by Americans as opposed to other foreigners.

27. In a speech on June 23, 1997, at Columbia University, then Prime Minister Ryūtarō Hashimoto said Japan had been tempted to sell U.S. Treasuries and buy gold on a number of occasions, mostly arising when the United States failed to stabilize exchange rates. In an editorial in the *Financial Times* the next day, this remark was characterized as a "veiled threat."

28. Vogel, *Freer Markets, More Rules*, and Steil, *Illusions of Liberalization*, argue that through the mid-1990s the power and preferences of Japanese (mostly MOF) bureaucrats determined a uniquely Japanese form of financial liberalization which included persistent or re-regulation. For purposes of this chapter, however, the broad similarities of pressures on both the Japanese and American banking systems, the similar rise of securitized corporate finance, the common experience of financial crisis and regulatory forbearance in response, and the enhancements in information and access available to investors constitute essentially the same process of liberalization.

29. Grimes's chapter in this volume describes this reversal of macroeconomic performance.

30. See Green, and other chapters in this volume.

31. C. Randall Henning, "U.S.-Japan Macroeconomic Relations in the Last Three Decades of the Twentieth Century" (Institute for International Economics, 2000).

32. Dwyer, "U.S.-Japan Financial Market Relations in an Era of Global Finance," notes that Japanese financial regulators in New York have offices across the street from the Federal Reserve Bank of New York, implying that there is an easy neighborliness between the two.

33. Steil, *Illusions of Liberalization*.

34. Anil Kashyap, "Discussions of the Financial Crisis," in Ryōichi Mikitani and Adam S. Posen, eds., *Japan's Financial Crisis and Its Parallels to U.S. Experience* (Institute for International Economics, 2000).

35. Ring-fencing means increasing supervisory scrutiny and discouraging other banks from having unreserved exposure to the banks under monitoring. Exclusion from the discount window forces the Bank of Japan (in this case) to provide upfront the extra liquidity for the U.S. operations of these banks. Both of these measures significantly constrain the ability of banks to conduct business.

36. Adam S. Posen, "Introduction: Financial Similarities and Monetary Differences," in Ryōichi Mikitani and Adam S. Posen, eds., *Japan's Financial Crisis and Its Parallels to U.S. Experience* (Institute for International Economics, 2000), pp. 7–8. This is a mainstream view in economics. Cargill, Hutchison, and Ito, *Financial Policy and Central Banking in Japan*; Friedman, "Japan Now and the United States Then"; Glauber and Kashyap, "Discussions of the Financial Crisis"; Hoshi and Kashyap, *Corporate Financing and Governance in Japan*; and Shimizu, "Convoy Regulation, Bank Management, and the Financial Crisis in Japan," all make similar assessments.

37. See the references in Friedman, "Japan Now and the United States Then," and Glauber and Kashyap, "Discussions of the Financial Crisis," for some of the criticism of U.S. mistakes.

38. The various annual publications of the American-dominated IMF and the Organization for Economic Cooperation and Development were quite explicit on these points, including references to past U.S. errors.

39. Eisuke Sakakibara, "U.S.-Japanese Economic Policy Conflicts and Coordination during the 1990s," in Ryōichi Mikitani and Adam S. Posen, eds., *Japan's Financial Crisis and Its Parallels to U.S. Experience* (Institute for International Economics, 2000), p. 181.

40. Ibid., p. 182. Interestingly, though Sakakibara is on record in numerous places as an advocate of exchange rate intervention as a policy tool, he admits that most of the interventions of the 1990s failed to have the desired or any lasting effect.

41. Ibid. Sakakibara claims that this reform was only possible because the U.S. government became more pragmatic following the Russian bond default and the Long-Term Capital Man-

agement collapse bringing the crisis home. He blames the U.S. puritanism on bank reform for the Japanese public's reluctance to inject public capital into the banks. Jeffrey Shafer, "The International Aspects of Japanese Monetary Policy," in Ryōichi Mikitani and Adam S. Posen, eds., *Japan's Financial Crisis and Its Parallels to U.S. Experience* (Institute for International Economics, 2000), strenuously contradicts this view of U.S. government intentions.

42. Shafer, "International Aspects of Japanese Monetary Policy," among others, recalls the disappointment that American officials felt in 1996–97 having their private advice to the MOF not to raise the consumption tax ignored. This experience may have contributed to some of the public tack and tone emerging from the U.S. Treasury for changes in Japanese policy in the late 1990s, though the pressures from the Asian crisis were obviously the main factor.

43. Council on Foreign Relations, 2000, *Task Force Report: Future Direction for U.S. Economic Policy toward Japan* (www.cfr.org/p/pubs/Japan_TaskForce.html), appendix.

44. Catherine Mann, *Is the U.S. Trade Deficit Sustainable?* (Institute for International Economics, 1999), goes so far as to suggest that liberalization of financial and other business services, allowing for more exports from the United States, would significantly reduce the overall U.S. trade deficit.

45. This was clearly recognized as a possibility as early as the 1983 yen-dollar talks. See Henning, "U.S.-Japan Macroeconomic Relations in the Last Three Decades of the Twentieth Century," among others, for more recent discussions emphasizing the low returns to capital.

46. A concentration ratio of market share among the top five companies would be 60 percent in both life and nonlife.

47. This summary draws on the Insurance entry in ACCJ, *U.S.-Japan Business White Paper 2001*. Steven Vogel notes that once U.S. firms did dominate the third insurance sector, the U.S. government argued that Japan should not liberalize that sector before liberalizing the rest of the insurance market. This had some economic logic, but politically was viewed in Japan as an instance of hypocrisy by the United States (with some justification).

48. In fact it is another widely held myth that the American call for Japanese macroeconomic expansion at the time of the Louvre Accord led to the Japanese asset price bubble. Leaving aside the contradiction between these two myths about which nation had influence as U.S. public debt rose, this blaming of the bubble on U.S. pressure is unjustified. Suffice it to say that it is far from obvious that U.S. pressure produced the specific BOJ monetary policies held responsible for the bubble (given the timing), that those scapegoated monetary policies actually caused the bubble (given the fundamentals), and that the bubble had to have the impact it did on the Japanese economy (given transmission mechanisms). See Henning, "U.S.-Japan Macroeconomic Relations"; Toshiki Jinushi, Yoshihiro Kuroki, and Ryuzo Miyao, "Monetary Policy in Japan since the Late 1980s: Delayed Policy Actions and Some Explanations," in Ryōichi Mikitani and Adam S. Posen, eds., *Japan's Financial Crisis and Its Parallels to U.S. Experience* (Institute for International Economics, 2000); and Kashyap, "Discussions of the Financial Crisis."

49. Edward Graham and Paul Krugman, *Foreign Direct Investment in the United States, Third Edition* (Institute for International Economics, 1997).

50. Matthew Higgins and Clive Walcott, *Global Capital Flows: Capital Appears Ready to Flow Back into Japanese Equities* (Merrill Lynch, May 21, 2001).

51. The FSA made sure to sell off the other nationalized major Japanese bank, the former NCB, to a domestic purchaser, for example, even though there was a valid foreign bid.

52. Chapter 3 by Grimes in this volume ties lagged perceptions of macroeconomic performance to broader U.S.-Japan relations.

53. The economic recommendations proffered to emerging markets by the IMF and World Bank, and the course of Asian monetary cooperation, are also affected by the perceived relative benefits of the American and Japanese financial systems. Chapter 7 by Searight in this volume addresses these two points from an international institutions perspective, emphasizing the institutions' independent role in forming these outcomes.

54. This is quite clearly the opposite outcome of the debate over the means of industrial production, where the Japanese model has largely remained triumphant, even as Japanese growth has receded.

55. Though even some American officials will be sympathetic to the view that exchange rate levels and volatility can (damagingly) diverge from values justified by fundamentals, they are less likely to believe anything can be done about it. See Richard H. Clarida, "G3 Exchange Rate Relationships: A Recap of the Record and a Review of Proposals for Change," Working Paper 7434 (Cambridge, Mass.: National Bureau of Economic Research, December 1999); and C. Randall Henning, *Currencies and Politics in the United States, Germany, and Japan* (Institute for International Economics, 1994).

56. Taylor (2000) is a recent, econometrically sophisticated argument that sterilized intervention does work for the most part. Kathryn Dominguez and Jeffrey Frankel, *Does Foreign Exchange Intervention Work?* (Institute for International Economics, 1993) is the standard work indicating that only unsterilized intervention, that is, backed by the promise of domestic monetary policy changes, will succeed.

57. Sakakibara, "U.S.-Japanese Economic Policy Conflicts and Coordination."

58. The literature on this subject is vast. For reasonably balanced economic treatments, see Hoshi and Kashyap, *Corporate Financing and Governance in Japan*; Mitsuhiro Fukao, *Financial Integration, Corporate Governance, and the Performance of Multinational Companies* (Brookings, 1995); and W. Carl Kester, "Industrial Groups as Contractual Governance Systems," *Oxford Review of Economic Policy*, vol. 8, no. 2 (Autumn 1992), pp. 24–44.

59. Fukao, *Financial Integration, Corporate Governance, and the Performance of Multinational Companies*, p. 3.

60. W. Carl Kester, "American and Japanese Corporate Governance: Convergence to Best Practice?" in Suzanne Berger and Ronald Dore, eds., *National Diversity and Global Capitalism* (Cornell University Press, 1996), p. 123. To be fair to Fukao, in *Financial Integration, Corporate Governance, and the Performance of Multinational Companies*, he predicted (p. 69) as well that reallocation of capital and labor to new opportunities from declining industries, for example, would be more efficient under American-style corporate governance than under the Japanese system.

61. Among many others, see: *Why the Japanese Economy Is Not Growing* (McKinsey Global Institute Reports, July 2000); Richard Katz, *Japan: The System That Soured* (M. E. Sharpe, 1998); and David L. Asher and Robert H. Dugger, "Could Japan's Financial Mount Fuji Blow Its Top?" Working Paper 00-01 (MIT Japan Program, web.mit.edu/mit-japan/Products/wp00-01.html).

62. Again, Hoshi and Kashyap, *Corporate Financing and Governance in Japan*, collects much of the research to date. Recently, some authors have begun to speak of Japan's economic success in the entire postwar period as coming despite its financial system, and the U.S. financial system making up for other weaknesses in education and labor markets. See Posen, *Restoring Japan's Economic Growth*, chap. 6, for references, particularly to the work of David Weinstein and his coauthors.

63. See, for example, Stephen Cohen and John Zysman, *Manufacturing Matters: The Myth of the Post-Industrial Economy* (Basic Books, 1987); Michael Dertouzos, Richard Lester, and Robert Solow, *Made in America: Regaining the Productive Edge* (Massachusetts Institute of Technology Press, 1989); Eileen Appelbaum and Rosemary Batt, *The New American Workplace: Transforming Work Systems in the United States* (Cornell University Press, 1994).

64. Sandra Black and Lisa Lynch, "What's Driving the New Economy: The Benefits of Workplace Innovation," Working Paper 7479 (Cambridge, Mass.: National Bureau of Economic Research, 2000); Jessica Cohen, William Dickens, and Adam S. Posen, "Have New Human Resource Management Practices Lowered the Sustainable Employment Rate?" in Alan Krueger and Robert Solow, eds., *The Roaring 90s* (New York: Russell Sage, 2002); and Paul

Osterman, "Work Reorganization in an Era of Destruction: Trends in Diffusion and Effects on Employee Welfare," *Industrial and Labor Relations Review*, vol. 53, no. 2 (1998), pp. 179–96.

65. New venture capital funds include investments by Chase, GE Capital (on its own and in conjunction with Sumitomo Bank), Goldman Sachs, Soros, and Warburg Pincus. Gratitude to Bowman Cutter for discussion of the changing American investors' perspective to amplify the quantitative data.

66. Robert Z. Lawrence "How Open is Japan?" in Paul Krugman, ed., *Trade with Japan: Has the Door Opened Wider?* (University of Chicago Press, 1991); Helen Milner, *Interests, Institutions, and Information* (Princeton University Press, 1994); and Schoppa, "The Social Context in Coercive International Bargaining," all give theoretical perspectives on and examples of such alliances.

67. ACCJ, *U.S.-Japan Business White Paper 2001*.

68. This volume's chapter 9 on technology by Vogel and Zysman details how such sectors as semiconductors became points of conflict because the United States wanted to keep them alive domestically.

69. None of this denies that some trade disputes, antidumping cases, and political tensions between the United States and Japan will be driven by traditional protectionist lobbies. The main concern here is what is the desired and likely agenda among trade policymakers on both sides of the Pacific within the realm of their discretion that remains after legislators' constituent interests are met.

70. Not discussed here is the learning (and frustration) felt by many American participants in previous U.S.-Japan trade negotiations, such as the SII talks, which also has fed this shift.

71. Council on Foreign Relations, *Task Force Report: Future Direction for U.S. Economic Policy toward Japan* (2000). See www.cfr.org/p/pubs/japan_taskforce.html. In the spirit of full disclosure, the author of this chapter was a signatory to the task force report and contributed to the drafting of the document.

72. National Defense University, *The United States and Japan: Advancing toward a Mature Partnership* (Washington: Institute for National Strategic Studies Special Report, October 2000). See www.ndu.edu/ndu/sr_japan.htm.

73. When financial matters were first made a significant part of the U.S.-Japan trade agenda, they were either specified in terms of American market share like other sectors, or they were seen as instrumental to getting Japanese imports up and the trade deficit down. Looking forward, the financial issues will be largely specified in terms of changes in Japanese domestic regulation as instrumental to increasing Japanese growth, without explicit trade targets. Such a move toward rulemaking is itself consistent with the general thrust of deregulation in the American style (see Vogel, *Freer Markets, More Rules*) and therefore with convergence.

74. Gratitude to Daniel Tarullo for forcing the consideration of this possibility.

75. FSA Commissioner Shōji Mori told Shinsei Chief Executive Officer Yasuhiro Masamoto that Shinsei "should behave in line with other Japanese banks." See Jason Singer and Phred Dovrak, "Japan Begins Pressing Shinsei to Lend to Shakiest Borrowers," *Asian Wall Street Journal*, September 26, 2001, p. 1.

76. While not at liberty to cite the officials and dates, the author of this chapter has personally been accused in meetings of participating in such a conspiracy since the release of a working paper version of this chapter and the publication of an op-ed advocating inward FDI. See Robert E. Litan and Adam S. Posen, "Open Japan's Banking Industry," *Asian Wall Street Journal*, August 10, 2001, p. 6.

77. Posen, "Japan 2001—Decisive Action or Financial Panic."

78. This would of course have a short-term contradictory effect on the Japanese economy, but it also is necessary to return to sustainable growth, and is better than the alternative. Fiscal and monetary policy can be used to offset the deflationary impact. See Posen, "Japan 2001—Decisive Action or Financial Panic."

79. Kashyap, "Discussions of the Financial Crisis," p. 109: "Throughout the 1990s, the major Japanese banks were simultaneously among the largest banks in the world, and the least profitable. This situation cannot continue much longer . . . at this point, the banks have virtually no competitive advantage vis-à-vis the other global banks; put differently, it is hard to think of a product or service line in which the Japanese banks could compete head-to-head with the world leaders and win much business."

80. Posen, *Restoring Japan's Economic Growth*, chap. 4, sets out the economic logic of such a crisis in detail, and how 1997–98 teetered on the brink of such an occurrence.

CHAPTER NINE

Technology

STEVEN K. VOGEL AND
JOHN ZYSMAN

In thirty-odd years Japan rose from military devastation to technological leadership. By the 1980s analysts, academics, and commissions on both sides of the Pacific proclaimed that Japan had surpassed the United States in many areas of high technology, and Japanese manufacturers were outperforming their American competitors in world markets in high technology as well as in televisions and automobiles.[1] Japan's rise as a technological power had a profound impact on the American psyche, fueling a public debate over American decline, prodding the government to revamp trade and industrial policies, forcing industry to revise strategies, and provoking a political backlash against Japan. It shifted the U.S.-Japan trade agenda toward high technology, and generated some of the most heated bilateral disputes of the postwar period.

Yet a funny thing happened just as Americans and Japanese were both declaring Japan's victory in a bitter battle for technological leadership—the Americans mounted a comeback. This reversal of fortune transformed the bilateral agenda once again, but this time the transition eased bilateral tensions as the two countries reverted to their comfortable postwar roles of leader and follower.

This chapter addresses two sets of questions. First, how can these shifts in technological leadership be explained? How does one account for the Japanese challenge and the U.S. resurgence, and what should be expected for the future? Second, how do technological advances and changes in technological leadership affect U.S.-Japan relations? How have they shaped bilateral relations over the past fifty years, and how are they likely to redefine these relations in the years to come?[2]

National Institutions and Technological Advantage

In addressing the first set of questions, this chapter builds on two basic propositions about how national institutions interact with technological change. First, it contends that technological change in the postwar era should not be viewed as exogenous to U.S. institutions, to Japanese institutions, or to the rivalry between the United States and Japan. For small countries with limited technological capabilities, it makes sense to view technological change as an external force to which government and market actors must respond. But the United States and Japan are themselves drivers of technological change, just as much as they are in turn affected by it. Moreover, the U.S.-Japan rivalry has profoundly affected the evolution of technology in both countries and in the world. U.S. technological leadership provided the foundation for Japan's technology challenge; Japan's challenge fueled America's technological resurgence; and the U.S.-Japan rivalry has propelled both countries further ahead of the rest of the world.

Second, this chapter contends that national governance systems strongly influence technological development, technological capability, and economic performance. National governance systems refer to the institutional arrangements that structure national political-economic systems and the market dynamics these arrangements induce.[3] These include the complex web of government policies (such as regulation or industrial policy), political institutions (political parties, bureaucratic agencies), and market institutions (financial systems, labor relations systems, interfirm networks) that together shape corporate strategies.[4]

Although the U.S. and Japanese governance systems have both evolved over the postwar period they have consistently differed in several important ways. The Japanese government does more to protect and promote domestic industry, and less to foster competition. The Japanese bureaucracy is more powerful, more centralized, and more autonomous from short-term political pressures. And the Japanese private sector is characterized by more long-term cooperative relationships between firms and labor, between firms and banks, and between different firms.[5]

National governance systems and national technological trajectories powerfully shape marketplace outcomes, but they do not determine these outcomes in any automatic way. The match or mismatch between capacities and tasks is not mechanical or simple. This chapter contends that propositions about how governance systems affect technological capability or economic performance should be viewed as contingent upon a country's stage of growth, its relationship to the international economy, its sectoral specialization, and the dominant technological paradigm at the time. When comparing the Japanese governance system to the U.S. system, for example, one cannot reach any meaningful conclusion about the overall superiority of one over the other. Instead, this chapter advances several contingent propositions. The Japanese system was more successful at the catch-up stage than at the mature stage; when the economy was insulated from international markets than when it became more exposed; in automobiles and consumer electronics than in aeronautics and software; and in the heyday of the lean production paradigm than in the Wintelist era (see discussion below).

These contingent propositions help to explain variations in U.S. and Japanese technological strength over time: specifically, Japan's rise to technological power from the 1960s through the 1980s, and the United States' resurgence since the 1990s. These shifts in technological leadership have corresponded with shifts in the dominant technological paradigm. Japanese institutions fostered the lean production paradigm that favored Japanese firms, and American institutions fostered the Wintelist paradigm that now favors American firms. Japanese institutions better fit the lean production system, while U.S. institutions better match the Wintelist era. This is no accident, of course, for Japanese and American institutions helped to foster the two paradigms in the first place.

Beyond these generalizations, this chapter disaggregates national capacities for technological development further, in two ways. First, it recognizes that the fit between governance structures and technology varies considerably across sectors. Zysman made this case with reference to France in the 1970s, and Herbert Kitschelt has applied it to Japan.[6] Kitschelt suggests that Japan excels in sectors characterized by medium to long production runs and amenable to incremental production improvements, such as office machines, appliances, consumer electronics, and electronic components. Japan lags in sectors that require huge public investments in basic research and breakthrough innovation such as aerospace, biotechnology, and software.

Second, the chapter suggests that the fit between governance structures and technology varies by function as well as by sector. That is, one can generalize that the auto sector requires incremental production improvement whereas biotechnology requires breakthrough innovation. So on balance Japanese production innovation produced a competitive advantage in automobiles, whereas American investments in science, biosciences, and science-based engineering generated an advantage in biotechnology. In practice, however, both sectors involve both sets of skills. So it may be more useful to suggest that the United States has a greater ability to: foster labor mobility; finance new ventures via equity markets; breed entrepreneurs; promote competition; support basic research; and generate breakthrough innovation. Meanwhile, Japan has a greater ability to: forge labor-management cooperation; provide stable finance via the banking system; train engineers; manage competition; and achieve incremental improvements in production. One can then apply these generalizations about advantages in functions to specific sectors or subsectors as appropriate.

Furthermore, different governance systems are not simply more or less effective in cultivating certain technological capabilities, but they shape distinct national technological trajectories. At the aggregate level, the United States and Japan have both succeeded in achieving technological leadership with very different governance systems. Even at the sectoral level, there is often more than one best practice.

These qualifications will become critical later in this chapter's assessment of Japan's ability to catch up or surpass the United States in the information technology (IT) sector. The chapter argues that U.S. institutions give the United States an advantage in many but not all of the functions important to the IT sector. Japanese institutions preclude Japan from following the American route to IT dominance, yet they could enable Japan to regain leadership via a very different trajectory of technological development.

Japanese Challenge

In the early postwar years, the U.S. government sought to help rebuild the Japanese economy so that Japan could emerge as a powerful bulwark against communism in the Pacific. It actively encouraged American firms to transfer technology to Japan and to import Japanese components. It tolerated Japanese protection while maintaining open markets at home, and ignored all but the most powerful U.S. industry demands for trade relief.

Meanwhile, American companies were willing to sell their technology to Japan because they did not view Japanese producers as a competitive threat. Most were more than happy to accept licensing and royalty payments rather than attempting to sell products directly or setting up manufacturing operations in Japan. They were not interested in trying to penetrate the Japanese market due to low expected demand and high barriers to imports and foreign direct investment. Those technology companies that did establish a major presence in Japan, such as IBM and Texas Instruments, only succeeded after negotiations with Japanese authorities in which they agreed to transfer technology in exchange for market access.[7]

U.S. industry launched its first trade complaint in a technology sector in 1959, when the Electronics Industry Association (EIA) demanded restraints on imports of low-cost Japanese transistors. The government ultimately denied the petition in 1962 on national security grounds. It judged that American firms still dominated the defense market and were fully capable of meeting a future surge in demand.[8] U.S. television manufacturers began to request trade relief in the early 1960s, and the Japanese responded by setting up an orderly marketing system to restrain exports. The U.S. government did not view Japan as a major threat in high-technology sectors until the 1980s, however, when Japan's phenomenal export success became a major source of bilateral tension.

The Japanese challenge to U.S. technological supremacy was rooted in incremental improvements in production processes, not revolutionary innovations. The shifts from U.S. to Japanese leadership and back rest on changes in the dominant production paradigm from mass production (Fordism), to lean production (the Toyota system), to a new paradigm introduced later in this chapter (Wintelism). American innovation paved the way for the Japanese challenge. In consumer electronics, the U.S. research and development system generated a series of innovations, beginning with the invention of the transistor in 1947 and continuing with routers and the foundations of the Internet.[9] Over time, however, Japanese government policy and private sector institutions interacted to generate comparative advantage in key sectors. The Japanese government policy of protection and promotion, combined with the strategic allocation of credit, drove Japanese companies toward high levels of investment, constant improvement of production processes, and ruthless competition for market share.[10] Japanese firms reformulated production and design processes into a "lean" production system that simultaneously eliminated inventories, facilitated constant quality improvements, and reduced costs. The challenge to traditional American manufacturing became an onslaught by the mid-1980s as lower and declining real costs in Japanese manufacturing combined with an overvalued dollar to fuel Japan's phenomenal export success in consumer electronics, automobiles, and high technology.[11]

American producers had difficulty responding. U.S. corporations had invested in achieving leadership in the Fordist mass-production paradigm. They were not simply reluctant to write off this investment and transfer to the next production paradigm, but they could not conceive of a new paradigm under which cost and quality were complements rather than alternatives.[12] U.S. producers gradually recognized that they could not maintain leadership through innovation alone, for the market advantages of innovation are lost if the innovating firms are not world-class producers. After a considerable lag, they finally began to adjust to the Japanese challenge, modifying domestic production systems and developing cross-national production networks.

Japan's rapid ascent to technological leadership in production not only presented the United States with a psychological shock, but also imposed some very tangible damage. In the semiconductor sector, for example, the U.S. industry reported $2 billion in losses and 25,000 lost jobs in 1985 and 1986, and almost all American producers abandoned the random access memory (RAM) business altogether. This fueled a wave of national introspection, generated enormous popular resentment, and provoked a massive political response.[13]

By the 1980s, the challenge in high-technology sectors displaced textiles and automobiles as the core agenda in U.S.-Japan trade relations. This in turn shifted the U.S. negotiating strategy from protecting the U.S. market to opening the Japanese market, and from removing overt Japanese trade barriers to addressing more structural impediments to trade. Executives in the U.S. high-technology sector had nothing but disdain for their counterparts in smokestack industries who sought protection from the government. They demanded antidumping measures and access to the Japanese market, not protection. Most U.S. government officials remained committed to a free trade line. The government was torn between an ideological commitment to free trade principles and political pressures demanding relief. Its uneasy compromise was to stake out a position in favor of free and fair trade.[14] In practice this took the form of American outrage against unfair Japanese practices. Japanese resented the Americans' moralistic tone, and felt they were simply being made scapegoats for the United States' inability to compete.

Semiconductor Accord

In the 1980s the United States and Japan sparred over trade issues in a wide range of high-technology sectors, including telecommunications equipment and supercomputers (see table 9-1).[15] The fiercest and most important battle centered on the core component for the high-technology sector, the microchip. Japanese producers achieved incremental improvements in production processes that allowed them to achieve higher yields (lower defect rates), especially in the more standardized productions such as dynamic random-access memories (DRAMs), and eventually to outpace the Americans in the race for higher memory capacity. The Japanese industry was dominated by large vertically integrated electronics firms that were both major producers and users of semiconductors. The U.S. industry, in contrast, was dominated by merchant producers who specialized in selling components and did not assemble finished electronic products themselves. IBM and AT&T, the largest users in the United States, manufactured chips for their own use but were prohibited from selling them on the open market by U.S. antitrust restrictions. The Japanese industry structure gave it several advantages: Japanese producers had deeper pockets for investing in new facilities and weathering price wars; they had the flexibility to cross-subsidize across business lines; and they had greater control over their own sales because they were major users themselves and they were linked to other users through industrial group (keiretsu) ties. In effect, Japan's top electronic firms could shut out American producers from the Japanese market by producing their own semiconductors and leveraging relationships with keiretsu affiliates.[16]

The Japanese semiconductor industry's surge in world markets in the mid-1980s (figure 9-1) generated an unprecedented political response from the United States. In 1985 the Semiconductor Industry Association (SIA) initiated a Section 301 petition against Japan for unfair trading practices; Micron Technology charged Japanese producers with dumping 64K DRAMs; the Justice Department opened an antitrust investigation into predatory pricing by Hitachi; three more U.S. companies filed dumping charges against Japanese producers of erasable programmable read-only memories (EPROMs); and the Commerce Department launched its own dumping case in 256K DRAMs.[17] The two sides then began talks designed to address these issues in a more comprehensive way, and ultimately negotiated the Semiconductor Trade Agreement of July 1986. The agreement sought to constrain Japanese producers from dumping in U.S. markets and to enhance U.S. access to the Japanese market. The Ministry of International

Table 9-1. *Major U.S.-Japan High-Technology Trade Disputes, 1980–2000*

Date	Issue and outcome	Cooperation	Tension
1980	**First NTT procurement agreement**	Low	Medium
	Opens public procurement to foreign companies		
1986	**MOSS electronics**	Medium	High
	Protects semiconductor designs, lowers tariffs, allows U.S. participation in Japanese research and development projects		
1986	**MOSS medical and pharmaceuticals**	Medium	High
	Standardizes drug approvals, clarifies pricing for reimbursements		
1986	**MOSS telecommunications**	High	High
	Allows foreign carriers to provide services over the core network		
1986	**Semiconductor trade agreement**[a]	Medium	High
	Regulates semiconductor pricing, sets target of 20% foreign market share in Japan in a side letter		
1987	**Supercomputers**	Low	Medium
	Opens bidding process		
1987–89	**FS-X codevelopment**[a]	Low	High
	Agreement to codevelop support fighter aircraft in 1987, renegotiated in 1989		
1990	**Supercomputers**	Medium	Medium
	Clarifies bidding rules		
1990	**Cellular phones**	High	Medium
	Opens Tokyo-Nagoya market, allocates spectrum for Motorola system		
1990	**Satellites**	High	Medium
	Sets procurement procedures		
1991	**Semiconductors**	Medium	Medium
	New agreement sets target of 20% foreign market access in Japan		
1991	**Liquid crystal displays**	Low	High
	Antidumping suit against Japan, imposes stiff antidumping duties		
1994	**Cellular phones**	High	High
	Nippon Idou Tsushin (IDO) agrees to add cell sites and voice channels so the Motorola-based system can expand service		
2000	**NTT interconnection agreement**[a]	High	Low
	Lowers interconnection fees by 20% over two years		

a. Case study is covered in this chapter.

Trade and Industry (MITI) would encourage Japanese producers to price according to cost and monitor Japanese pricing practices, and the two governments would take prompt action if they found dumping. In effect MITI seized control over the industry and established a price floor for semicon-

Figure 9-1. *Worldwide Semiconductor Market Share, 1982–2000*

Percent

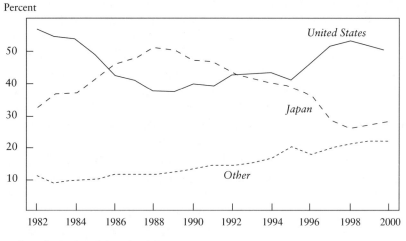

Source: Semiconductor Industry Association.

ductors. Meanwhile, MITI pledged to encourage Japanese users to buy American semiconductors and to assist American producers in penetrating the Japanese market. Japanese negotiators refused to commit to a specific market share target in the agreement itself, but pledged to work toward a goal of 20 percent foreign market share in an infamous side letter to the agreement. American officials took the side letter as a commitment, whereas Japanese officials denied that the letter even existed until a Japanese journal obtained a copy of the letter and published it.[18]

In 1987 American producers charged that Japan was not abiding by the agreement. Congress voted to recommend retaliation for Japan's failure to comply with the price floor agreement; the Defense Department issued a report warning of U.S. dependence on Japanese semiconductors; and the administration announced that it would impose $300 million in punitive tariffs on Japanese exports.[19] With foreign market share in Japan still well below 20 percent, the two sides extended the agreement in 1991. Although analysts dispute the economic impact of the agreement, the evidence suggests that the price floor failed because it padded profits for Japanese producers and increased costs for U.S. users, while the market access accord succeeded in enhancing foreign market share in Japan.[20]

The Semiconductor Agreement was not only the most contentious trade dispute of the 1980s, but it also set the scene for the primary confrontation of the following decade: the conclusion of the Framework Talks in

1993–95. Both sides learned important lessons from the experience of the Semiconductor Agreement—only different lessons. Japanese negotiators concluded that they should never agree to "managed trade" in the form of commitments to specific market share. Many Americans concluded the opposite: that the United States must insist not only on changes in regulations and procedures, but on concrete results. The Clinton administration came to office with a commitment to taking a tougher stance on trade with Japan. With the end of the cold war, many Clinton advisers felt the United States no longer needed to compromise its economic interests to maintain harmony with its military allies. Meanwhile, the Japanese saw an unprecedented opportunity to take the high road in trade talks, accusing the Americans of proposing managed trade while they were simply defending free trade principles.[21] This became the central point of contention during the Framework talks, as the U.S. side pressed for an agreement to monitor results with quantitative indicators and the Japanese side opposed anything that might imply managing trade flows.

FS-X Dispute

Japan's rise to technological power not only redefined economic relations, but also began to affect security relations by the 1980s. Although Japanese technological leadership centered on commercial rather than military applications, commercial technology had surpassed military technology in many areas. The world had shifted from an era characterized by spin-offs from military to commercial applications to one of "spin-ons" from commercial technology to military uses. The U.S. Department of Defense grew increasingly concerned about American reliance on Japanese electronic components in the early 1980s. In 1983 it negotiated an agreement establishing mechanisms for Japanese technology to flow to the United States for military use.[22] Meanwhile, leaders on both sides started to grasp the implications of Japanese technological leadership for international politics.[23] The United States had become more dependent on Japan for maintaining its own military leadership; third countries stood to gain a military advantage from access to Japanese technology, or to lose out from a lack thereof; and Japan's growing technology base enhanced Japan's ability to emerge as a major military power in its own right.[24]

In this context the United States and Japan launched their most ambitious attempt at military technology cooperation, the codevelopment of Japan's next-generation support fighter, the FS-X.[25] Japanese government officials and arms manufacturers were committed to maintaining and enhancing Japan's military technology base. Although they purchased a substantial amount of military hardware from the United States out of technological and political necessity, they also sought to license U.S. technology and to develop their own weapon systems. They were especially eager to develop a major weapon system on their own. Although they recognized that this would be more costly than purchasing a system off-the-shelf from the United States, and that they might not even match the capabilities of an American system, they felt that the benefits of cultivating Japan's military industrial base would far outweigh these costs. U.S. government reports compiled amidst the FS-X controversy generally assessed the situation in the same way: Japan would spend more and develop an inferior weapon system, but it would make substantial gains in its capacity to integrate complex aircraft systems (military or civilian) in the process.[26] Given the rising bilateral trade deficits and the United States' overwhelming comparative advantage in manufacturing weapon systems, the U.S. government pressed hard for Japan to purchase an American plane. Many U.S. officials assumed that they would never be able to convince Japan to buy an American plane off-the-shelf, so they were willing to accept Japanese production under license.

After protracted negotiations, the two sides compromised on codevelopment in 1987. Japanese manufacturers would not simply produce a U.S. plane under license, but would jointly develop a new plane based on the American F-16 that would incorporate Japan's best dual-use (commercial-military) technology. The two sides signed a memorandum of understanding (MOU) in 1988 that stipulated that the U.S. side would get 40 percent of development work and set out guidelines for the two-way flow of technology. The negotiations over the details of this arrangement proved to be extraordinarily contentious. The two sides were vying not only for the economic benefits of doing the production work, but also over the technological benefits that would come out of the project. Some American officials became increasingly alarmed that the Japanese were trying to redefine the project as Japanese indigenous development, and this eventually set off a full-fledged political furor.

In 1989 U.S. Congress members pressed the administration to renegotiate the MOU. After a heated debate within the United States plus further negotiations with Japan, Congress ultimately approved a revised agreement whereby the United States would be able to withhold the critical software codes. The two sides also established clearer guidelines for technology transfer, and guaranteed the United States a 40 percent share of production work (in addition to development work). In the process the U.S. government delayed the project by at least a year and outraged the Japanese. After the renegotiation, the two governments and the American and Japanese contractors continued to spar over the terms of collaboration: How much technology would flow from the United States to Japan and vice versa, which side had proprietary rights to which technology, and how the two would share development and production work.[27] Ultimately, the project cost much more and took much longer than originally anticipated, and produced a weapon system that failed to live up to expectations. The FS-X, now renamed the F-2, has the dubious honor of being the world's most expensive fighter at about 12 billion yen per plane. The contractors were plagued with recurring problems with the wings, and only completed development and delivered the first F-2 in September 2000. Both governments are now much less optimistic about the prospects for collaboration on military technology projects in general, and for Japan-to-United States technology flows in particular.

Nevertheless, the United States and Japan have agreed on yet another ambitious collaborative project: to research and develop theater missile defense (TMD) systems. The U.S. government had been trying to enlist Japan's financial and technological support for missile defense for several years, but the Japanese only committed themselves reluctantly in 1998 after North Korea stunned them by launching a trial rocket over Japanese territory. Japanese officials remain ambivalent about the project because they judge that TMD research and development, unlike FS-X codevelopment, will provide few benefits to Japan in terms of upgrading technological capabilities. Moreover, legal constraints and political opposition could impede Japan's ability to actually deploy a TMD system. If the U.S. and Japanese governments do not handle this project better than the FS-X, they could end up increasing bilateral tensions without achieving any significant technological or military benefit.[28]

U.S. Resurgence

The American resurgence as the world leader in high technology, like the earlier Japanese challenge, was built on a shift in the dominant production paradigm. Japanese production innovation created the lean production era. The lessons from that era were soon diffused among companies throughout the advanced industrial countries. The Wintelist era that has now emerged was in turn created by a wave of American firm-led innovations in strategy, structure, and production. In this new era final assemblers (such as IBM or NEC) no longer assert vertical control over markets, but share control with players throughout the value chain, from software firms (Microsoft) to component suppliers (Intel) to telecommunications equipment manufacturers (Cisco).[29] The automobile industry gave way to electronics as the core sector of the economy, and mechanical processes gave way to digital electronics as the core technology—or at least autos and mechanical engineering had to share primacy with computers and electrical engineering. The dominant firms now specialize in one part of the value chain (such as assembly, components, or software), and the assemblers combine efficiency and flexibility via cross-national production networks rather than through vertically integrated production systems.

In the earlier period, large assemblers dominated by exercising vertical control over manufacturing and technology. They either used this control to compete on price and quality with open standards, or to lock in customers and capture rents with closed standards. In consumer electronics, they generally shared open standards: that is, the technical specifications that define the system architecture and enable the pieces of the system to inter-operate remained in the public domain. In telecommunications and early mainframe and minicomputers, the dominant firms maintained closed standards, meaning they owned the relevant technical information as intellectual property. In the Wintelist era, however, producers work with "open but owned" systems built to restricted standards. This means that producers own the key product standards as intellectual property, but make them available to other firms that design complementary or competing components, software, or final products. The standards are licensed rather than published, and they are typically restricted in terms of the designation of licensees, permissible uses, or technical specifications.

The U.S. government fostered the emergence of the Wintelist paradigm by sponsoring basic research, providing a critical launch market for the electronics sector, and creating the original system that developed into the Internet. Moreover, U.S. antitrust policy prevented AT&T and IBM from dominating the electronics sector, permitting the rise of independent merchant semiconductor firms and spurring a pattern of cross-licensing technology across the sector. This in turn propelled the disintegration of the value chain, as manufacturers could specialize in assembly and leverage the benefits of working with a diverse set of component suppliers. Eventually specialization at one point of the value chain fostered specialization at other points, from materials to software through to system integration. The government also deregulated telecommunications markets, thereby creating a diverse group of large, sophisticated, and aggressive new players in the market. These new players became some of the critical users driving innovation under the new paradigm. They either built their own private or virtual networks or forced traditional carriers to adapt to their demands. The American governance system enabled a technological revolution that built on user-driven innovation in a system characterized by open standards.

This new technological paradigm played to American advantage. The core technology shifted toward the United States' subsectoral advantages: from memory chips to microprocessors and from hardware to software. The paradigm moved toward the United States' functional advantages, as innovation became more important and incremental production improvement became less critical (see the discussion of sectoral and functional advantages above). The United States benefited from being the locus of innovation because it was able to set new global technological standards and U.S. firms interacted with each other in local networks of innovation such as Silicon Valley. Meanwhile, U.S. firms finally began to close the gap with the Japanese in manufacturing systems. In the 1970s and 1980s U.S. semiconductor firms could not keep up with Japanese firms that emulated their technology and achieved higher quality, higher volume, and lower costs in production. In the Wintelist era, however, the U.S. innovators have the edge even if the Japanese maintain an advantage in production technology because the innovation cycle has accelerated and designs have become more complex (see figure 9-1).[30] By the late 1990s, expert commissions were reporting that the United States had achieved a substantial lead over Japan in many areas of technology, and that it appeared to be extending that lead.[31]

Meanwhile, Japan confronted the opposite situation: the technological paradigm shifted away from areas of its sectoral and functional advantage, and the governance system that had served it so well in the past now impeded adjustment. Japan's heavy regulation of the telecommunications and finance sectors forestalled the development of large dynamic users of telecommunications services that could drive innovation in the Wintelist era. Japan's low labor mobility, lack of entrepreneurs, and lack of venture capital financing became liabilities in an era in which innovation and applications are more important than manufacturing systems. To make matters worse, Japan was mired in a prolonged economic crisis that further constrained its ability to adjust to the shifting technological paradigm.[32]

NTT Interconnection Agreement

The U.S. technological resurgence has combined with U.S. economic strength and Japanese weakness to transform U.S.-Japan economic relations at the turn of the century.[33] Although bilateral trade deficits remain, U.S. officials simply do not pay the same attention. Domestic trade groups no longer demand relief from Japanese imports in the same way. Many of the most vulnerable U.S. industries have either retreated or moved production offshore. Meanwhile, the United States faces challenges from a more diverse set of competitors, including China, South Korea, and Taiwan. Given Japan's economic crisis, U.S. policymakers are genuinely ambivalent about whether they should continue to stress market access issues with Japan, shift more to macroeconomic concerns, simply leave market pressures and domestic political forces to push Japan to liberalize, or stop beating up the Japanese altogether and start helping them save their economy.

In this new context, the administration shifted to a much lower-profile approach to trade talks with Japan after 1995 under the rubric of the Enhanced Initiative on Deregulation. Japan launched its own deregulation program in the 1980s, and raised it to a top priority in 1993. The initiative sought to complement Japan's own deregulation process with bilateral talks to address those deregulation measures with the greatest impact on foreign market access. The U.S. government set its own sectoral priorities within these talks and monitored progress on an annual basis. In recent years U.S. government officials have increasingly preferred to leverage Japan's own internal pressures for reform rather than to resort to the classic outside pressure (*gaiatsu*) strategy.

Under the Enhanced Initiative, the United States took up the question of Japanese telecommunications regulation and specifically the interconnection fees Nippon Telegraph and Telephone (NTT) charges to its competitors. This case demonstrates how the United States and Japan continue to spar over domestic institutional differences in the IT era, but with much less fanfare and friction than in the past. The U.S. government was concerned that Japan was not living up to its commitments under a World Trade Organization (WTO) accord on telecommunications, and that high interconnection charges would make it difficult for American telecommunications and related service firms to expand in the Japanese market. U.S. negotiators contended that NTT set interconnection charges at rates from two to ten times higher than NTT's counterparts in other countries. High interconnection rates not only cut into competitors' profits and made it harder for them to match NTT prices, but virtually precluded competitors from challenging NTT's near-monopoly in local service. This in turn meant that NTT could leverage the benefits of cross-subsidization, using local service profits to finance cuts in long-distance and Internet charges. The Ministry of Posts and Telecommunications (MPT) disagreed with the United States over technical issues regarding the calculation of these charges and the pace of their reduction. The ministry had strongly supported competition in telecommunications since privatizing NTT in 1985 and opening the market to competition.[34] In 1998, however, the ministry made a pact with NTT and its political supporters whereby the government would break up NTT into one long-distance company and two regional operating companies and allow NTT into the international service market. In reaching this compromise, ministry officials assured NTT that the operating companies would be able to make a reasonable profit within three years. After this settlement, some ministry officials became less aggressive in promoting competition and more protective of NTT. In July 2000 the two sides finally came to an agreement whereby NTT would reduce interconnection charges by 20 percent within two years and make additional cuts in 2002. Meanwhile, the Japanese government began to set the stage for yet another elaborate political deal to enhance competition without crippling NTT by reorganizing NTT once again.

In the end the interconnection agreement lacked all of the acrimony and high-profile politics of the semiconductor and FS-X disputes. In fact many top policymakers in Washington barely took notice. The Japanese government had effectively retarded Japanese entry into next-generation networking by moving so cautiously in promoting telecommunications competition and restructuring NTT. This hampered American firms' ability to compete with NTT, but it threatened U.S. interests much less than the Japanese surge in semiconductor markets or the potential emergence of Japan in the aerospace sector. NTT has not been a competitive threat outside Japan, although NTT DoCoMo (discussed further below) could change that. Japanese firms are still inclined to favor domestic suppliers, but American dominance in the equipment for next-generation networks means that U.S. companies are willing to tolerate these practices.

The George W. Bush administration has sought to take a more accommodating stance than its predecessor on trade issues with Japan. It places a higher priority on strengthening the bilateral security relationship than on achieving concessions on trade issues. It also prefers to build on a strategy that began to emerge toward the end of the Clinton period, leveraging domestic Japanese pressures rather than resorting to traditional pressure tactics.[35] Nevertheless, U.S. vulnerability to an economic free fall in Japan has incited some U.S. officials to press Japan more directly for economic reforms.[36]

The Future

Although the future evolution of technology cannot be foreseen, one can identify critical questions, describe possible scenarios, and assess how these scenarios might affect U.S.-Japan relations in the future. The critical question is whether the United States will maintain its technological lead or Japan will catch up or retake the lead. This in turn hinges on two things: the future evolution of the technological paradigm, and the ability of the Japanese government and Japanese firms to adapt to this evolution.

The Japanese expansion into world markets followed a wave of production innovations in complex manufacturing. Japanese strategies of industrial finance and the managed relationship between Japanese domestic markets and international markets helped to cultivate a surge in industrial production, and this facilitated the wave of innovations loosely labeled as lean production. Likewise, the American comeback was facilitated by innovations that shifted the terms of competition in electronics, by adaptations to new market conditions, and by production outsourcing and reorganization that muted many Japanese advantages. After Japan's asset bubble burst in 1990, Japanese firms found it hard to respond to the new competitive challenges from American companies.

What follows after lean production and Wintelism? Is another shift in the terms of competition on its way? If one comes it is likely to emerge from the evolution of the new communications networks. Will that evolution favor American firms, as seems to be the case now, or will it favor Japanese companies? The leading-edge users in the major industrial countries will determine the configuration of the new networks, and thereby create the terrain on which the next-generation competition takes place With respect to the next technology paradigm, three questions are central. First, how will land-based broadband integrate with mobile data networks? The traditional response would be that this depends on the leading-edge applications (the "killer apps") that emerge. The content provision—such as streaming video, for example—might provide the demand that sets the network architecture. Yet intense point-to-point communication would favor alternate network architectures, such as a world of video chat rooms, for example.[37] If that is the case, will the communication architecture be a variant of the

Japanese DoCoMo system (discussed below) that rests on short messaging, or of a new architecture that might extend America Online (AOL) chat room and instant messaging technology into a broadband universe? Throughout the first phase of the Internet, an open end-to-end architecture allowed leading-edge users to define the architecture.[38] That favored the United States, where deregulation facilitated private network innovation. In the future, however, providers might drive innovation rather than leading-edge users. Second, will the network of the future rely on open or closed standards? The Internet employs an open standard, and its success was built on the user-driven innovation that an open standard allows. But DoCoMo has demonstrated the possibility of a successful closed standard. Third, what will the next-generation network look like? Will it be a patchwork of private systems on the model of the current Internet, or a more centralized and unified network bringing fiber optic cable to the home?[39] The specifics of network evolution will influence which competitive system establishes global leadership.

NTT DoCoMo's success in mobile communications, with its wildly popular i-mode telephone with Internet access, provides a critical test case for the future of Japanese technological leadership. NTT's mobile subsidiary, DoCoMo, has crafted a distinctive model for the mobile Internet that had attracted 30 million subscribers by November 2001, and brought it record-breaking profits and an astounding share price.[40] DoCoMo provides "always on" service to compatible mobile handsets. That is, users do not need to dial up the Internet because the connection is continuous. It also offers the convenience of paying for Internet services through the telephone bill, and the security of DoCoMo's screening of both users and service providers.

DoCoMo's strategy defies the Wintelist logic.[41] DoCoMo has prospered in an insulated market with an assured position, and DoCoMo itself— rather than the users—has driven innovation. DoCoMo already dominated Japan's mobile telephone market prior to introducing i-mode. It benefits from its connection to NTT, Japan's dominant telecommunications carrier, and from close ties with Japanese handset manufacturers. The government has supported DoCoMo by facilitating the coordination of technical standards, sponsoring research and development, subsidizing infrastructure investment, and allocating spectrum to DoCoMo for free. Moreover, DoCoMo's i-mode system is closed in two senses: it relies on a proprietary technical standard (its own packet-switching technology) and it controls the network. When users request a URL via i-mode, DoCoMo servers translate the request, transmit the material across traditional fixed-line networks, and pass the requested page back to the user across their wireless connection. DoCoMo controls the start menu users view on their phones. Being listed and available via this menu distinguishes about 1,200 privileged official i-mode content providers (as of mid-2001) from about 30,000 unofficial ones.

DoCoMo now faces new challenges as it moves on to third-generation (3G) wireless and expands into global markets. It has taken the lead in 3G wireless, beginning free trials in May 2001 and launching commercial service in October 2001. Its 3G service provides data transfers of up to 386 kilobits a second, forty times faster than i-mode, allowing users to make video telephone calls or to transfer large data files.[42] DoCoMo began to expand into international markets in 2000, with a series of partnerships and joint ventures including the acquisition of a 16 percent stake in AT&T Wireless announced in December 2000.[43]

In the end, DoCoMo may not be able to supersede the Wintelist logic, and it may have to loosen control over both technical standards and network content in order to expand. DoCoMo announced a partial move in this direction in March 2001 with a three-stage plan. It will publicize the standards for inclusion in the i-mode menu; set up a third-party organization to certify Internet services not listed on the i-mode menu and to collect fees for these services; and then open the i-mode network to Internet service providers by 2003.[44] Nevertheless, DoCoMo retains some distinctive advantages that remain salient in the 3G era: a strong financial position, a dominant market position in its home market, substantial government support, and strong ties to some of the leading handset manufacturers.

Ultimately, Japan's ability to adapt to the emerging technological paradigm will also depend on political leadership and government policy. Here the Japanese record over the past ten years is not promising. The Japanese bureaucracy appears to have lost confidence in itself and legitimacy in the eyes of the public. Meanwhile, politicians have focused on the turmoil of ongoing political realignment rather than attempting to fill this void. Moreover, existing institutions generate incentives against fundamental change. For example, NTT's powerful political status makes it more difficult for Japan to move boldly forward with procompetitive regulation. This is only further compounded by NTT's alliance with the powerful union *Zendentsū* and the Ministry of Finance, which has its own stake as partial owner of NTT.

The government and the private sector are acutely aware that they lag the United States in the all-important IT sector, and they have mobilized to address this gap.[45] The government's IT Strategy Council unveiled an ambitious reform program in December 2000 designed to propel Japan to global leadership in the IT sector by 2005. The plan combines substantial liberalization of the telecommunications market, heavy investment in the telecommunications infrastructure, improvements in the legal apparatus to support electronic commerce, and measures to promote electronic government. Yet government policies to date remain too timid both in liberalizing markets and in financing infrastructure, and too closely linked to the ruling party's goals of promoting pork-barrel projects in outlying areas. Japan's sorry record of policy innovation in the 1990s, however, does not preclude the possibility of greater dynamism in the future.

The United States and Japan have adjusted themselves back to their familiar postwar roles of technological leader and follower, greatly reducing bilateral friction. If Japan remains behind, one can expect bilateral trade relations to be smoother in the next twenty years than they have been in the past twenty. Even if Japan catches up or surpasses the United States, however, a second Japanese technological challenge will not be as destabilizing as the first one. For one thing, it would not have the same psychological impact. More importantly, U.S. leaders have learned a valuable lesson from the cycle of Japanese challenge and U.S. resurgence: the United States and Japan may have different national governance systems, but Japan's distinctive institutions do not all translate into unfair advantages. Some of them bestow unfair disadvantages as well.

Notes

1. For example: Department of Defense, Office of the Undersecretary of Defense for Acquisition, "Report of the Defense Science Task Force on Defense Semiconductor Dependency" (February 1987); Department of Defense, Office of the Undersecretary of Defense for Acquisition, "Electro-Optics and Millimeter Wave Technology in Japan" (May 1987); Ministry of International Trade and Industry, "Trends and Future Tasks in Industrial Technology: Summary of the White Paper on Industrial Technology" (September 1988); and Namiki Nobuyoshi, ed., *Nichibei no sangyō hikaku (Comparing U.S. and Japanese Industry)* (Tokyo: Nihon Keizai Shimbun, 1985). For further details, see Steven Vogel, "Japanese High Technology, Politics, and Power," Research Paper 2 (Berkeley Roundtable on the International Economy [BRIE], March 1989), pp. 5–41.

2. Technological change is defined broadly to include shifts in production paradigms, such as the advent of lean production systems, as well as specific product innovations, such as the invention of the transistor.

3. Zysman employs the concept of "the institutional structure of the political economy" to depict the links between the institutional arrangements of finance, labor, and goods markets and the dynamics of competition and economic performance that result. See John Zysman, *Governments, Markets, and Growth: Financial Systems and the Politics of Industrial Change*

(Cornell University Press, 1983); and "How Institutions Create Historically Rooted Trajectories of Growth," *Industrial and Corporate Change*, vol. 3 (1994), pp. 243–83.

4. Michael Porter, *The Competitive Advantage of Nations* (Free Press, 1990); Giovanni Dosi and Richard Nelson, "An Introduction to Evolutionary Theories in Economics," *Journal of Evolutionary Economics*, vol. 4 (1994), pp. 153–72.

5. See Chalmers Johnson, *MITI and the Japanese Miracle: The Growth of Industrial Policy, 1925–75* (Stanford University Press, 1982); Richard Samuels, *The Business of the Japanese State: Energy Markets in Comparative and Historical Perspective* (Cornell University Press, 1987); Masahiko Aoki, *Information, Incentives, and Bargaining in the Japanese Economy* (Cambridge University Press, 1988); Daniel Okimoto, *Between MITI and the Market: Japanese Industrial Policy for High Technology* (Stanford University Press, 1989); Chalmers Johnson, Laura Tyson, and John Zysman, eds., *Politics and Productivity: The Real Story of Why Japan Works* (Cambridge: Ballinger, 1989); Michael Gerlach, *Alliance Capitalism: The Social Organization of Japanese Business* (University of California Press, 1992).

6. John Zysman, *Political Strategies for Industrial Order: State, Market, and Industry in France* (Berkeley: University of California Press, 1977); Herbert Kitschelt, "Industrial Governance Structures, Innovation Strategies, and the Case of Japan: Sectoral or Cross-National Comparative Analysis?" *International Organization*, vol. 45 (Autumn 1991), pp. 453–93.

7. Clyde Prestowitz, *Trading Places: How We Are Giving Our Future to Japan and How to Reclaim It* (Basic Books, 1989), pp. 30–32; and Dennis Encarnation, *Rivals beyond Trade: America versus Japan in Global Competition* (Cornell University Press, 1992), pp. 36–96.

8. Kenneth Flamm, *Mismanaged Trade? Strategic Policy and the Semiconductor Industry* (Brookings, 1996), pp. 128–32.

9. This section builds on Stephen Cohen, Bradford DeLong, and John Zysman, "Tools for Thought: What Is New and Important about the 'E-conomy'" Working Paper 138 (Berkeley Roundtable on the International Economy [BRIE], February 2000).

10. Johnson, Tyson, and Zysman, *Politics and Productivity*.

11. See Laura Tyson, *Who's Bashing Whom? Trade Conflict in High-Technology Industries* (Institute of International Economics, 1992), especially pp. 17–31, for data showing Japan's rising competitiveness in high-technology sectors in the 1980s; and C. Fred Bergsten and Marcus Noland, *Reconcilable Differences? United States-Japan Economic Conflict* (Institute of International Economics, 1993), pp. 88–89, for the shifts in U.S. and Japanese revealed comparative advantage in high-technology sectors from 1971 to 1990.

12. Stephen Cohen and John Zysman, *Manufacturing Matters: The Myth of the Post-Industrial Economy* (Basic Books, 1987).

13. Both American and Japanese views of the bilateral relationship grew significantly more negative in the 1980s, especially 1984 through 1987. See figure 1-1 in the introduction to this volume.

14. Steven K. Vogel, "The 'Inverse' Relationship: The United States and Japan at the End of the Century," in Robert J. Lieber, ed., *Eagle Adrift: American Foreign Policy at the End of the Century* (Longman, 1997).

15. Table 9-1 follows the definitions of cooperation and tension given in the introduction to this volume. The levels of cooperation and tension in the table represent subjective assessments, and are offered for illustrative purposes only.

16. Michael Borrus, *Competing for Control: America's Stake in Microelectronics* (Cambridge: Ballinger, 1988), pp. 99–117; Tyson, *Who's Bashing Whom?* pp. 85–101.

17. Bergsten and Noland, *Reconcilable Differences?* p. 129.

18. Prestowitz, *Trading Places*, pp. 37–38.

19. Department of Defense (February 1987); Bergsten and Noland, *Reconcilable Differences?* pp. 130–31.

20. Tyson, *Who's Bashing Whom?*; Bergsten and Noland, *Reconcilable Differences?*

21. Vogel, "'Inverse' Relationship."

22. See Department of Defense, Office of the Undersecretary of Defense for Research and Engineering, "Industry-to-Industry International Armaments Cooperation Phase II—Japan" (June 1984).

23. In this context, Akio Morita and Shintarō Ishihara published a controversial book in which they stress how Japan's high-technology prowess enhances its geopolitical clout: *"Nō" to ieru nihon* (Tokyo: Kōbunsha, 1989), later translated into English as Shintarō Ishihara, *The Japan That Can Say No* (Simon and Schuster, 1991).

24. Vogel, *Japanese High Technology*.

25. On the FS-X, see Prestowitz, *Trading Places*; Vogel, *Japanese High Technology*; Richard Samuels, *"Rich Nation, Strong Army": National Security and the Technological Transformation of Japan* (Cornell University Press, 1994); Michael Green, *Arming Japan: Defense Production, Alliance Politics, and the Postwar Search for Autonomy* (Columbia University Press, 1995); and Mark Lorell, *Troubled Partnership: A History of U.S.-Japan Collaboration on the FS-X Fighter* (New Brunswick, NJ: Transaction Publishers, 1996).

26. Prestowitz, *Trading Places*.

27. Lorell, *Troubled Partnership*.

28. Michael Swaine, Rachel Swanger, and Takashi Kawakami, *Japan and Ballistic Missile Defense* (RAND, 2001).

29. This section builds on Michael Borrus and John Zysman, "Wintelism and the Changing Terms of Global Competition: Prototype of the Future?" Working Paper 96B (Berkeley Roundtable on the International Economy [BRIE], February 1997).

30. The authors thank George Scalise for this insight. Japan's declining comparative advantage was evident in other high-technology sectors as well. For example, from 1990 to 1998 the share of Organization for Economic Cooperation and Development (OECD) country imports coming from Japan declined from 17.7 percent to 10.9 percent for computer equipment, and from 23.1 percent to 5.8 percent for communications equipment: *OECD Information Technology Outlook* (OECD, 2000), p. 27.

31. See, for example, Department of Defense, Office of Japan Affairs, "Maximizing U.S. Interests in Science and Technology Relations with Japan" (National Academy Press, 1997).

32. This chapter does not mean to suggest that the mismatch between Japanese institutions and the new technological paradigm caused Japan's economic crisis. As Adam Posen notes, failures of macroeconomic policy and banking regulation are more directly responsible: "Unchanging Innovation and Changing Economic Performance in Japan," in Richard Nelson, Benn Steil, and David Victor, eds., *Technological Innovation and National Economic Performance* (Princeton University Press, forthcoming).

33. See the Green, Grimes, and Searight chapters, as well as the conclusion, in this volume.

34. Steven K. Vogel, "Creating Competition in Japan's Telecommunications Market," Japan Information Access Project Working Paper (May 2000); Steven K. Vogel, *Freer Markets, More Rules: Regulatory Reform in Advanced Industrial Countries* (Cornell University Press, 1996), pp. 137–66.

35. Michael Williams and Peter Landers, "A Kindler, Gentler Way to Pry Open Japan," *Wall Street Journal* (January 11, 2001), p. C1; David Sanger, "O'Neill Offers a New Approach to Japan," *New York Times* (February 6, 2001), p. C1. For the intellectual justification for this approach, see Leonard Schoppa, *Bargaining with Japan: What American Pressure Can and Cannot Do* (Columbia University Press, 1997).

36. Gerard Baker, "Japan's Ills Force New Approach by U.S.," *Financial Times* (April 4, 2001), p. 9.

37. Cohen, DeLong, and Zysman, "Tools for Thought"; Michael Kleeman, "E-Commerce and Network Architecture: New Perspectives," in BRIE-IGCC E-conomy Project,

E-Commerce and the Terms of Competition in Industries (Brookings, 2001); and Andrew Odlyzko, "Content Is Not King," *First Monday*, vol. 6 (February 2001).

38. François Bar, Stephen Cohen, Peter Cowhey, Brad DeLong, Michael Kleeman, and John Zysman, "Access and Innovation Policy for the Third-Generation Internet," *Telecommunications Policy* 24 (2000), pp. 489–518.

39. Michael Kleeman, "Kleeman's Wonderful World of Next Generation Networks," manuscript (2000).

40. *Asia Week* (June 22, 2001).

41. Bar and others, "Access and Innovation Policy"; Mark A. Lemley and Lawrence Lessig, "The End of End-to-End: Preserving the Architecture of the Internet in the Broadband Era," Working Paper No. 207-UC Berkeley Law and Economics Research Paper No. 2000-19 (Stanford Law School John M. Olin Program in Law and Economics, 2000); David Bach and John Zysman, "E-Commerce: What Will the Next Generation Look Like?" manuscript (2001); and Ben Ansell and David Lancashire, "Third Generation Wireless Deployment: Regional Lessons and International Repercussions," manuscript (2001).

42. *Asia Week* (June 22, 2001).

43. "A Big Deal for Tiny Screens," *Wall Street Journal* (December 1, 2000), p. B1.

44. AsiaBizTech (March 27, 2001). See www.nikkeibp.asiabiztech.com/wcs/frm/leaf?CID=onair/asabt/moren/126612 (July 2001).

45. For example, OECD, *OECD Information Technology*, p. 83, reports that only 25.8 percent of Japanese households (versus 42.1 percent of U.S. households) have PC access and only 14.9 percent (versus 26.2 percent) have Internet access.

CHAPTER TEN

Final Thoughts: Whither U.S.-Japan Relations?

STEVEN K. VOGEL

T his final chapter builds on the analysis in the body of the volume to address a single all-important question: How will the future of U.S.-Japan relations differ from the past? To project into the future on the basis of the past, one must choose between two basic alternatives: either identify current trends that will continue, or describe current patterns that will break. The trick, of course, is to discern which trends will continue and which patterns will break. Based on an analysis of the factors that generated the current patterns and trends in the first place, five trends are likely to continue in the next ten years, but three patterns will break.[1] To begin, the breaks follow:

1. U.S.-Japan relations will be less stable.

As noted in this volume's introduction, one is struck by the continuities in the U.S.-Japan relationship over the past fifty years even more than by the changes. Given the dramatic shifts in the global balance of power, one would have expected a bolder redefinition of the bilateral relationship. Given the enormous shift in the relative economic power of the two countries, one would have expected a more substantial rebalancing of roles. Michael Green and Keith Nitta explain this stability, but they do so in quite different ways. Green stresses that the United States and Japan had a common interest in preserving the core features of the San Francisco system, and the cold war framework provided a powerful incentive for the two to cooperate. Nitta stresses how the San Francisco system coalesced into foreign policy paradigms in both countries that clarified roles and harmonized expectations, and thereby enhanced stability.

Nevertheless, Green and Nitta suggest that the postwar framework has become less constraining in recent years. Green notes that the United States and Japan were forced to work much harder to preserve this framework in the 1990s than they did in the cold war era. When the two sides made a special effort, as they did under the Nye Initiative in the mid-1990s, they were able to shore up the San Francisco framework. When they were less vigilant, as in the early and late 1990s, the security relationship became more precarious. Nitta points more ominously to a period of paradigm drift. The doctrines that governed postwar foreign policy in the two countries have eroded, making behavior less predictable and relations less stable.

This suggests that the factors surveyed in this volume will be more important in the future. Shifts in the relative power of the United States and Japan and in the Asian regional balance of power have only required minor adjustments in the past (see chapter 2 by Green), but they could be more destabilizing in the future. Japan's dramatic postwar rise to economic power had relatively little impact on the overall structure of the relationship (see chapter 3 by Grimes), yet Japan's ability or inability to recover from its current economic crisis may reorient the relationship more profoundly. In the absence of a stable international balance of power and a strong consensus on foreign policy goals in the two countries, domestic politics, international organizations, media coverage, financial integration, and technological progress will all influence the relationship more directly than they have in the past.

This does not mean that U.S.-Japan relations will necessarily be more tense or conflictual. Rather, it merely suggests that the relationship will be more fluid and more open to redefinition. The San Francisco system kept certain features of the relationship virtually locked into place. The United States maintained a steady military presence in Japan; the United States took primary responsibility for Japan's defense and only relied on Japan for narrowly defined military roles and missions; and Japan's foreign policy was subordinated to that of the United States. These features are now more open to readjustment than ever before.

The terrorist attacks on the World Trade Center and the Pentagon in September 2001 have accelerated the process of redefining the U.S.-Japan relationship. The Japanese government quickly announced a seven-point plan to support the U.S.-led war on terrorism that stretches the limits of the

San Francisco framework. It pledged to provide rear area support for U.S. forces, including transport, supply, and medical support services, and to strengthen security for U.S. military facilities in Japan. The Diet then passed legislation to allow Japanese forces to provide support beyond those geographical areas directly surrounding Japan, and to authorize Japanese forces to defend U.S. bases in Japan. The government also agreed to increase intelligence sharing with the United States and to provide economic assistance to Pakistan and other countries to reward their cooperation with the U.S.-led military effort. In the short run, the war against terrorism—like the earlier cold war—will strengthen U.S.-Japan security cooperation and push both governments to keep disagreements on other issues from undermining this cooperation. It is not likely to forge a new framework, however, that will be as stable and enduring as the San Francisco system. It has sparked a transition in U.S.-Japan relations that will continue for many years. As the United States and Japan negotiate these changes, they can now contemplate a wider range of options than they have since 1951.

2. *Security relations will be more contentious.*

The overall level of bilateral tensions will not increase, but the locus of tensions will shift, with friction increasing on the security side and diminishing on the economic side. The postwar period was characterized by greater cooperation and harmony on security and greater conflict and tension on economic issues. That pattern may be about to reverse itself.

As noted above, U.S. and Japanese leaders increasingly are questioning the core features of the San Francisco system. They are likely to generate considerable friction as they renegotiate this grand bargain. In Japan opinion leaders from both right and left are showing signs of increasing nationalism and resentment toward the United States. Prime Minister Junichirō Koizumi has called for constitutional revision so that Japan can take greater responsibility for its own defense. Shintarō Ishihara, the enormously popular governor of Tokyo, has publicly denounced Japan's dependence on the United States and its deference to the U.S. government on foreign policy. The Democratic Party, Japan's leading opposition party, calls for deep cuts in U.S. forces including the eventual removal of the marines. Citizens in Okinawa and other areas with U.S. bases demand a renegotiation of the Status of Forces Agreement (SOFA), and a reduction or outright withdrawal of American forces from Japan.

Meanwhile, the George W. Bush administration has charted out ambitious plans for upgrading the U.S.-Japan security alliance, including a recalibration of the division of labor between the two countries. It hopes to persuade the Japanese government to expand its own defense capabilities and to increase its role in collective security; enhance U.S.-Japan joint development of a new Theater Missile Defense (TMD) system; cooperate more closely on technological development, joint exercises, and planning; and further specify procedures for military cooperation in the event of a regional conflict.

The war on terrorism has increased the likelihood that Japan will cooperate with U.S. plans for strengthening the alliance. Even so, the Japanese government faces some formidable economic and political constraints. The process of redefining the U.S.-Japan alliance will require some protracted and difficult negotiations over the terms of the transition. To put this in terms of the language presented in this volume's introduction, the war on terrorism is likely to increase U.S.-Japan cooperation in the security sphere, but to increase tension as well.

Moreover, the United States and Japan may confront other challenges in the years to come, any one of which could destabilize the alliance. For example, the reconciliation or reunification of the two Koreas could prompt a wholesale revision of U.S.-Japan security arrangements. A China-Taiwan conflict could bring to the surface U.S.-Japan differences over how to deal with China.

This volume does not claim that bilateral security relations will necessarily deteriorate, for this ultimately depends on how the two governments manage their relations. The end of the cold war and the erosion of postwar paradigms means, however, that domestic political developments and shifts in the regional balance of power are more likely to disrupt U.S.-Japan security relations than they have been in the past.

3. Economic relations will be less contentious.

William Grimes as well as Steven Vogel and John Zysman show how Japan's rise to economic and technological power generated enormous tension in the 1980s and early 1990s, and the U.S. economic resurgence and the Japanese recession have since reduced this tension. Although the U.S. economy may slow and the Japanese economy may revive in the years to come, the two countries will not return to 1980s levels of tension in economic relations. As Grimes notes, the United States and Japan are both mature economies, so the gap in economic performance between the two is likely to be small. In any case, a Japanese economic resurgence would not have the same shock effect as Japan's phenomenal postwar economic rise. In addition the U.S.-Japan savings gap that underlay many bilateral disputes in the 1980s and 1990s is likely to narrow, given a shrinking U.S. budget deficit, an exploding Japanese budget deficit, and the aging of the Japanese population.

Moreover, as Adam Posen explains, the internationalization of finance is driving a partial convergence of U.S. and Japanese economic institutions, reducing the potential for future conflict over differences in the two economic systems. U.S. and Japanese industry have also become much more closely integrated through direct investment, joint ventures, and various forms of collaboration in research, production, and distribution (see chapter 3 by Grimes). This suggests that U.S. and Japanese industry will have less conflicting interests on bilateral trade issues, and a greater stake in maintaining harmonious trade relations. In addition, as Leonard Schoppa notes, the domestic faction within Japan supporting economic liberalization has expanded in recent years, and this will make it considerably easier for the two countries to cooperate on trade issues.

Beyond these three breaks, this volume identifies five trends that will continue or even accelerate. These trends still represent change rather than stasis in U.S.-Japan relations, but the change is continuous rather than discontinuous:

1. Japanese foreign policy will become more independent from the United States.

This does not mean that Japanese foreign policy will become truly independent, but that it will become relatively less dependent. Over the postwar period, Japan has emerged from near total dependence on the United States in 1951 to become a full participant in the international community and a major power in its own right. It began to experiment with a more autonomous foreign policy under Prime Minister Yasuhiro Nakasone in the 1980s, and it diverged from the United States on issues ranging from development aid to the Asian financial crisis in the 1990s. As Amy Searight notes, Japan has been especially assertive in staking out its own position within international organizations.

Japanese government officials have muted their criticism of U.S. foreign policy to date, but they may become more assertive in pressing their own positions in the future. They clearly differ with the United States on China, believing that the United States and Japan must focus on engaging China, not containing it. They fear that the Bush administration's hard line on China-Taiwan issues and its commitment to missile defense could provoke China. And they feel that U.S. criticism of Chinese human rights violations is simply counterproductive. They are concerned about the U.S. government's propensity for unilateralism on issues such as missile defense, the

Anti-Ballistic Missile (ABM) Treaty, and the Kyoto protocol on greenhouse gases. In addition they question the United States' penchant for military intervention in far-flung conflicts such as the Kosovo crisis.

2. Bilateral relations will become more embedded in multilateral relationships.

The United States and Japan relied very heavily on bilateral channels throughout the postwar period. The United States crafted the Asia-Pacific security structure on a hub-and-spoke network of bilateral alliances, with the U.S.-Japan relationship as the linchpin. On trade issues the United States favored bilateral negotiations rather than multilateral channels. As Amy Searight demonstrates, however, the U.S.-Japan relationship has become increasingly embedded in international institutions in recent years, especially on economic issues. This does not mean that bilateral conflict and cooperation will disappear, but that some of it will shift to the multilateral arena. This should reduce bilateral tensions overall, although it will also increase the potential for bilateral conflict within these multilateral organizations. On the security side, bilateral alliances are not likely to give way to a multilateral framework any time soon. With the demise of the cold war system, however, the U.S.-Japan relationship is now more sensitive to changing relations with other Asia Pacific countries, especially China. Likewise, the Asian region is slowly becoming more integrated, primarily through dense networks of trade and investment, but also through formal institutions such as Asia-Pacific Economic Cooperation (APEC) and the ASEAN Regional Forum (ARF). This suggests that the U.S.-Japan relationship will become more interwoven with broader multilateral relationships, such as U.S.-Japan-China or Japan-South Korea-China relations, and more linked to regional institutions.

3. Bilateral relations will become more pluralistic.

To an astonishing degree, a small elite of politicians, bureaucrats, diplomats, and intellectuals dominated the bilateral relationship during the postwar period. This has gradually changed over time, however, and this trend is likely to accelerate in the future. As Laurie Freeman notes, the mass media have become increasingly powerful and more independent players in U.S.-Japan relations. In the future, the new media will further transform the relationship, empowering nonelite groups and individuals. In addition, as Adam Posen demonstrates, financial institutions and industrial corporations have become more powerful in dictating outcomes, such as market access and levels of investment, that were primarily structured by government actors in the past. Local governments are becoming more important

actors in the bilateral relationship, with local leaders such as former Okinawa governor Masahide Ōta and Tokyo governor Shintarō Ishihara
playing a significant role in foreign policy. U.S. and Japanese nongovernmental organizations (NGOs) are creating their own dialogue and forging
partnerships. Meanwhile, cultural exchange, tourism, and personal diplomacy are rising. This suggests that U.S. and Japanese government officials
will have to develop much more sophisticated strategies of working with the
media, industry, and citizen groups to realize their goals.

4. The U.S.-Japan agenda will expand.

Throughout most of the postwar period, the United States and Japan
focused almost exclusively on a core agenda centered on security and trade.
This volume has noted how some issue areas, such as technology and
finance, have increased in importance in recent years. The volume has paid
little attention to other areas, such as energy, the environment, human
rights, and immigration. This selection of topics is justified because these
other issues have not been central to the relationship in the postwar period.
In the future, however, the agenda will continue to expand, with these non-
core issues increasing in importance. On balance, this is likely to improve
relations between the two countries because it deflects attention from areas
of conflict and increases opportunities for cooperation. In fact the United
States and Japan initiated a Common Agenda program in the 1990s to
work on such global problems. Their mutual preoccupation with trade and
security issues limited their ability to push forward the agenda, but the two
countries will have opportunities to move further in this direction in the
years to come. At the same time, however, the expansion of the agenda can
also generate new possibilities for conflict. The United States and Japan
may have a common interest in the protection of whales and the reduction
of greenhouse gases, for example, but they have very different positions on
how to achieve these goals.

5. Military power will decline in utility.

In the past the security alliance has dominated the U.S.-Japan relationship, and U.S. preeminence in military power has largely defined the
(unequal) terms of the relationship. In the future, however, security relations
will no longer overshadow economic relations, and military power will no
longer overwhelm other kinds of power in the same way. This does not
mean that security relations are no longer important. In fact the bilateral,
regional, and global balance of power will continue to be the most critical
factor shaping the relationship. Security relations will probably increase in
their importance in the bilateral agenda in the near-term future, as the

United States and Japan work together in the war on terrorism and strive to enhance their alliance. Rather, this volume is making two more specific claims. First, the bilateral agenda is expanding (see point 4 above) into new areas in which military advantage is of little use. As neoliberal theorists argue, military power is less dominant because it is irrelevant to a growing proportion of the international relations agenda. A military advantage is critical in deterring security threats, but less useful when negotiating treaties on intellectual property rights or setting new standards for carbon dioxide emissions. Second, new actors (see points 2 and 3 above) are deepening and broadening the relationship beyond its military foundation. The rise of new actors such as international organizations and nongovernmental organizations brings new dimensions to the relationship where military power no longer dictates outcomes.

The evidence assembled in this volume suggests that future U.S.-Japan relations will differ from the past in these eight ways. The authors of this volume readily concede, however, that American and Japanese politicians, bureaucrats, business people, journalists, and ordinary citizens have considerable freedom to define the future of this relationship for themselves. In fact, if U.S. and Japanese leaders better understand the new challenges they face at the beginning of the twenty-first century, then they will be that much better able to cope with these challenges.

Note

1. The conclusions presented here build on the individual chapters and reflect discussions among all of the chapter authors. Individual authors may differ, however, on some of the specific predictions.

Contributors

LAURIE A. FREEMAN is assistant professor of political science at the University of California, Santa Barbara, and the author of *Closing the Shop: Information Cartels and Japan's Mass Media* (2000).

MICHAEL J. GREEN has been a senior fellow at the Council on Foreign Relations and is the author of *Arming Japan: Defense Production, Alliance Politics, and the Postwar Search for Autonomy* (1995). Since contributing to this volume, he has become director of Asian affairs at the National Security Council.

WILLIAM W. GRIMES is assistant professor of international relations at Boston University and the author of *Unmaking the Japanese Miracle: Macroeconomic Politics, 1985–2000* (2001).

KEITH A. NITTA is a doctoral candidate in political science at the University of California, Berkeley, where he is working on Japanese educational reform.

ADAM S. POSEN is senior fellow at the Institute for International Economics and the author of *Restoring Japan's Economic Growth* (1998).

LEONARD J. SCHOPPA is associate professor of political science at the University of Virginia and the author of *Bargaining with Japan: What American Pressure Can and Cannot Do* (1997).

AMY E. SEARIGHT is assistant professor of political science at Northwestern University and is currently writing a book on Japanese trade policy.

STEVEN K. VOGEL is associate professor of political science at the University of California, Berkeley, and the author of *Freer Markets, More Rules: Regulatory Reform in the Advanced Industrial Countries* (1996).

JOHN ZYSMAN is professor of political science at the University of California, Berkeley; codirector of the Berkeley Roundtable on the International Economy (BRIE); and the author of *Governments, Markets and Growth: Financial Systems and the Politics of Industrial Change* (1983) and many other works.

Index

Abe, Masahiro, 66
Acheson, Dean, 12, 72
Afghanistan, 21, 111, 183
Aizawa, Seishisai, 67
America OnLine (AOL), 256
Anti-Ballistic Missile (ABM) Treaty, 266–67
APEC. *See* Asia-Pacific Economic Cooperation
ARF. *See* ASEAN Regional Forum
Armacost, Michael, 82, 150
Armitage-Nye Report (*2000*), 227
Asahi Shimbun, 132, 140
Asanuma, Inejirō, 108
ASEAN (Association of South East Asian Nations), 168, 179, 181
ASEAN Regional Forum (ARF), 168, 188, 267
Ashida, Hitoshi, 77, 100, 103–04, 105
Asia: communism in, 71–72; containment program, 72, 73; economic organization, 90; financial crisis, 28, 45, 55, 135, 180, 215, 230; financial miracles, 180; financial networks, 267; GATT membership, 167; press coverage, 134; regional organizations, 163–64, 168; security, 88, 99,

188; as trading partner, 52; views of Japan, 173
Asian Monetary Fund proposal, 180, 181
Asian Wall Street Journal, 222
Asia-Pacific Economic Cooperation (APEC): Japanese role, 172, 174, 178–79, 192; as regional trade agreement, 167–68, 267; U.S. role, 171, 174
Association of South East Asian Nations. *See* ASEAN
AT&T, 245, 251, 257
Australia, 164, 178
Automobile industry: high-tech challenge, 244, 251; international cooperation, 57; Japanese advances, 239; production improvement, 242; trade negotiations and disputes, 52, 59, 116, 178, 186; U.S. interest in Japanese producers, 225–26; U.S. sanctions and tariffs, 118, 195n30, 195n31

Balance of power: effects on media and information, 129, 133, 136, 140, 142, 152; multiple dimensions, 3; realist view, 189; role of domestic

rearmament, 105–07; renewal and revisions,15, 29, 77, 99, 107–10; settlement and ratification, 100, 104–06, 109, 118–19, 123n17, 123n22; terms, 100–06, 123n29, 187; view of the U.S., 109; Yoshida, 100, 102–07; Yoshida Doctrine, 63, 65, 74, 79

U.S. News & World Report, 142

USSR. *See* Union of Soviet Socialist Republics

van Wolferen, Karel, 149
Verba, Sidney, 126–27
Vietnam, 21
Vietnam War, 16, 111
Vogel, Ezra, 80
Vogel, Steven, 121, 205
Voicestream, 220

Wall Street Journal, 141
Waltz, Kenneth, 189
Washington Post, 141
White, Theodore, 140
World Bank, 24: changes in, 167; dispute litigation, 178; Japanese participation, 161, 172, 173, 179–82, 187, 190, 192; legalization, 169, 178, 192; role, 162; U.S. role, 180, 192. *See also* International organizations
World Trade Organization (WTO), 89,

118: binding power, 169,178, 186; changes in, 186–87, 191, 192; dispute resolution, 176, 178; effects, 190–91; expansion, 167; Financial Services Agreement, 217; Japanese participation, 190; legalization, 175, 186; Seattle meetings, 191; telecommunications accord, 253; U.S. role, 186. *See also* General Agreement on Tariffs and Trade; International organizations

Yamaichi Securities, 207–08
Yoshida, Shigeru: approval of peace and security treaties,100, 102–05; on constitution, 14; defense role, 111; foreign policy, 65; rearmament, 105–07; U.S. military bases, 123n14; Yoshida Doctrine, 11, 13, 74–80, 105
Yoshida Doctrine: adjustments (*1960*), 15, 31; containment and, 70, 74; economic and strategic factors, 13–14, 63, 74–80, 83, 105; modified version, 89; nationalism, 90; weakening of, 64, 85–86

Zendentsū, 257
Zoellick, Robert, 226
Zucker, Harold G., 128
Zysman, John, 241